Lord Beaconsfield

THE CROWELL HISTORICAL CLASSICS SERIES

UNDER THE EDITORSHIP OF *Herman Ausubel*

Lord Beaconsfield by Georg Brandes
WITH AN INTRODUCTION BY SALO W. BARON

Queen Elizabeth by Mandell Creighton
WITH AN INTRODUCTION BY G. R. ELTON

William Stubbs on the English Constitution
EDITED BY NORMAN F. CANTOR

Impressions of Russia by Georg Brandes
WITH AN INTRODUCTION BY RICHARD PIPES

IN PREPARATION

Americans of 1776 by James Schouler
WITH AN INTRODUCTION BY RICHARD B. MORRIS

The First Two Stuarts and the Puritan Revolution
by Samuel R. Gardiner
WITH AN INTRODUCTION BY WILLSON COATES

Hume by Thomas Henry Huxley
WITH AN INTRODUCTION BY ALBERT HOFSTADTER

Life of Andrew Jackson by William Cobbett
WITH AN INTRODUCTION BY MARCUS CUNLIFFE

ری ری ریرے رے رے

Lord Beaconsfield

A STUDY

BY Georg Brandes

ری ری ریرے رے رے

WITH AN INTRODUCTION

BY Salo W. Baron

THOMAS Y. CROWELL COMPANY

Established 1834   New York

GEORG BRANDES AND
LORD BEACONSFIELD

◆§ If a personality like Lord Beaconsfield, or Benjamin Disraeli as he was known until he reluctantly accepted a peerage at
the age of seventy-two, were to appear today on the American
political scene and aspire for the offices of Secretary of the Treasury and President of the United States, he would be considered an
utter maverick. And yet in nineteenth-century Britain, Disraeli was
able to serve several times as chancellor of the exchequer and prime
minister.

Neither his personal appearance nor his earlier career predisposed the electorate in his favor then, nor would they do so
today. Although quite handsome, he must have consciously antagonized even his young aristocratic friends when he appeared in
society wearing "green velvet trousers, a canary-colored waistcoat,
low shoes, silver buckles, lace at his wrists, and his hair in ringlets."
Nor was his political career advanced by his early reputation as a
widely read author of romantic and semimystical novels. We
certainly have had entertainers elected to the United States Congress, but they usually gave up their artistic careers before entering
politics and apparently felt that the two did not mix. But Disraeli
continued writing while in Parliament. In fact, as late as 1870,
in the interval between two terms as prime minister, he published a
novel *Lothair* which, because of his political eminence, became an
immediate best-seller. He himself could boast that his book was
"more extensively read by the people of the United Kingdom and
the United States than any work that has appeared in the last half-
century."

His political views would also make him most unpopular with the majority of Americans or Englishmen today. A professed "imperialist," he belonged among Britain's most important Empire-builders. True, he envisaged the British Empire not as a source of colonial exploitation by England's ruling classes, but rather as the divinely ordained instrument for the great task of what Rudyard Kipling was to call later "the white man's burden." It was he who engineered Queen Victoria's assumption of the title Empress of India and the transfer of Indian soldiers to Europe in preparation for a possible conflict with Russia. He consciously wished to make Britain an Asiatic as well as a European power, evoking jeers from opponents that he wanted to remove the Empire's capital from London to Delhi. Disraeli was particularly conscious of Russia's straddling the two continents (we know that even today the Soviets demand, over Red China's protests, full partnership in conferences of Asian and African nations), and he considered it his major duty to stem Tsarist expansion into Iran and the Ottoman Empire. Had he headed a British Cabinet after the Second World War, he certainly would have acted as did his disciple, Winston Churchill, and refused to preside over the liquidation of the British Empire.

Disraeli was an outright "colonialist." He believed that Britain's colonial peoples would require a long period of tutelage by the British government to instruct them in modern statecraft and a civilized way of life. He ridiculed the assumption that even the Egyptian constitution could easily be patterned after the English institutions which had grown during many centuries. Doubtless, such insistence on "gradualness" today would be like waving a red flag before most of the developing nations. Even some contemporaries ridiculed Disraeli's notion of England's civilizing function among her African allies. Among the hundreds of Disraeli caricatures which appeared in *Punch* (a selection of more than one hundred was republished in a volume while he was still alive) one of 1870 shows the Sultan of Zanzibar in a discussion with the British leader about the abolition of slavery. The caption reads in part: "But remember O Sheikh Ben Dizzy, Conservative Party very strong in Zanzibar!"

This allusion to Disraeli's lifelong Conservative allegiance must likewise be understood in its peculiar meaning. The British Tories never were so reactionary as were most of their Continental confreres or as are those fragmentary groups which now campaign in the guise of an American Conservative Party. Under Disraeli's leadership, in particular, the British Conservatives espoused many programs favoring the common man. Disraeli himself saw in the alliance between the landed aristocracy and the urban "lower classes" the necessary counterweight to the Whigs representing the middle classes and, particularly, the industrial and banking plutocracy. This approach antagonized some of his friends, while his enemies derided his combination of conservatism and radicalism. Disraeli proudly admitted that he was indeed "a Conservative to preserve all that is good in our constitution, a Radical to remove all that is bad." But as in his colonial policies, he believed that the conditions of the common man could be improved by government action. He was, indeed, a believer in the maxim that much should be done for the people but very little by the people. Yet at a crucial juncture in British history it was he who in 1867 helped push through an unwilling Parliament the so-called Household Suffrage Bill which vastly extended the popular franchise. He never regretted this move, although the enlarged electorate in the very first election voted him and his party out of office by a substantial majority.

Underlying his convictions was Disraeli's basic denial of the natural equality of man. Far from being a believer in the doctrine of evolution and the survival of the fittest, which he often dismissed with a shrug, he declared that "though Nature will never ultimately permit this theory of natural equality to be practiced, the preaching of this dogma has already caused much mischief, and may occasion much more." His repudiation of this "dogma" is best illustrated by his reiterated arguments in favor of the then much-debated Jewish Emancipation. Unquestionably he greatly contributed to that final act of admission of Jews to Parliament enacted in 1858. The first Jewish deputy enabled through that act to take his seat among England's lawgivers, Nathaniel Rothschild, was, despite his Whig orientation, formally introduced by Disraeli. But unlike most champions of Jewish emancipation, Disraeli contended that Jews deserved equality of rights not because they were *equal* to other men, but rather because they belonged to a superior race. In his "political biography" of Lord George Bentinck, the Tory leader, published in 1852, Disraeli eloquently described the survival of the Jewish people against tremendous odds:

Egyptian Pharaohs, Assyrian kings, Roman emperors, Scandinavian crusaders, Gothic princes, and holy inquisitors have alike devoted their energies to the fulfillment of this common purpose [of destroying it]. Expatriation, exile, captivity, confiscation, torture on the most ingenious, and massacre on the most extensive, scale, with a curious system of degrading custom and debasing laws which would have broken the heart of any other people, have been tried, and in vain. The Jews, after all this havoc, are probably more numerous at this date than they were during the reign of Solomon the Wise, are found in all lands, and, unfortunately, prospering in most. All of which proves that it is in vain for man to attempt to battle the inexorable law of nature, which has decreed that a superior race shall never be destroyed or absorbed by an inferior.

He did not deny the presence of a disproportionate number of Jews among the Continental leaders of socialist and other radical parties particularly during the Revolutions of 1848 (we need but remember that Karl Marx was living in London), but he placed the blame entirely on the endless persecutions the Jews had suffered. He claimed that, through their deep attachment to the conservative principles of religion, family, and property, Jews were a naturally conservative group. Only the relentless rebuffs they experienced made them turn to extremist parties bent upon the overthrow of regimes which had so constantly maltreated them.

Such doctrines of racial superiority might have made Disraeli acceptable as a politician today to the White Citizens' Councils in

America or the champions of *apartheid* in South Africa. If he had been more keenly aware of the debates conducted in the 1870s in Germany and France, he would have realized that similar arguments in reverse were giving rise to the racial antisemitism of a Wilhelm Marr or Richard Wagner. Yet this lifelong belief in the superiority of the Jewish race was for him an important source of strength. From the outset he had to fight his way up the social and political rungs. He knew that he owed his conversion to Christianity at the age of twelve to the stubbornness of the Jewish elders of the Spanish-Portuguese Congregation in London who had elected his father, Isaac D'Israeli, to their board. When the latter, a typical Voltarian skeptic and essayist, declined the election, they fined him the maximum amount provided in the congregational statutes. Without this conflict Isaac might never have severed his nominal association with that congregation and his children might have grown up as Jews.

Benjamin's enemies never forgot this "blemish" on his personality, underscored by his typically Mediterranean physiognomy. His perennial rival, William Gladstone, was not alone in describing him as "a foreigner with not a drop of English blood in his veins." Thomas Carlyle glibly called him the "superlative Hebrew Conjurer." Gloating over his electoral defeat in 1880, the historian Edward A. Freeman wrote a letter to a German colleague which the latter described as "shouting and dancing at the deliverance from the yoke of Jewry." Caricaturists of *Punch* and a host of political pamphleteers rarely failed to exaggerate Disraeli's "Jewish" appearance and behavior. He, for his part, was too proud to deny or minimize his Jewish descent. Turning the tables on his enemies, he insisted on the superiority of his own ancestry over that of the highest English aristocracy whose forebears had been but "Baltic pirates" or had enriched themselves by robbing monasteries during the Reformation and by draining the wealth of India. Time and again he prided himself on being a Jew; in fact, a total Jew of both Sinai and Calvary, since Christianity was but "Judaism for the multitude."

In these circumstances few observers at the beginning of his career would have predicted that he might achieve supreme power through the then aristocratically dominated Tory party in England. The odds against him must have appeared even greater than they would with respect to a similarly exotic figure in American politics today. Even in retrospect Lord Morley, commenting on Disraeli's mockery of the British Philistine and his aloofness and detachment from hollow conventions, had to admit: "How on earth such a man ever became an extremely popular Prime Minister I can never tell."

Yet his great brilliance and sharp wit, often compared even by his enemies with those of Voltaire, as well as his extreme steadfastness in the face of recurrent defeats brought him to the top. He took in his stride, for instance, his early failures to secure a parliamentary seat, just as he later managed to serve as chancellor of the exchequer or prime minister without a majority in Parliament. It was only toward the end of his life (from 1874 to 1880) that he enjoyed solid parliamentary backing and widespread popular approval.

Most importantly, Disraeli was less a political theorist than a pragmatic statesman who readily adjusted his policies to changing international and domestic exigencies. If he more or less consistently backed the landowning class in which he saw the backbone of British greatness—he feared that exclusive concentration on mercantile endeavors might cause England's ultimate downfall as it did that of Venice or ancient Tyre—he nevertheless accepted the popular verdict when free trade became a dominant element in British domestic and foreign policy. Among his numerous prophetic foresights not the least were his serious misgivings about the ensuing damage to British agriculture. As it turned out, twentieth-century England had to abandon free trade, and, despite numerous protectionist measures, she has faced recurrent crises in her attempt to preserve the value of the pound.

In general, as Georg Brandes rightly observes, Disraeli "does not appeal to ideas but to precedents, not to principles but to Bolingbroke or to Shelburne; he does not quote Shakespeare but Hansard; he desires, above all things, to be national and historical." Living in the United States, Disraeli would undoubtedly have invoked other precedents; he might have been as ardent a Jeffersonian here as he was a dedicated Tory in Victorian England. Not that he was unprincipled and wholly opportunistic as alleged by his enemies or even by such fellow conservatives as Lord Salisbury, who once called him "a mere political gamester." There was, in fact, much more consistency in Disraeli's general outlook and even in his successive political measures than in those of his far more doctrinaire counterpart, William Gladstone. But he was a realist who carefully weighed the possibilities and, while in his novels he could yield to flights of fancy, in practical politics he sought the attainable.

However, what he considered attainable appeared to many contemporaries wholly utopian. For example, long before Theodor Herzl, he regarded as a definite possibility the restoration of the Jews to Palestine through both political action and practical upbuilding. Not only the heroes of his early novels, Contarini Fleming and David Alroy, but also Lothair could contend, to cite Fleming, that "the political regeneration of the country to which I am devoted may not be distant, and in that great work I am resolved to participate." Such an opportunity seemed to emerge during the crisis in the Eastern Question of 1877–78. Disraeli may indeed have been the author of an anonymous German pamphlet, *Die jüdische Frage in der orientalischen Frage,* recently discovered in Vienna, which contained proposals for the reconstruction of a Jewish nation in the Holy Land. It was attributed to him by a leading Austrian statesman, Baron Johann Chlumecky, who claimed to have translated it from the English at the request of the British ambassador in Vienna. Disraeli abandoned this project, however, during the negotiations at the Congress of Berlin, in which he was to play a dominant role. He not only checked Russia's expansion into the Balkans but he also secured for Great Britain the island of Cyprus as an important strategic outpost protecting her lifeline to India.

Quickly realizing the new situation, Disraeli withdrew his pamphlet (which may have been intended as a mere trial balloon) and suppressed most of the existing copies. Even in his frustrations this political realist thus showed how far he was ready to go in bridging the chasm between his cherished dreams and existing realities.

Not surprisingly, Disraeli's fascinating and complex personality attracted many biographers during his lifetime and afterwards. Among them was Georg Brandes, whose volume, written in 1878 and translated into English two years later, from the outset carved for itself a special niche. Of course, the ramified correspondence conducted by Disraeli, a facile and persuasive writer, particularly with his sister Sarah, a lifelong confidante, was not available to Brandes. Most of these letters were published after Disraeli's death and were to be used to good advantage in the classic six-volume biography by William F. Monypenny and George E. Buckle (1910–20). Nor were the documents assembled in the Public Record Office and the enormous literature written on almost every aspect of Victorian life during the last ninety years accessible in the 1870s. Yet, by his penetrating psychological interpretation, long antedating the modern literary biography as written by an André Maurois, Brandes was able to examine Disraeli's motivations much better than did many of his successors.

Brandes was not a political theorist; he was in the main an historian of literature, whose multi-volume work, *Main Currents of Literature in the Nineteenth Century*, was becoming a classic before he tackled *Lord Beaconsfield*. But precisely because he used Disraeli's novels to better advantage than anyone else in order to dig more deeply into the recesses of their writer's mind, he was able to shed light also on the political behavior of that "Asian mystery" who so greatly puzzled other contemporaries.

Understandably, Brandes had an ambivalent attitude toward Disraeli's "Semitism," which had antagonized many of Britain's politicians, historians, and men of letters. Against the chorus of condemnation by such diverse personalities as William Thackeray, George Eliot, and Matthew Arnold, Brandes evinced considerable sympathy for this British statesman who, by the very flaunting of his Jewish antecedents, forced his way into the highest echelons of the aristocracy and the world of politics. Brandes, whose middle names were Morris Cohen, had himself experienced the effects of anti-Jewish discrimination in 1872: Against general expectations, he had failed to become professor of esthetics at the University of Copenhagen, the University preferring to leave the chair vacant because it could not find any candidate even remotely comparable to Brandes as a scholar and lecturer.

On the other hand, writing his *Lord Beaconsfield* in Berlin during the first upsurge of racial antisemitism after 1873, the Danish biographer could not quite tolerate Disraeli's "Semitism" in which he sensed but another facet of the same fallacy. Like many liberals of the day, he indulged the belief that the Jewish question would quickly disappear if only the Jews would "accept the all-embracing modern religion of humanity." He saw in Disraeli "not only a distinguished representative of Judaism, but . . . the last Jew." History has shown that both men had tried to oversimplify a problem which, as Wilhelm von Humboldt had observed long before them, some of humanity's best minds had despaired of solving.

It is remarkable that Brandes, the literary historian, had relatively little to say about Disraeli as a writer. Although his book follows the pattern of Disraeli's literary creativity and devotes a chapter to each major novel and essay, Brandes employs few strictly literary criteria and only tangentially deals with Disraeli's prose and literary techniques. Nor does he try to place him within the framework of contemporary English literature, in which Disraeli had achieved high standing. After all, while still in his early twenties, the novelist had received a laudatory letter from Goethe and a favorable review from Heine. William Thackeray, who had little use for Disraeli's political views and in fact exposed the latter's *Coningsby* to public ridicule in a satirical counterpart entitled *Codingsby*, later spoke admiringly of the "literary hero who at twenty years of age astonished the world with his brilliant story of 'Vivian Grey'; who in a little time afterwards and still in the youthful period of his life, amazed and delighted the public with the wondrous tale of 'Alroy.' "

Brandes realized that the Disraelian novel, however artistically conceived and executed, was only a vehicle for the exposition of the political, theological, and social ideas of the author, who had early in his career declared through the mouthpiece of one of his romantic heroes that he would rather be a Caesar than a Homer, a Napoleon than a Shakespeare. It is, indeed, Brandes's permanent merit to have distilled from the endless dialogues in Disraeli's tales his basic teachings in their progression through the years. He understood the difficulties of writing a biography of a personality so changeable and scintillating as Lord Beaconsfield's. In such cases, he declared, "mere literary criticism must become psychological, and psychology must embrace the emotions of the individual soul and the spirit of the age." Armed with these ideas, Brandes succeeded in relating Disraeli's literary art and his all-embracing passion for the "art of politics."

SALO W. BARON

New York City
November, 1965

CONTENTS

Lord Beaconsfield

INTRODUCTION

❧ It is usual to draw a decided distinction between politicians and literary men. There seems to be a great gulf between the men of letters and the men of action. Every one can bring forward instances to show that distinguished *savants*, orators, poets, and professors have shown a want of common sense or political ability if they have left the paths of literature for the career of a statesman. We have often seen political theorists condemned to play but a subordinate part, or to exercise but a temporary influence, in the parliament of their country, and humanitarian poets, like Lamartine, who have wearied the national assembly with their lyrics, and whose political career has been confined to a single great moment. As a rule, then, eminent literary ability precludes political action, and, *vice versa*, political action suppresses the development of literary powers. Practical politicians, therefore, often somewhat undervalue those who come to politics fresh from the ranks of literature; while, on the other hand, men of speculative tendencies and refined culture are apt to have something of the same feeling towards the men of eminent administrative or diplomatic talents; and when, like Renan, for example, they see their fine-spun political theories rejected, they find compensation for their wounded pride in the idea that shrewd and worldly wise mediocrity, in most cases, suffices for the politician.

Nevertheless, there is an aspect under which leading statesmen become literary characters, and fall within the sphere of the literary critic. Within certain limits, every political magnate has a literary side. At any rate, there are his speeches and letters, and Carlyle has shown how much insight may be gained from the letters and speeches of even so illiterate a statesman as Cromwell.

These productions have also, for the most part, a direct literary value; for a superior man, whatever his education may have been, generally finds expression for his thoughts in a way peculiar to himself: he is original, that is, he is in possession of the secret, often withheld from many an author by profession, of characterizing or caricaturing a person or subject by some mimic or graphic word.

Still, in spite of the contrast between theoretical and practical men, a long series of exceptions has shown that literary and political talents may be found united. The political historian is sometimes transformed into the practical politician, and there are still more instances of the transition from politics to history. Cicero and Thiers were at once eminent authors and statesmen, Julius Cæsar and Frederick the Great were both men of literary tastes, and were at the same time politicians and military geniuses.

Artistic, and still more poetic, gifts are, in the case of leading statesmen, very rare, the rarest of all. Cavour was a good speaker; Bismarck is an excellent speaker, but he is not a born orator, nor was Cavour, who was entirely without artistic training; near the close of his life, after a visit to Tuscany, he said, "I have discovered in myself a taste which I did not know that I possessed—the taste for art," a saying which accords with what he used to say when conversation turned to this subject: "I cannot make a sonnet, but I can make Italy." Scarcely any one would suspect Bismarck of secret poetical productions; a romance or a poem from him sounds still more improbable than a sonnet by Cavour. Yet there are so many literary productions by his hand, that a shrewd critic might try to delineate his character from them; but it would be anything but exhaustive: it is only in his actions that we see the whole man; the chief characteristics of a statesman such as he is are concealed from the eyes of the literary critic.

It is all the more interesting for the critic, when by a solitary chance, one of the leading statesmen of Europe is also a distinguished author, a poet, and a politician, who has portrayed his own character and given us his ideas in his works. The critic hereby gains an insight, seldom granted him, into the psychology of such a personage. Each work by his hand is an instrument which he has fabricated for us himself, wherewith we may penetrate into the workshop of his ideas; each book that he has written is a window through which we may look into his mind. Each train of thought which he has revealed to us, every character he has devised, every feeling that he has described, contains, partly, a series of confessions which he has consciously laid bare, and which must be carefully examined, as well as a series of involuntary confessions running parallel to them, which may be detected; only no attempt should be made to extract them by force, or you would be apt only to extract what you had yourself put in. If the critic be on his guard, both as regards himself and the author, these literary productions will afford him more than mere literary insight; for the ideas and sentiments expressed belong to the statesman, and not to him in his character of novelist alone; they are the outcome of his whole character as a man, which is the common source and deepest spring of his political and literary gifts.

It will be my endeavour to apply a literary-critical method to the present Prime Minister of England. The study of the statesman Lord Beaconsfield, through the novelist Benjamin Disraeli, is attractive to me. Complete materials for the task I do not possess, as I write of a man still living, and whom I have only seen and heard from a distance, as many others have seen and heard him, and for knowledge of whom not a single special source is open to me. After careful perusal of what already exists on the subject, I hope that my method of treating it will be found new. Lord Beaconsfield's writings have not yet been made the subject of conscientious study, unbiassed by party spirit. The portrait of the author has been painted in turn by Whigs and Tories, political foes and political friends, and hate or partisanship has mingled the colours. To me Disraeli is neither an object of admiration nor dislike, but simply a highly original and interesting character; and after long study of it, I have not been able to resist the desire to reproduce it on paper.

I

THE FAMILY

◆§ It is only in royal and ancient noble families, in which the records of a long series of ancestors have been carefully preserved, that it is possible to trace with certainty the qualities inherited by an individual, and to follow the combinations and transformations which the mental faculties of the race have experienced in the course of time. Of the ancestors of eminent personages we generally know too few, and of the personages themselves too little, to study the process of the formation of their characters in the family.

Benjamin Disraeli is a descendant of one of the Jewish families compelled by the Spanish Inquisition to leave the Peninsula towards the end of the fifteenth century. These families, who, although expelled from Palestine, had never wandered from the originally civilized countries of ancient times—those in the Mediterranean basin, and who had never been exposed to a rigid climate uncongenial to the race, formed for a long time the natural aristocracy of the Jewish people. They had resided, happy and respected, partly in the large cities, partly on their estates in Aragon, Andalusia, and Portugal, for the acquisition of landed property was not then denied to them. Fanaticism afterwards deprived them, by one blow, of all their rights and hopes. Lord Beaconsfield's ancestors, therefore, took refuge in the Venetian Republic, and, according to a family tradition, as soon as they trod the soil of Venice, renounced their Spanish name, and "from gratitude to the God of Jacob, who had led them through unexampled trials, and unheard-of dangers," took the name of d'Israeli, by which the family was henceforth to be known. It grew and flourished without let or hindrance for more than two hundred years.

Towards the end of the eighteenth century, a member of the

family resolved to send his youngest son, Benjamin, to England, which seemed then to secure religious liberty to the Jews, and offered a favourable opening for commercial undertakings on a large scale. Religious liberty, however, was neither of long standing nor complete in England. The Jews had been expelled from the country long before they had been driven from Spain or Portugal. They were only tolerated from the reign of William the Conqueror to that of Richard Cœur de Lion; cruel persecutions then broke out, until, in 1290, the accusation which we meet with during all the Middle Ages, that they used the blood of slaughtered Christian children at their Easter sacrifices, caused them to be so ill treated and plundered that they finally had to leave the country.

A ballad in Percy's "Old English Ballads" shows that the popular fancy was constantly occupied with the banished race; these fellow-countrymen and murderers of the Redeemer, though the people had never seen them, became bloodthirsty monsters in their eyes; and in English literature, Marlowe's Barabbas and Shakespeare's Shylock are memorials of the superstitious disgust and terror which they inspired up to the period of the Renaissance. The "Jew of Malta" was, to a certain extent, the pattern for his fellow in the "Merchant of Venice." There was good reason, in both cases, for laying the scene in the countries bordering on the Mediterranean, for there were scarcely any Jews in England. But it was with less reason that in both dramas the southern Jew is represented as a type of cruelty; for while on the stage in England he poisoned his daughter and whetted his knife to slay his creditor, thousands of the race, of both sexes, in Spain and Portugal, chose rather to suffer martyrdom at the stake than to abjure the faith of their fathers. The most sorely tried martyrs of that age were represented on the English stage as murderers and hangmen.*

It was not until the time of the Commonwealth that, protected by Cromwell himself, though not by any law, the Jews began to return to England. Under George II, the Minister, Lord Pelham,

---

* "Studienreisen in England," p. 272, von Jul. Rodenberg. "Curiosities of Literature," introd., by Isaac d'Israeli.

was favourable to them, and during his ministry, Benjamin d'Israeli, the grandfather and namesake of Lord Beaconsfield, became, in the year 1748, an English citizen, without civil rights. His wife, who belonged to a family which had suffered much from persecution, and who was vain and ambitious, was ashamed of her Jewish origin, and by an ignoble, but not uncommon association of ideas, transferred her embitterment at belonging to a despised caste from the oppressors to the oppressed. Meanwhile, her energetic husband quickly made a fortune, bought an estate, laid out a garden in the Italian style, entertained company, ate macaroni prepared by the Venetian consul in London, played whist, sang canzonets, and, "in spite of a wife who never forgave him his name, and a son who thwarted all his plans," he lived vigorous and happy till he was nearly ninety years of age.

In seeking precursors of the characteristics of the grandson, our attention is involuntarily arrested by the picture which he himself has given us of his grandfather. He was a man of warm blood, sanguine, enterprising, and successful, with a temperament never ruffled by disappointment, and a brain ever fertile in resources, even when one disaster followed quickly upon another.

It had always been the hope of this ambitious and practical merchant, who was, in 1815, a rival of the house of Rothschild, to found a finance dynasty; but this favourite scheme was frustrated by the exclusively literary tastes of his only son. Isaac d'Israeli (as he wrote his name) grew up misunderstood by both his parents, and without ever having a good word from his mother, who foresaw a life of humiliation for her son. His first poem excited real terror in his parents' house. He was sent to school in Amsterdam, in order that he might forget his poetic fancies; but the schoolmaster, a negligent man, lived and moved in the atmosphere of the eighteenth century, and had a large library of the authors of that age, which young d'Israeli eagerly devoured. Before he was fifteen he had read Voltaire, and tried his strength on Bayle; at eighteen he returned to England, a disciple of Rousseau. His stay at home was but short. His father told him that he had decided to send him away again—this time to a large mercantile house at Bordeaux. The incorrigible literary son answered that he had written a great poem against trade as the ruin of mankind. Instead of Bordeaux, he contented himself with going to Paris, where, until 1788, he spent his time in libraries and among *savants*. In England, he soon after began to publish poetical attempts, as well as those annals, or rather anecdotes of literature, which made his name as an author, though they are remarkable neither for spirit nor accuracy.

The character of the quiet man of letters and bookworm forms in many respects a marked contrast to that of his son. At first sight, it is like the contrast between a learned Benedictine monk in his quiet cell, and a restless tribune, whose life is passed amidst the turmoil of the forum. Isaac d'Israeli was of a shy and retiring nature; in his youth he was inclined to melancholy; in manhood he was a collector; as an old man he was given up to contemplation, too critical to be satisfied with his own performances, and too retiring ever to gain confidence in himself. Not even his growing reputation could give it him, for he best knew his own shortcomings, and he felt an inward schism between himself and the spirit of the age. In a literary point of view, he stood in England beneath a waning star; he was a disciple of Pope and Boileau. Nevertheless, he saw the necessity, even by reason of his early enthusiasm for Rousseau, of giving more scope and freer play to nature and passion in poetry, without, on the other hand, possessing the powers of mind which would have enabled him to anticipate the coming change in English poetry. When the great naturalistic revolution in the literature of England was proclaimed and carried out by others, he was no longer young or pliant enough to take part in the movement. He lived for literature, but when he was young literature was old, and when he was old it had renewed its youth. The results of this discrepancy were, on the one hand, the continual secret distrust of his own powers, which is a weakness; on the other, utter absence of vanity, always rare, and especially so in an author. Neither the weakness nor the virtue was inherited by his famous son. The simple bookworm produced a self-confident bravado, who has had both adroitness enough to conform to the powers that be, and power so to transform the tendencies of the age, that they have taken the stamp of his mind and will.

Even in outward things there is a contrast between father and son. Isaac d'Israeli lived in seclusion. When at home, although a married man, he generally spent the whole day and evening in his library; his only diversion in London was going from one bookseller's to another. It would be scarcely possible to imagine a greater contrast than his son, who bears the complete stamp of a man of the world. But the contrast is still more striking when they are compared in their relations to politics. The father not only never took part in politics, he did not even understand them. It is clear that the son did not inherit his practical political vocation from his father.

And yet nature was experimenting with Isaac d'Israeli's mind, and laying the foundations for larger abilities. First, his literary studies and tastes were of great importance for his son. Nothing tends more to easy and rapid acquisition of faculty in the use of language than a literary forerunner in the race. Then some of the deepest primary faculties in Benjamin Disraeli's mind are obviously derived from his father. He was, in many respects, a genuine child of the eighteenth century, and everything in his son's mind which is in unison with the character and style of that age was inherited in a direct line. In a literary point of view, the father was not much more than a living lexicon of authors, but a lexicon of the times of the Encyclopædists; he had early laid aside the prejudices of his contemporaries, in order to imbibe their philosophy, and was a decided, though quiet free-thinker, destitute of a creed both in the literal or intellectual sense of the word. In 1833 he published a work called "The Genius of Judaism," in which he ridicules, from a deistic standpoint, the Israelitish constitution of the Mosaic laws and regulations about health and food, regarded as revealed and eternal truth. He long entertained a project of writing a history of the English free-thinkers. He was all his life an unprejudiced sceptic, with a tendency to sarcastic wit.

This keen and negative quality is also the first to show itself

in the son. The mystical and romantic Benjamin Disraeli begins as
a satirist. The first part of "Vivian Grey," "Popanilla," "Ixion in
Heaven," and "The Infernal Marriage," are so many satires in the
spirit of the eighteenth century. "Vivian Grey" is a type for
Beaumarchais; "Popanilla," a fantastic journey in Swift's style; the
family descent of the two mythological tales is to be traced
to no less a person than Lucian; they would certainly not disgrace
Voltaire, of whom they remind one, and might, without profana-
tion, be set to music by Offenbach, so blasphemous are they against
the gods of Greece. We should not understand anything of the
character of Benjamin Disraeli if we overlooked the fact that even
his theories and fantasies, which bear the strongest impress of the
great romantic reaction, had been, without exception, disinfected
by born scepticism and early developed critical faculty. Even in
his castles in the air, you do not find the malaria arising from the
Maremmas of superstition and prejudice; they are the Fata
Morganas of the desert, the products, consciously constructed, of
an arid and fiery fantasy; by careful observation they may be easily
distinguished from the structures of dreamland and reverie, which
owe their existence to *naïve* and thorough mysticism.

Not only the critical and negative, but also the positive, romantic, Conservative tendencies of Benjamin Disraeli are derived from
his father. The old *littérateur*, although Radical in a religious sense,
had an instinctive liking for the Tory way of thinking. He was
attracted by the house of Stuart; he laboured for five years on his
work on the reign of Charles I, and received for it an Oxford
diploma, with the dedication, "Optimi regis optimo vindici;" he
considered his work on James I a literary matter of conscience. In
both cases it was his conviction that he was the vindicator of men
who had been misunderstood, but it was not mere accident that
they were both crowned heads who coveted absolute power, and
were defeated in the struggle with Puritanism and parliament. The
son has followed in his father's footsteps in these sympathies; in
sundry passages in his writings he has broken a lance for the
Stuarts; he has adopted and defended the title of "martyr" for

Charles I, and he even says, in "Sybil," that never did a man die
a hero's death for a greater cause—the cause of the Church and
the poor. That these two unpopular monarchs of former times were
dissenters from the dominant religion has, perhaps, conduced to
ensure sympathy with authors who sprung from a dissenting body.
It is plain, however, that the younger Disraeli, however little Conservative when he first appeared as a politician, was not influenced
by political Radicalism in the parental home. With the Voltairean
opinions which then prevailed in good society, he received, much
earlier, some germs of decided Toryism, germs which were en-
veloped in a certain spirit of opposition to the popular conception
of the political history of England, but which, under favourable
circumstances, were strong enough to develop themselves.

We know too little of Disraeli's mother to judge what qualities
he may have inherited from her. She died after forty-five years
of married life, in her seventy-second year. He seems to consider
that he derived his faculties exclusively from the paternal side. And
we find in the practical energy and enterprising character of the
grandfather, the complement of the purely literary and contempla-
tive nature of the father, which seems to be necessary to weld and
polish the practical and literary gifts of a descendant of the race
into a two-edged sword.

As the son of Isaac d'Israeli, the future statesman was born not
only with a certain range of qualities, but in a somewhat excep-
tional social position. Authors then enjoyed higher consideration
in Great Britain than now, and the elder d'Israeli had a popular
and respected name. Besides his colleagues, among whom the poet
and epicure Samuel Rogers was his friend, he was acquainted with
many of the enlightened politicians and aristocrats of the day.
The son, therefore, from his youth saw many distinguished men
and women in his father's house, and the father's name opened
many an aristocratic house to the son. The advantage generally
enjoyed by the born aristocrat alone of having in early youth made
acquaintances and connections which are otherwise the reward
of long years of labour, was richly enjoyed by the young Disraeli.

In his youthful works there are now and then traces that he was
not unaware of the advantage of having such a father. Vivian Grey
likes to hear his famous father praised; in the "Young Duke"
Disraeli dwells on the benefit, even to a boy, of having a living
proof that the family blood is good for something, and says:
"There is no pride like the pride of ancestry, for it is a blending
of all emotions." And while the author seems involuntarily to be
comparing his lot with that of the aristocracy, he continues: "How
immeasurably superior to the herd is the man whose father only is
famous! Imagine, then, the feelings of one who can trace his
line through a thousand years of heroes and of princes!" *

Disraeli's singular pride of ancestry goes far beyond pride in his
distinguished father; but while his descent was necessarily only a
disadvantage to him in a worldly point of view, and was the chief
obstacle in his path, his position as his father's son gave him the
start in the course offered him by destiny in the great European
race for fame and distinction.

* "The Young Duke," p. 88.

NOTE: The edition referred to throughout is Lord Beaconsfield's Novels
and Tales in 10 vols. Great pains have been taken to find all the quotations,
but as in many cases no references are given in the original work, a few very
short ones have eluded me, and may not be quite verbatim.—TR.

II

BOYHOOD

◆§ Benjamin Disraeli himself gives 1805 as the year of his birth, but he really seems to have been born on 21st of December, 1804.* His mother, Maria Basevi, bore first a daughter, Sarah, then three sons, of whom he was the eldest. He was received into the Jewish community; but when his father afterwards separated himself from it—if report speaks truly—he gave his friend Samuel Rogers leave to take him to church and have him baptized. Rogers was totally indifferent to religion, but it seemed to him a pity—so it is said—that this fine, intelligent boy should be excluded by his creed from the most important civil rights and highest social advantages. Anyhow, the baptism took place in the parish of St. Andrews, on 31st of July, 1817. In the church registers, Benjamin Disraeli is spoken of as "about twelve years old."

He was sent to a private school at Winchester, and was afterwards placed for a short time in a lawyer's office. All desired information as to his inner life in his boyhood and early youth may be found in his novels. We learn from "Vivian Grey" and "Contarini Fleming," which contain unmistakable autobiographical elements relating to these years, what we should expect, that in this early period of Disraeli's life humiliations abounded as well as triumphs. In both books the hero is the decided favourite among the boys, from his abilities, his boldness, and his talents as a leader, and is acknowledged, so to speak, unanimously, as the cleverest and most original boy in the school. His English essays and verses are admired and copied. In short, he is the popular hero, while he regards his schoolfellows as beings whom he is resolved to rule. But behind all this popularity, the possibility of a general hatred is con-

* Picciotto: "Sketches of Anglo-Jewish History," p. 300.

cealed, not only the envy which always pursues success, but fierce ill will of a special kind, brutal in its origin, and cruel in its exercise —in a word, the hatred of race. When the usher's dislike to Vivian Grey first breaks out, he uses the expression, "seditious stranger;" and no sooner has the word been given, than his schoolfellows join in with, "No stranger! no stranger!" * This expression does not find its motive in the book, for in no sense of the word can Vivian Grey be called a stranger in the school. The word has obviously crept into the novel from some reminiscence of the author's childhood; only it was not the word used in reality, which more decidedly pointed to a foreign nationality, and sounded far more contemptuous.

On this subject, "Contarini Fleming" comes still nearer the truth, in which the hero, with his southern appearance and Italian descent, finds himself unhappy among his fair half-brothers in the north. "They were called my brothers, but Nature gave the lie to the reiterated assertion. There was no similitude between us. Their blue eyes, their flaxen hair, and their white visages, claimed no kindred with my Venetian countenance. Wherever I moved I looked around me, and beheld a race different from myself. There was no sympathy between my frame and the rigid clime whither I had been brought to live."†

If we add to the Venetian type the still deeper Israelitish stamp, and to the national contrast the religious prejudice as it existed in an English school in 1820, we shall be able to form an idea of Disraeli's feelings when he emerged from his father's house into boy's estate, and found that he was not looked upon as an equal, but as a "foreigner" of lower caste. Such an impression in those early years is one of the deepest which can be received—one of those never effaced from sensitive and aristocratic minds. To feel yourself disgraced without being conscious of any fault! To be looked down upon because of your appearance, your father, your people, your religion, your race! A poor boy among rich ones, an illegitimate child among legitimate, a Catholic among Protestants, a de-

---

* "Vivian Grey," p. 9.   † "Contarini Fleming," p. 5.

formed boy among well-grown schoolfellows, feels himself, each in his own way, thrust aside and humiliated. But a Jewish boy in a Christian school of the old-fashioned sort felt something of what all these feel put together. He learnt for the first time that he was a Jew, and all that the name implies. He discovered that he was not reckoned as one of the people among whom he lived, had no part in the deeds of their forefathers or in their history, but was an isolated being: and yet was constantly thrown with others, whom he did not know and had never seen before; who regarded him as ugly, nay, even repulsive; to whom his mode of speaking was ridiculous, nay, even repugnant; and who pointed at him the finger of scorn. In the reading lessons, a Jew was inevitably a ridiculous, vulgar, or mean and avaricious person, a cheat, a usurer, or a coward. And in the same class, or one close by, there was sure to be another boy of Jewish origin, whose countenance was branded with the mark of slavery, abject and degraded to the last degree, made to be a scapegoat and clown; and at every blow struck at this poor wretch, he felt his own cheek burn, and every dastardly act of his was felt to be his own shame. Even when, by severe struggles, he had won comparative immunity for himself, he had not the slightest power to protect his brother Jew, or to secure this caricature of himself from general contempt and brutality. And why should he suffer all this? Not at home, but at school did he find the answer. His people, who once in far distant ages were the blest and chosen people, were now cursed and rejected, were suffering the penalty for a crime committed by their fathers nearly two thousand years ago. O ignominy! Unconsciously and against his will, to belong to this despised and accursed nation! Was not his grandmother at Enfield in the right in denying her kinship with them; and was it not the most natural thing in the world to hate them himself, and thus to acquire the right to be considered an exception?

But this question could not be seriously entertained; for see all these scornful looks, these mocking, disdainful glances; listen to this calling of names behind your back, to these challenges which must be accepted and outbidden. In both the above-named youthful novels of Disraeli, the hero has in his school days a great decisive fight with a boy put forward by the hatred of a whole clique. In both he considers that a great wrong has been done him, and in both he takes revenge. But in his method of doing it, the character of the author is revealed no less plainly than that of the hero. Vivian Grey revenges himself on the faithless comrades who have left him in the lurch with a tyrannical teacher, by a method projected in cold blood and relentlessly carried out. In the next half-year he gains favour with this teacher, employs him first as an instrument of torture for the other boys, and in the end gives him up to them as a victim, while he keeps them off from himself with a loaded pistol. He leaves the school, saying that if he could devise a new and exquisite method of torture he would apply it to this teacher, who was the first to apply the word "stranger" to him. Contarini Fleming revenges himself with less forethought, but not the less completely. He does it in a boxing match with a much bigger boy; he falls upon him like a wild beast, and throws him to the ground. Consider the following passage:—"He was up again in a moment; and indeed, I would not have waited for their silly rules of mock conduct, but have destroyed him in his prostration. But he was up again in a moment." *

How characteristic is this turn! Contarini does not respect the accepted rules of the combat, any more than Vivian shrinks from deception as a means; thirst for revenge in both cases is so keen that it causes all other considerations to be forgotten. Read Contarini's account of it:

"Again I flew upon him. He fought with subtle energy, but he was like a serpent with a tiger. I fixed upon him: my blows told with the rapid precision of machinery. His bloody visage was not to be distinguished. I believe he was terrified by my frantic air.

"I would never wait between the rounds. I cried out in a voice of madness for him to come on. There was breathless silence. They were thunderstruck. . . . Each time that he came forward I made

* "Contarini Fleming," p. 37.

the same dreadful spring, beat down his guard, and never ceased working upon his head, until at length my fist seemed to enter his very brain; and, after ten rounds, he fell down quite blind. I never felt his blows; I never lost my breath.

"He could not come to time. I rushed forward; I placed my knee upon his chest. 'I fight no more,' he faintly cried.

" 'Apologize!' I exclaimed—'apologize!' He did not speak.

" 'By heavens, apologize!' I said, 'or I know not what I shall do.'

" 'Never!' he replied.

"I lifted up my arm. Some advanced to interfere. 'Off!' I shouted. 'Off, off!' I seized the fallen chief, rushed through the gate, and dragged him like Achilles through the mead. At the bottom there was a dunghill. Upon it I flung the half-inanimate body.

"I strolled away to one of my favourite haunts. I was calm and exhausted; my face and hands were smeared with gore. I knelt down by the side of the stream, and drank the most delicious draught that I had ever quaffed." *

The sweetness of the draught was in the revenge—complete revenge. One sees the natural character of this first brood of Disraeli's boys. There is not one drop of the milk of human kindness in their blood—no higher law than an eye for an eye in their souls. It seems as if these young fellows had suffered too cruelly in early childhood to be able to restore their equanimity in any other way than by procuring inviolability for themselves by methods equally cruel, and by quaffing long and repeated draughts of revenge.

* "Contarini Fleming," p. 37.

III

YOUTHFUL AMBITION

&ampampamp Benjamin Disraeli was, by the general consent of his contemporaries, as a boy and youth, very handsome. He had long,
raven-black locks; eyes sparkling with spirit and intelligence; a
good nose; a mouth round which there was a restless, nervous
play; and a complexion striking from its romantic paleness. He
was everywhere found attractive, and often petted both by men
and women. Men were delighted with his shrewd questions and
witty replies; and from women he seems to have early learnt what
he said in his first book, when scarcely twenty years of age, that
the only rival which a clever man has to fear is a precocious boy.

What was going on meanwhile in the restless mind which was
revealed by this expressive exterior? Wild dreams, passionate affections, longings for knowledge, and paroxysms of thirst for learning. Disraeli shows himself in his earliest works so amazingly
precocious in worldly wisdom, in fashion, and in penetrating,
sarcastic observation, that an inattentive reader might take him for
a purely outward-bound character, who had, so to speak, over-
leapt that first stage of development, in which a youth is self-
engrossed, searches deep into his own heart, weighs his capabilities
in secret, and tries the elasticity and extent of his powers. But he
could not really have escaped any of it; it only appears so because he passed through all these stages with great rapidity as a
boy, while with many Germanic natures it occupies the first
lustrum of manhood. Neither vague dreams, fantastic visions of the
future, doubt, nor lassitude were spared him. "Contarini Fleming"
is witness that he was acquainted with it all; but the result of the
ordeal was as favourable as it was rapidly attained. His brain was
fertile, and gave birth to dreams, fancies, schemes, intrigues, which

in their turn gave birth to new ones. He was full of courage; he was not only undaunted, he sought for adventures, and the intriguer in his brain was the born ally of the adventurer in his breast. The result of his self-examination was absolute confidence in his powers and in his future. *Forti nihil difficile*, the words which Disraeli inscribed upon his banners at his first election, were, long before they were formulated into a motto, the watchword which coursed with the blood in his veins.

This confidence in himself is a feature of his character. While gifted people, doubtful of themselves have to contend with an ever-recurring discouragement, and characters in which the moral element predominates are always trying to make new conquests in order to gain self-esteem, and cannot feel it before they have earned it, young Disraeli felt sure of his abundant resources, lost no time in listening to the moral lectures of the inward monitor, allowed life and destiny—which with its smiles and frowns, soon seemed to him the most impressive of moralists—to take care of his education, and, from his first entrance on man's estate, he felt himself to be an object of respect to himself and of value to others.

Wherever a fund of talent exists, there is a certain force which impels it to develop itself, and prevents the individual from standing still by continual excitement of the faculties. The love of gain, of acquisition, was a force of this kind with Disraeli's immediate ancestors; love of action and zeal for reform are frequent forms of it with persons of literary or political tastes. Let us inquire what was the original motive power in his case.

There is a very convenient psychological-critical method which has often been applied to the present Prime Minister of England, which consists of identifying him with one of the creations of his own brain, and boldly ascribing to him every sentiment and every dishonourable thought of this character; but criticism requires more delicate instruments than such biographers employ.

It is not in the rough outlines of a work, still less in the moral quality, greater or less, of the characters described, that criticism finds vouchers for the *ego* of the author; but in casual expressions, turns of thought which serve as exemplifications; in the choice of metaphors; in lyrical outbursts, which do not belong to the course of the narrative, but which will make way for themselves because they fill the soul of the writer, and he is unable to restrain them.

Suppose, for example, that an author has been early struck with the impossibility of knowing the human soul from books, and wishes to illustrate the opinion by instances; we may be sure that the first examples which come to his lips will be those with which his own experience has furnished him. Disraeli exemplifies it as follows:—"A man may be constantly searching into the hearts of his fellow men in his study, and yet have no idea of the power of ambition or the strength of revenge." Ambition is the first example that occurs to him; and it is this passion which, in all his early writings, is the source of the joys and sorrows of all the characters.

In "Vivian Grey" he says: "For a moment he mused over Power; but then he, shuddering, shrank from the wearing anxiety, the consuming care, the eternal vigilance, the constant contrivance, the agonizing suspense, the distracting vicissitudes of his past career. Alas! it is our nature to sicken from our birth after some object of unattainable felicity, to struggle through the freshest years of our life in an insane pursuit after some indefinite good, which does not even exist! . . . We dream of immortality until we die. Ambition! at thy proud and fatal altar we whisper the secrets of our mighty thoughts, and breathe the aspirations of our inexpressible desires. A clouded flame licks up the offering of our ruined souls, and the sacrifice vanishes in the sable smoke of Death." *

One hears both the soaring flight and the melancholy of ambition in this lament. Will it succeed? Will my powers be equal to it? We find these questionings now and then in Disraeli's earliest works, but far more frequently as to the issue than as to his own powers. In "The Young Duke" there is a page where the narrator suddenly steps out of the book, and, with youthful want of self-restraint, entertains the reader with an account of the place where he writes, of himself, and his inner life:

* "Vivian Grey," p. 356.

"Amid the ruins of eternal Rome I scribble pages lighter than the wind, and feed with fancies volumes which will be forgotten ere I can hear that they are even published. Yet am I not one insensible to the magic of my memorable abode, and I could pour my passion o'er the land; but I repress my thoughts, and beat their tide back to their hollow caves. . . .

"For I am one, though young, yet old enough to know Ambition is a demon; and I fly from what I fear. And Fame has eagle wings, and yet she mounts not so high as man's desires. . . .

"Could we but drag the purple from the hero's heart; could we but tear the laurel from the poet's throbbing brain, and read their doubts, their dangers, their despair, we might learn a greater lesson than we shall ever acquire by musing over their exploits or their inspiration. Think of unrecognized Cæsar, with his wasting youth, weeping over the Macedonian's young career? Could Pharsalia compensate for those withering pangs?

"View the obscure Napoleon starving in the streets of Paris! What was St. Helena to the bitterness of such existence? The visions of past glory might illumine even that dark imprisonment; but to be conscious that his supernatural energies might die away without creating their miracles: can the wheel or the rack rival the torture of such a suspicion?" *

This direct address is out of all connection with the book, and forms, with its pathetic lyrical flight, a remarkable contrast to the fashionable, and, now and then, affected frivolous tone of the novel. The words were keenly felt, and it was hard to suppress them. As one who is possessed of some secret cannot sometimes deny himself the satisfaction of giving a hint of it in some way not observed by others, though his interest is deeply involved in its concealment, the young author apparently could not refrain from producing an effect by tearing the mask of the elegant author from his face in one passage of his books, and suddenly disclosing to the reader his real visage, furrowed by the sufferings and temptations of ambition.

Ambition as such is not immoral; it is in itself neither moral nor

* "Young Duke," p. 82.

immoral, but natural, and it only receives a moral impress from its
means and ends. It varies according to whether its object is chiefly
fame or power. In Disraeli's case, desire for fame and love of power
were both direct products of his self-esteem, though they were
scarcely of equal strength. In case of need, he would rather have
contented himself with power without fame, than with fame without power. It appears to me that if he had had his choice, whether
to be the powerful president of a secret tribunal, or a Tasso feted
at Ferrara, he would have chosen the former. But the two objects
have certainly never been separated in his aspirations, although he
felt his relations towards them to be different. He saw fame before
him as if he could grasp it, extort it by his talents; there was,
therefore, no need to gain over or flatter any one; he would,
perhaps, attain it best by challenges on all sides. Power was far off,
very far, and was only to be attained step by step; the path was
slippery and tortuous; but he was firmly resolved to spare no
pains, to shrink from no humiliation, no trial of patience, that
might lead to the goal. And the goal was an actual one. While
honour is in its very nature relative, indefinite in quality, and you
may always long for more, the power to which a man may hope
to attain is something definite. Young Disraeli longed at all events
for the highest power, and if, with his southern blood and fantastic
tendencies in boyhood, we may conjecture that he dreamed of dark
conspiracies and secret societies, before long the brilliant and safe
position of a prime minister presented itself to him as the real
object of desire. No sooner did he begin to write than he began
to portray prime ministers, and with equal imaginative faculty
and political sagacity.

The two novels in which they occur, "Vivian Grey" and
"Contarini Fleming," both bear the stamp of psychological
biographies, and each is the complement of the other. They contain
forecasts of his own training, both as a politician and a novelist.
Vivian Grey, the hero of the earlier work, is a young man inclined
to politics, with talents for authorship; Contarini Fleming, on the
contrary, is an imaginative youth, with talents for politics; both

have a passion for power and fame. But that to Disraeli power appears to be the chief good, is betrayed most clearly in the career of the novelist, in which we should not, *a priori*, have expected to find love of power so strongly accented.

The task which, according to his own statement, Disraeli set himself in "Contarini Fleming," was to portray the development of a poetic character; he aimed at giving us his "Wilhelm Meister," with this difference—that his hero was to mature for poetry, and Goethe's for the realities of life. Ambition is often a part of the poetic nature, but it may be latent, and only betray itself in discreet and quiet ways. Goethe's "Meister" is only ambitious in this way. But let us hear the poet in Disraeli describe himself as a schoolboy. "Indeed, existence was intolerable, and I should have killed myself had I not been supported by my ambition, which now each day became more quickening, so that the desire of distinction and of astounding action raged in my soul; and when I recollected that, at the soonest, many years must elapse before I could realize my ideas, I gnashed my teeth in silent rage, and cursed my existence." *

Years go by, and the poet, whose father is a distinguished politician, has suffered his first defeats and won his first spurs. In moments of self-confidence, he saw his genius and destiny struggling for life or death, and the struggle ended with his "sitting on a brilliant throne, and receiving the laurel wreath from an enthusiastic people." But politics are always almost as attractive to him as literature; through his father's influence he is appointed to the post of under secretary of state, and gains a decided triumph in the councils of the nation by his decision and presence of mind. Would it not be said, on reading the following outburst, that this poet, contrary to the intention of the author, showed more political than poetical ambition, and a greater desire for power than for a famous name?—"I felt all my energies. I walked up and down the hall in a frenzy of ambition, and I thirsted for action. There seemed to me no achievement of which I was not capable, and of which I was

* "Contarini Fleming," p. 33.

not ambitious. In imagination I shook thrones and founded empires. I felt myself a being born to breathe in an atmosphere of revolution."*

At this moment his father comes to him and prophesies that he will become prime minister in the country in which they live (Scandinavia), and perhaps still more than that, which may mean in a country of more importance. The father is mistaken in his son's powers, for he soon returns to literature; but the mistake seems to us only too natural, for we do not often find a thirst like this for power and action in a poet, and by endowing him with these qualities Disraeli has unconsciously betrayed how universal he considers them. In the novel, the father and son discuss the question whether deeds or poetry, the fame of a statesman or the fame of a poet, is to be preferred, and the son decides for poetry; but it can scarcely be doubted that it is the father who expresses Disraeli's own opinion when he declares for the opposite view. In his preface to "Curiosities of Literature," by his own father, Disraeli afterwards said that an author may have a deeper influence over his contemporaries than a statesman, and that a book may be a greater thing than a battle or a congress. This was true, and it was his honest opinion; yet he did not mean or feel that it was true in his own case. He felt far more deeply what he made Contarini Fleming's father say, that a poet's lot was a sad one, and fame after death a poor compensation for the persecutions and deprivations in which the lives of the greatest poets have been passed. He early promised himself not to be content with posthumous fame. He never seriously doubted that action was above writing poetry, and Count Fleming speaks from his own heart when he says: "Would you rather have been Homer or Julius Cæsar, Shakespeare or Napoleon? No one doubts. Moralists may cloud truth with every possible adumbration of cant, but the nature of our being gives the lie to all their assertions. We are active beings, and our sympathy, above all other sympathies, is with great action."†

I have said that by endowing a poet in his youth with love of

* Ibid., p. 176.   † "Contarini Fleming," p. 155.

power, he betrayed his belief in the universality of the passion. Twelve years later, when he knew better than to give the public any picture of himself than such as would serve his ends, he writes again: "Fame and power are the objects of all men." He calls "thirst for power and desire for fame" the forces which call us out of social obscurity, and ambition the "divinity or the demon to which we all offer so many sacrifices." Power and fame are certainly not the objects of all men; they were not the objects of Franklin, Kant, or John Stuart Mill. It was not thirst for these things which called men like Spinoza or Newton from obscurity into immortality. All great men have not offered sacrifice to ambition. Washington sacrificed nothing to it, nor has Garibaldi. But in utterances like these the speaker unconsciously gives us contributions to his own psychology.

The first motive of his actions, then, was to raise himself, to quench the raging thirst for distinction. The source of this thirst was a born love of dominion, of ruling and influencing other men. A saying of Disraeli's in "Tancred" refers to this tendency when he is defending an ambitious Syrian emir from the charge of having only selfish aims: "Men certainly must be governed, whatever the principle of the social system, and Fakredeen felt born with a predisposition to rule." *

All depends on what it is that is sacrificed to this passion. And there can be no doubt that Disraeli soon came to the conclusion that it would not do to bargain and haggle too scrupulously. He was not made for a Stoic. Even his Vivian Grey stumbles, in his ambitious reflections, on the problem how it happens that so many great minds are thrust aside and misunderstood, and solves it by saying that these rare characters are too much engrossed with themselves to be able to study others. The cool and sagacious youth draws the following conclusion from it:—"Yes; we must mix with the herd; we must enter into their feelings; we must humour their weaknesses; we must sympathize with the sorrows that we do not feel, and share the merriment of fools."†

I certainly should not apply these words to the author him-

* "Tancred," p. 369.   † "Vivian Grey," p. 18.

self, if I had not found the same idea expressed in writings in which he speaks in his own name. Even in these he considers it justifiable to advocate views and sentiments which you do not share, in order to retain power, and to guide a movement which might otherwise have worse issues. In "The Crisis Examined," 1834, he says: "The people have their passions, and it is even the duty of public men occasionally to adopt sentiments with which they do not sympathize, because the people must have leaders."* A duty it never is, and it can only be justified in cases of urgent necessity; but if words such as these are not necessarily evidences of want of morality, they are undoubtedly the language of love of power.

That a man like Benjamin Disraeli was ambitious is only the secret of a Polichinello, a fact too generally acknowledged to need proof. But the term "ambitious" is but an empty word; it only expresses the abstract quality in which everything depends on the quantity and the method. The study of the man's early writings shows to what extent and in what way he was ambitious.

Ambitious, then, he was. And with this irresistible longing for power and mastery, he saw mountains of obstacles rise up between him and his desires. He was unknown, he was a commoner, without influential connections. England was a thoroughly aristocratic country, and full of prejudices, and he was—the son of a Jew. He had, it is true, been by accident formally introduced into the Christian Church, and thus the absolute obstacle to his political career was removed. But the baptized Jew was no nearer the goal than the unbaptized, the tokens of race and hatred of the race remained. One born a Jew the prime minister of a great Power! It was absurd; unheard of, since Joseph ruled Egypt as the favourite of Pharaoh. England was ruled by aristocrats, and what was he? A pariah.

A pariah—but why? And here query after query arose. Was, then, this mixed population of Saxons and Normans, among whom he had first seen the light, of purer blood than he? Oh no, he was descended in a direct line from one of the oldest races in the

* "Benjamin Disraeli, Earl of Beaconsfield," vol. I. p. 121.

world, from that rigidly separate and unmixed Bedouin race, who had developed a high civilization at a time when the inhabitants of England were going half naked, and eating acorns in their woods. He was of pure blood; and yet, strange to say, they regarded his race as of lower caste, and, nevertheless, they had adopted most of the laws and many of the customs, which constituted the peculiarity of this caste in their Arabian home. They had appropriated all the religion and all the literature of his fathers. They had acknowledged this literature to be sacred, inspired by God Himself, and this religion to be a revelation which might be supplemented, but could never be abolished. They divided their time by Jewish methods. They rested on the Sabbath, in accordance with a Jewish law, and it was observed by them scarcely less literally or fanatically than in the ancient land of the race. They considered it to be a virtue, even a duty, continually to study the history of his ancestors, and taught it to their children before teaching them the history of their own country. Week by week they sang in their churches the hymns, laments, and praises of the Jewish poets; and finally, they worshipped the Son of a Jewish woman as their God. Yet, nevertheless, they excluded with disdain from their society and their parliament, as if they were the offscouring of the earth, the race to which they owed their festivals, their psalms, their semi-civilization, their religion, and their God. He racked his brains. He was not a child who took legends for realities; he was a sharp-sighted youth, brought up by a sceptical *savant* in an eighteenth century library, who, when a boy, had learnt French out of Voltaire. His father had himself put the works of the great Frenchman into his hands, because, as a boy, he seemed disposed to lose himself in fantasies; and he had devoured the hundred volumes, had read them with laughter, with profound admiration, and bitter tears over the fate of humanity. It had been a revelation to him; the world's history had been transacted before his eyes—pedants and priests and tyrants; the folio volumes by blockheads, the funeral bells of inquisitors, the prisons of kings, and the wearisome, stupid system of deceit and

misgovernment which had so long sat as a nightmare on the breast
of nature—in a word, all our ignorance, all our weakness, and all
our folly presented themselves to his view. He did not need to ask
himself whether orthodoxy came forth unscathed from this long
indictment against the enemies of thought. But what was that
to him? Those who despised the Jewish race were always just
those who accepted revelation, while the Voltaireans had always
pleaded for toleration. Besides, he did not look at the question at
all from this dogmatic point of view. He took a practical view
of it. The Asiatic race to which he belonged had in an intellectual
sense conquered Europe, and the quarters of the world peopled by
Europeans. Northern Europe worshipped the Son of a Jewish
mother, and gave Him a place at the right hand of the Creator;
southern Europe worshipped besides, as Queen of Heaven, a Jewish
maiden; this was all the difference between the two religious parties
who agreed in contemning his people. He was proud of his descent
from a race which, scattered, banished, martyred, plundered, and
humiliated for thousands of years, by Egyptian Pharaohs, Assyrian
kings, Roman emperors, Scandinavian crusaders, Gothic chiefs, and
holy inquisitors, had still held their own, had kept their race pure,
and remained to this day irrepressible, inexhaustible, indispensable,
full of energy and genius. When he fell into this train of thought,
it seemed to him as if he were living through the whole history of
the race, and as if the whole race lived in him—all the departed
children of Israel in him, Disraeli; all those who had fallen asleep,
those who had died in obscure misery, insulted, tortured, burnt at
the stake—they lived in him and should receive satisfaction through
him. And what was it, then, with which this people were reproached now? With rejecting Christ and hating Him: He hate
Christ?—the fairest flower and the eternal pride of the Jewish race,
the son of the chosen royal family of the chosen people! Nay, no
one hates his own flesh and blood, and he was the kinsman of
Him whom his race was accused of hating. He, too, sprang from
a noble family among the people which was the aristocracy of
mankind.

Dreams! Idle dreams! He was really a pariah among the aristocracy of his country—aristocracy as they were called. Fine aristocrats, indeed! ancient nobility! A few of the most distinguished of them could, with difficulty, trace their pedigree back for eight hundred years to a troop of Norman knights, whose fathers were wreckers, Baltic pirates, to whom the elements of civilization had been communicated by priests who taught them the religion of Asia; and to whom did the rest of the great families owe their wealth and their nobility? The rank was often derived from some cunning chamberlain, who contrived to perform eye-service for some tyrannical king; or to some former club-house waiter, who had bought the title of baron, and the wealth had mostly one and the same source—plunder; only with this difference, that some fortunes had been made by sacrilege and plunder of monasteries during the Reformation so called, others by draining India during the so-called colonization of that country.*

And now to have to exclaim with the hero of his first book: " 'Curse my lot! that the want of a few rascal counters, and the possession of a little rascal blood, should mar my fortunes!' "†

* "Sybil," pp. 11, 89; "Tancred," p. 427.   † "Vivian Grey," p. 18.

IV

CHARACTERISTICS

✍ Let us imagine this passionate impulse to make way for himself, the first symptom of which is always a desire to attract attention, grafted upon a genuine Oriental temperament, and we shall not be surprised that Disraeli first exhibited himself in the curious character of a dandy.

The age had something to do with it. He was a youth when George IV was king, of whose pink suits and white silk waistcoats his contemporaries read long descriptions, and whose inventions in shoe-buckles and hat shapes were as much discussed as the inventions of *mitrailleuses* by other monarchs. And Disraeli entered the literary circles of good society at the time when Byron, not long before his death, was the idol of the clever English youth, and appeared to them to be poetry incarnate, as well as a model of anti-Philistinism. But Byron was the first instance in England of a mixture of romanticism which set all rules at defiance, and of coxcombry dictating the fashion. He had almost an equal desire to write verses which should be on everybody's tongue, and to excite astonishment by social caprices at variance with all the usages of society, and to introduce new ones. If George IV and he had nothing else in common, they were agreed in their admiration of Beau Brummell, the lion among the London dandies; and many of Disraeli's writings bear witness to the deep impression which had been made upon him in former years by Byron's person and poetry. His ideal of life at that period may be characterized by an expression of his own in one of his early works, "half passion, half fashion." * Nothing could be further from his thoughts than to adopt Goethe's well-known saying about good society:

* "The Young Duke," p. 224.

"It is called good when it affords no occasion for the least romance."* On the contrary, the life of the elegant world had for him all the poetry which it generally has for those originally excluded from it, and all the charm which it has for those to whom it is an object of ambition. This precociously polished youth—who did not for a moment doubt that he was, in mind and native nobility, the equal of lords and dukes, nay, rather their superior—felt himself instinctively attracted by the flutterings of the "golden youth," in the sunshine of fortune, and he early made it a speciality to describe high society. The type of "The Young Duke," published at the age of twenty-three, but obviously written before, is that which may be briefly described as the Pelham type: the young man of the world, endowed with abundant means, whose follies seem likely to ruin him, until it turns out that he is at bottom an honourable and chivalrous character, capable of renouncing all his follies and love of display, to marry a young and noble girl, who first disdains, then loves and forgives him. Bulwer's "Pelham" appeared in 1828. "The Young Duke" was written during the same time at Rome, and was published during the following year. Disraeli, perhaps, looks down at his man of the world from a more lofty height than Bulwer; he never holds him up to admiration; he likes him, and describes him with indulgence. Much is forgiven him because he is so thoroughly aristocratic, so in accord with his rank, so fashionable.

A dandy was at that time in England (as a few years later a romanticist was in France) a being who, from his appearance, his dress, and his mode of wearing his hair, laid claim to be regarded as a mortal out of the common run. With his Oriental love of show, Disraeli overstepped the line observed by the greatest dandies. He was handsome, and he knew it. We must imagine him not as he is as an old man, but as in his youthful portraits, with a wild, melancholy, poetic expression in the Byron style; with his beautiful thick hair parted on one side, so that the long glossy

* . . . mann nennt sie die gute
Wenn sie gum kleinsten Gedicht keine Gelegenheit giebt.

locks hung down low; with a broad, limp shirt-collar falling over the careless neck-tie; a velvet coat of unusual cut, lined with white silk; a waistcoat embroidered with flowers in gold; the hands half concealed with embroidered ruffles; the fingers covered with rings; the breast adorned with an armour of gold chains; and dancing shoes on his feet; in his hand an ivory cane, the handle inlaid with gold, carried by a silken tassel. *Voilà l'homme*, called Disraeli the younger, as he exhibited himself in London society, whose latest and brightest ornament he is, to an amused and astonished world! He is decked out like a woman, and more so than a woman of correct and refined taste.

Disraeli had the true appreciation of one who aspires to be a man of the world for the little finishing touches and advantages which stamp a young man as a man of fashion—especially when he not only rides the best horse, and drives the best cabriolet, but does it in such a way as to impose his own style on others instead of adopting theirs. We meet with this Brummell-worship in a number of Disraeli's novels. In "Vivian Grey," a German, Emilius von Asslingen, is introduced as an arbiter of fashion, who, without wealth or rank, and solely by following his own fantastic tastes without regard to anybody else, becomes the living model by which royal highnesses and dukes regulate their style. In "The Young Duke," the hero himself is a leader of fashion. In "Henrietta Temple," Disraeli introduces, under the fictitious name of Count Alcibiades de Mirabel, the leader of fashion in the England of that day, the well-known Count d'Orsay, and expresses without reserve his admiration for this reckless, amiable, and gifted Frenchman, who, with champagne in his veins, maintained his position all his life as dictator to the tailors and idol of the ladies. Better to be the first in the little empire of fashion than second in the political arena! Even Cæsar was a dandy in his youth.

In his earliest youth, then, Disraeli adroitly adopted the tone of the fashionable world; in society he was often silent, but was in the highest degree attractive when he told stories. He could use both flattery and banter, be cold and devoted at the right time and place; he could touch lightly on important subjects, and talk with humorous importance of trifles. To judge from his books, he has penetrated as deeply into the mysteries of the epicurean art as into that of the tailor. A man of the world does not only eat, he knows how to eat, and can not only drink, but make an impression by giving advice about the treatment of a Johannisberger or a Maraschino. A man of the world is not ashamed now and then to give a chapter from Brillat-Savarin. One finds in Disraeli valuable contributions to the physiology and æsthetics of the palate. His first descriptions of London high life swarm with hymns to ortolans: "Sweet bird! . . . all Paradise opens! Let me die eating ortolans to the sound of soft music!"—with odes to soups: "Ye soups! o'er whose creation I have watched, like mothers o'er their sleeping child!" * with the wildest expressions about the whiting, that "chicken of the ocean;" about the warm and sunny flavour of brown soup, the mild and moonlight deliciousness of white; about sherry with a pedigree as long as an Arab's, Rhine wine with a bouquet like the breath of woman. Wherewith can the flavour of a lobster salad be better compared than with the arts of a coquette? And how natural to conclude the comparison with a regret that a rendezvous with the lobster salad is not so harmless as that with the lady!

That is the style—a gastronomic humour springing from a lively and sensuous fancy, flavoured with a few drops of flippant, yet controlled, frivolity. It is the conversational tone of that day; in good society the sensuality inseparable from fiery youth must find vent in gastronomy; for good society, though it looks at sensuality itself through its fingers, does not permit some aspects of it to be mentioned. If you want to glorify sensual life within the limits prescribed by good society, you must sing the praises of soup. If you want to extol active life, you must treat every sort of sport with the gravity that it deserves. Sport banishes all superfluous care. "The sight of a pair of spurs is enough to drive away all thought of suicide."

* "The Young Duke," p. 33.

His father's library and London society were the first schools
through which young Disraeli passed; the short time spent in a
lawyer's office only initiated him a little into practical routine.
Strange to say, and characteristically enough, he had no university
training. Was he too practical to care for it, or too impatient to
submit to its restraints? One is ready to think it with the latter
when he speaks, in "Vivian Grey," of the "courage" which a
young politician has shown in immuring himself for three years in
a German university. But this much is clear, that the want of a
learned education has avenged itself, and perceptibly left something lacking in Disraeli's mind. It is all very well to despise the
wisdom gained from books, and to shrug your shoulders at pedants
and pedantry; but learning is not to be acquired from political
fantasies nor learnt in *salons*. Disraeli never learnt to respect
learning; he was not inoculated with it in early youth, when the
mind is open to such impressions; neither has he ever attained
scientific insight, for neither as a youth nor a man has he ever been
trained by scientific methods. In consequence of this, the germs of
fantasy and paradox, which were in his mind, were in conditions
only too favourable for growth. This also opened the way for a
curious, half-developed mysticism, a taste for the mysterious and
emotional, a curious preference for all unscientific knowledge and
ideas, if they have any historical or practical value, which are
opposed to reason. This is the explanation of Disraeli's employment
of the conjuring formulæ of the Cabbala as machinery in "Alroy,"
of his general habit of describing secret societies as potent forces in
history. If in the course of a story he can conceal himself behind
some mysterious apparatus, it has more interest for him than the
idea which underlies a cause or an action. When he is writing
of Jews, he represents them as connected together all over the
world as by a kind of freemasonry. When he is describing workmen, he loves best to present them in long robes, with masks on
their faces, ranged around a skeleton, initiating a novice into a
Trades Union by some hocus-pocus, as was the custom in the Holy
Vehm in mediæval Germany. He has described more than one of

the secret societies of European democracy with profound appreciation of the power exercised by them by means of some half-intelligible watchword; and through nearly all his works there runs a lively admiration of the Roman Catholic Church, with its active organization, mystical doctrines, magical means, and practical ends. With what pride he has referred to the fact, in more than one of his writings, that there were Jews among the first Jesuits, and how he respects the intelligence and power of the Jesuits! One asks involuntarily, whether he has half as much respect for all the philosophy and natural science of Europe put together, and feels that he regards a meeting of scientific men as of far less importance than a meeting of fanatical conspirators.

At the time when Disraeli entered life, all men with poetical or æsthetic tendencies had a common object of antipathy—the doctrine of utility. In the form of moralizing mediocrity, in which it had been presented to them, the German and Scandinavian romanticists heaped ridicule upon it. It was usually conceived of as a levelling tendency, as hatred of the beautiful and the good, and it was opposed in the name of poetry, religion, and heroism. But while, in the rest of Northern Europe, Utilitarianism had appeared in more or less vague and confused forms as enlightenment or rationalism, in England it was represented by no less a man than Bentham, who first gave the doctrine a system and a name, and his school became more and more a power.We find in Disraeli the well-known æsthetic dislike to utilitarianism, but with a local and individual peculiarity.

Although a plebeian by birth and a freedman by baptism, he was a born aristocrat, deeply impressed with the feeling that men and races are variously endowed. Utilitarianism appeared to him also to be a levelling tendency, and, as such, he hated and ridiculed it. He calls it an enemy to mountains as well as to monarchs. In "Popanilla" (1827) he makes a utilitarian philosopher propose to level the Andes on the ground that these monstrosities are decidedly useless, and, therefore, neither sublime nor beautiful. He even asserts, in the *Foreign Quarterly Review* (1828), that he has met with a personal enemy of Mont Blanc. This caricature of utilitarianism appears to him so telling that, a year later, he takes it up again in "The Young Duke." The duke, on a short journey, in which he travels incognito, meets with a passenger in a stage-coach, who, casting his eyes on the duke's park, declares that the park and its owner, as well as all the aristocracy, are useless, and ought to be abolished. The man extols an author who has made a spirited and vigorous attack upon the Andes, in which he shows the uselessness of everything which lifts itself up above the rest, and condemns these mountains as the aristocracy of the earth.

There is nothing specially English in this; the romanticists of all countries would have joined in it; but it is quite intelligible that the man who thought thus in his youth should not afterwards regard the Manchester theories with favour, and would never be tempted to put the material interests of England above her name and prestige. But what does appear to me absolutely peculiar in Disraeli is his dislike, concealed beneath jests over its prosaic side, to the scientific element in utilitarianism. It is repugnant to him because it overestimates abstract reason, and undervalues imagination. There is a line in "Coningsby" which expresses and explains Disraeli's antipathy with admirable brevity: "Mormon counts more votaries than Bentham." Let us duly consider this dictum. It merely states a statistical fact or what is supposed to be so; but one sees behind it Disraeli's contempt for a doctrine purely scientific, which cannot, therefore, be fanatical. It is placed in the mouth of a person in the book who is Disraeli's spokesman, and the train of thought is intended to show that neither physical nor economical, but mental causes, have occasioned the great revolutions in the history of the world. The origin of every great deed must, according to him, be sought in the imagination: a revolution takes place when the imagination of a people revolts against the Government, and he who appeals to the imaginations of men is a more powerful, and therefore a greater, more eminent man, than he who appeals to their interest—so certainly as imagination is more potent than reason.

This, as it seems to me, is the language and these the ideas of

a man destitute of learning. A more scientifically trained mind is
sure to regard with the greatest respect those undertakings and
institutions which bear a scientific stamp; and even if by historical
and philosophical self-culture he has accustomed himself to see
reason in phenomena like Jesuitism or Mormonism, his recognition
of power in the political organization of the one and in the religious
fanaticism of the other, is involuntarily mingled with contempt for
what is adverse to reason. In Disraeli's case there is not only no
trace of such contempt, but rather an admiring sympathy. He may,
on the other hand, compel himself to acknowledge the greatness
of pure reason; but what he by nature, and involuntarily, respects
is the catchword which electrifies the unreasoning masses.

Still, it is in this high value placed on the use of imagination,
conditioned by the lack of scientific training before mentioned,
that the originality of the man consists. There is some truth, something even profound, in this view of imagination as a political
motive power. It springs from his own peculiarly imaginative
temperament; and this mode of looking at things is to such an
extent the central point with him, that he who rightly apprehends
Disraeli's opinion of the part played by imagination in politics,
and his adroitness in turning it to account, possesses the key to his
mental powers as a novelist and a statesman.

The characteristic development of the idea in "Coningsby" is
as follows:—"How limited is human reason the profoundest in-
quirers are most conscious. We are not indebted to the reason of
man for any of the great achievements which are the landmarks of
human action and human progress. It was not reason that besieged
Troy; it was not reason that sent forth the Saracen from the
desert to conquer the world, that inspired the Crusades, that
instituted the monastic orders; it was not reason that produced the
Jesuits; above all, it was not reason that created the French Revolution. Man is only truly great when he acts from the passions; never
irresistible but when he appeals to the imagination. Even Mormon
counts more votaries than Bentham." *

What is here expressed as the opinion of Disraeli's mature

* "Coningsby," p. 240.

years, hovered vaguely before his eyes as a youth, and betrayed itself in his involuntary antipathy to Bentham and the Benthamites. He has been opposed to them all his life. At a later period, he aimed his blows at them as mere rational politicians, who had no eye for the lessons of history, or what was historically possible. At a still later stage, he opposed the stress laid in politics by their successors on material motives and calculations which logically led to the principle of non-intervention; but what was most repugnant to him in utilitarianism was the contempt expressed by its first advocates for imagination, not only in poetry, but as a constituent of human nature. Bentham's dictum, "All poetry is misrepresentation," challenged the poet in him; but the utilitarian contempt for imagination altogether, which he considered to be the inspiring motive power in every great act, incensed in the highest degree the future statesman.

For he was led by his own nature, as well as by his first researches into politics, to regard imagination as the decisive force in them. He perceived that it was not enough to handle existing circumstances adroitly, but that the statesman must have the gift of reckoning with the future. He must be able to forecast and prepare the future—must, so to speak, be able to handle it as his material. He saw, moreover, that the statesman must be able to generalize from the details collected by reading or experience, to enable him to form those comprehensive views, without which he is the mere slave of routine. But he found in the human mind no other faculty than political imagination to enable him to form this comprehensive view of the present, or to construe and prepare the future.

And it was this faculty which enabled him to see restless visions, to weave dreams, to forge plans and intrigues. When he looked into his own mind, he had assuredly no cause to lose heart or to doubt of his future. He possessed in an eminent degree the faculty on which all depended—imagination, and especially imagination applied to politics on a grand scale.

V

"VIVIAN GREY"

Why, then, the world's mine oyster,
Which I with sword will open.

With this motto on the title-page, Disraeli's first novel went forth into the world in the year 1826. And the contents of the book agreed with the motto. Vivian is the son of a distinguished author, lively, talented, irresistibly attractive, and engrossed from boyhood with the idea of making a career for himself. In society he is petted and patronized by a dozen women of fashion, but the apparently frivolous boy is an obstinate and indefatigable student, and when he has devoured a mass of historical reading, he takes to the study, "which is certainly the most attractive that exists, but for a boy the most dangerous," the study of politics. His first political reflection is simply this—How many great nobles only want brains to become ministers, and what does Vivian Grey want in order to become one? Nothing but the influence of such a noble. He thinks that when two people are to such an extent necessary to one another, they should act together, and concludes: "There wants but one thing more—courage, pure, perfect courage; and does Vivian Grey know fear?" * He answers his own query with a bitter and scornful laugh. Vivian is not scrupulous in the choice of his means. At a dinner-party at his father's house, he begins by flattering a blockhead of a nobleman, the Marquis of Carabas, and gains his lordship's favour by giving him a recipe for tomahawk punch, and another to the marchioness for her nervous parrot. The two men form a political alliance, and Vivian founds the "Carabas party" out of a set of narrow-minded, avaricious, and

* "Vivian Grey," p. 19.

envious landed nobles, in which he plays the part among the bluff earls of political Figaro. He has not only no doubt of success himself, but succeeds in instilling the same faith into others. "For it was one of the first principles of Mr. Vivian Grey, that everything was possible. Men did fail in life, to be sure, and after all, very little was done by the generality; but still all these failures and all this inefficiency might be traced to a want of physical and mental courage. . . . Now Vivian Grey was conscious that there was at least one person in the world who was no craven either in body or in mind, and so he had long come to the comfortable conclusion that it was impossible that his career could be anything but the most brilliant." *

It appears necessary to Vivian Grey to attract to the new party a real politician of great talent, who has retired into private life; and to this man, whom he regards as his equal, he makes no secret of his contempt for the other members of the party. Grey explains to Cleveland that he is not in the slightest degree duped by the Marquis of Carabas or any one else, but, though he has full confidence in his own abilities, he wishes to employ the power of others. Ought he to play the part of hermit in the drama of life only because his fellow-actors are sometimes fools, and, when opportunity offers, become clowns?

It must not be supposed that the cold and unscrupulous Vivian Grey gains the easy political victory that he expects. On the contrary, all his schemes are frustrated. As if the author had foreseen, with prophetic eye, the long series of disappointments and defeats that awaited him, he makes blow after blow fall upon his hero of romance. His noble allies leave him in the lurch on the first disaster, and load him with undeserved contumely. Cleveland, who imagines himself betrayed, insults him so grossly that Vivian is compelled to give him a challenge, and, to crown his misfortunes, kills his former friend in a duel. He has a serious illness, and, on his recovery, the best thing he can do is to make a long tour abroad in order to forget and be forgotten.

* "Vivian Grey," p. 44.

With this, the most remarkable part of the book in a psychological point of view, in which the scene is laid in England, comes to an end. The second and larger part treats of Vivian Grey's travels in Germany; his visits to German baths and courts, larger and smaller, of his travelling and love adventures, his intercourse with great nobles and reigning princes and ministers. This second part is considerably more mature than the first, and appeared a year later. Unfortunately, there is not a single thread to connect it with the first part. Vivian himself is not the same person; the work as a whole, has crumbled to pieces in the young author's hands. Nevertheless, "Vivian Grey" is a sparkling book; there is spirit in the dialogues, and wit in the reflections, which make it even now worth reading, and it produced an effect like the contact of flint and steel in English society. The cause lay not alone in the merits of the book—though such works, when the abundant English fictitious literature of the nineteenth century had no existence, were a rarity; nor was it alone the political matter which attracted attention; the main thing was that the fictitious dish which the young Disraeli had served up was spiced with the most appetizing of all condiments, scandal. In the descriptions of London society there were spiteful sketches of well-known personages, and when the report of this was spread, society of course had no rest until the real name of every single character was discovered. "Have you read 'Vivian Grey'?" "We are all in it together, no doubt." "I sent this morning for a Key to it." This was the colloquy in London drawing-rooms after the appearance of the book, just as it occurs in "Contarini Fleming," after the hero's first novel. A number of Keys came out, one of which, in 1827, ran through ten editions. Most of the guesses contained in them were undoubtedly very silly, but so much is clear, that the conversation in "Vivian Grey" overflowed with direct or veiled personalities.

In the mixture of truth and fiction which excited so much unæsthetic curiosity in Disraeli's first work there was something involuntary, which was to be attributed to the author's youth; but at the same time, one of his permanent characteristics was betrayed

in it, and it has been repeated nearly every time he has set pen to
paper as a novelist. In that character he never forgets the actual life
around him; he does not care for a purely imaginative effect; he
wants to strike in at the present moment, and in order to this
nothing comes amiss to him. He finds it hard to tear himself away
from the present political situation, even when he wishes to do so,
for his imagination is not a free bird, although a wild one; it is
the trained falcon who executes the behests of his ambition and
carries out his plans.

It has been stated almost as a certainty in England, that Disraeli,
at twenty, found the original of Vivian Grey in the looking-glass,
and the only youthful thing in the book has been said to be the
naïveté with which the author displays the hard-headedness of age.
There is, clearly enough, some personation of himself in Vivian
Grey, for there is not the slightest irony in the treatment of him;
but the hard-headedness is affected rather than *naïve*. The great
object of the young author was to make an impression on the
reader, and, therefore, he only described and exaggerated those
qualities which he considered the most imposing, and which, bad
or good, he was most ready to confess to. But everybody knows
that an ambitious youth of eighteen or twenty, when he wants to
be somebody, desires above all things to be the practised man of the
world, cool and calculating, whose heart has no influence over him,
or could, at any rate, only be touched by a glowing erotic passion,
while he is irresistible to every woman. He has a horror of all the
softer feelings, reverence and innocent admiration for persons or
ideas, as sheer nonsense. When you have not long escaped from the
nursery, you tremble at everything that reminds you of it, and if,
at that age the child within you weeps or indulges in vain hopes, it
fires the cheek with shame, and you feel ready to throttle him.
Disraeli's "Vivian Grey," especially the first part, is a product of
this state of mind; the author is *fanfaron de vice*, and instead of
showing himself *naïve*, as he really is, forces himself to affectation.
No acute reader will conclude from "Vivian Grey" that the emotional passages in his later works must be false, because that work

betrayed the author's true character; the critic will, on the contrary, draw conclusions about his earlier state of mind from the earnestness of feeling of those published but a few years later, and thus convince himself of the obvious affectation in "Vivian Grey," which Disraeli has ever since himself acknowledged.

The young author forms the groundwork of the character of his hero by making him a political adventurer. In his mouth there is nothing degrading in it. The English word "adventure" means, in its active sense, a "venture," and in its passive sense that may be said of it which Disraeli makes his Ixion write in Minerva's album, and it is repeated, word for word, by his *alter ego*, Sidonia, in "Coningsby:" "Adventures are to the adventurous." With his taste for the fantastic, and his sympathy with the aspiring, he always had a certain preference for adventures and those who meet with them. In the political sphere, certainly, an adventurer is not an attractive person. But if the position of affairs in England about the year 1826 is taken into account, it is easy to see that a gleam of adventure might lure a man on, who, without connections to help him, wanted to carve out a political career for himself. It was so customary for the younger scions of the ruling aristocratic families simply to represent their opinions, that he who tried to form his own at first hand, and make a start in life, seemed to be somewhat of an adventurer. But Disraeli made this adventurous feature too glaring; he sometimes made his hero a true Reineke Fuchs, to give the reader an idea of his own cleverness, than a Mephistopheles, to give them to understand that this *débutant* in life and literature was not to be trifled with. Thus Vivian Grey is really terrible, when, with calculating coolness, he revenges himself on the woman who has thrown him over, and who, from hatred of him, has become a poisoner; but he is not much more cruel than the author could be under some circumstances. If any one acquainted with Disraeli's writings will imagine Sir Robert Peel, twenty years later, as he writhed upon the Ministerial bench under Disraeli's cold and vengeful speech, he can hardly fail to be reminded of the glance "beaming like that of a happy bridegroom," with which Vivian Grey leaves Mrs. Felix Lorraine, when she sinks back in her chair, unmasked, disarmed, and entangled in a net from which she cannot escape, and breaks a blood-vessel from suppressed rage. The thirst for revenge is the same in the novel as in real life, only in the novel it is too much in the Franz Moor style.

The novel, as the reader will perceive, turns on politics; it is, so to speak, a rehearsal for real political chess moves, or the military manœuvres in which our officers are prepared for the tactics of war. Nature has but little place in this book; here and there we have a moonlight night or a mountain landscape, but they only form a melodramatic background for the struggles and perils of the adventurer. Nature is to Mr. Disraeli never anything but—what he characteristically calls her in two of his works—an Egeria, that is, a source of political inspiration. He has taken refuge with her when weary of politics, like the tired soldier in the Vivandière's tent. But he never loved her for her own sake. When Contarini Fleming is taking lessons in history from Numa Pompilius, he exclaims: "I, too, will take refuge with Egeria;" and he finds in a lonely vale embosomed in trees, the wise nymph of political inspiration, and day after day cannot tear himself away from the ever-recurring vision. In "Vivian Grey," Disraeli calls Nature the "Egeria of man," and adds with bitter humour: "Refreshed and renovated by this beautiful communion, we return to the world, better enabled to fight our parts in the hot war of passions, to perform the great duties for which man appeared to have been created—to love, to hate, to slander, and to slay." *

It cannot be denied that this view of Nature is original. How plainly the words reveal the restless haste with which the ambitious author quaffs a draught from the beauties of Nature, only immediately to turn his back upon her! The poet in him needs Nature, and sees in her a Muse; the politician only seeks a stimulant from her, at most only asks from her a sign, and thus for him she is transformed into a sort of political Muse, who, initiated into his plans and struggles, comforts him in misfortune, and crowns his victories with smiles.

* "Vivian Grey," p. 109.

The larger part of "Vivian Grey," in which the hero travels in Germany, does not, therefore, contain descriptions of nature, but in spite of much that is crude and wanting in good taste, in spite of a description of the Bacchanalian revels of the Rhenish counts, who are a match for Victor Hugo's "Burgraves," it contains many well-conceived contributions to the characteristics of the small German counts of that day and even much later. There is, for instance, a Grand-Duke of Reisenburg, who prides himself on having the best orchestra in the world, and who never misses a new thing at a theatre. He is equally proud of his scenery, and the historical accuracy of his decorations and costumes. When he has Rossini's "Othello" performed, Brabantio's house is a precise copy of the palace Sansovino or Palladio on the Grand Canal. Othello does not, as usual, appear dressed as a Moor, for the dramaturge on the ducal throne thinks it far more probable that an adventurer, who has raised himself to be general of the army and admiral of the fleet of Venice, would imitate even to affectation, the manners of his adopted country, and not venture to challenge the hatred of his Christian soldiers as a Moor wearing a turban. Disraeli was obviously thinking of the Grand-Duke of Saxe Weimar, but the passage reads just like a description of the ducal theatre of Meiningen of the present day.

But more interesting than this bit of description of Germany, is one of the chief characters in the book, the prime minister of bourgeois origin, Beckendorf. In him we meet for the first time in Disraeli's books with his ideal, so often met with afterwards, and most elaborately portrayed, under the name of Sidonia; a man with a "master mind," all-sufficient to himself, and, therefore, the born master of other minds. Beckendorf tells Vivian Grey, who is the sport of destiny, that there is no such thing as destiny; that man, far from being, as he is said to be, the creature of circumstances, himself creates circumstances, if he is a man of the right sort. Such a man has no other destiny, and not other Providence than his own genius, and circumstances must serve his genius like slaves; there is no peril, fearful as it may appear, from which a man may not extricate himself by his own energy, as the seaman, by firing a cannon, may disperse the waterspout which hangs over his head.

In vigorous words like these the idea of the influence of individual character upon destiny, which is a standing doctrine in Disraeli's writings, is thus early expressed. Compare with it the vindication of this faith written twenty years later: "It is not the spirit of the age," says Coningsby. "The spirit of the age," answers Sidonia, "is the very thing that a great man changes." "But what is an individual," asks Coningsby, "against a vast public opinion?" "Divine," is Sidonia's concise answer.*

In "Tancred," the last but one of Disraeli's novels, we find expressions no less strong, with the same tendency; it is evidently his firm belief, as it has been the belief of many other energetic men. It is a faith which does not favour the tendency of science in our day, to ascribe everything, characters as well as actions, to the spirit of the age, but it nevertheless still makes itself heard, and is, anyhow, of the greatest practical import. How far it was Disraeli's purpose to make his hero profit by the vigorous *sursum corda* which was addressed to him, we are not told; the probability is that he did not know what to do with the young fellow, and therefore broke the story off suddenly. I have already said that in riper years he did not overestimate his 'prentice work. He complains and offers it as his apology that translations and reprints have made the suppression of this affected boyish work impossible. Whether his verdict would have been so severe if the cynicism of the first part had not soon begun to be inconvenient to Disraeli, is a question I am unable to answer.

Only a year after he had given his first romance to the world, he followed it by a smaller, quite different, and more amiable one, the political satire "Popanilla."

* "Coningsby," p. 119.

VI

"POPANILLA"

⋅§ "Popanilla" is a jest beneath which neither bitterness nor pathos lies concealed; the satirical darts fly in every direction, fantastically and free, not as if with a wish to advocate any very definite political views, and therefore to cast ridicule on the opposite party.

In the Indian Ocean is situated the Isle of Fantaisie, undiscovered by European circumnavigators or missionary societies; the climate is fine, the soil fruitful; the inhabitants, innocent of civilization, pass their lives in a simple paradisaical state. One of them, named Popanilla, finds, while seeking a precious lost lock of hair on the shore, a box of books which has been cast ashore from a shipwrecked vessel. The books contain nothing but useful knowledge —philology, hydrostatics, history, politics, all written in a utilitarian spirit; and Popanilla, who, by means of them, discovers to his dismay that his people, whom he had considered some of the best in the world, are a lot of useless barbarians, resolves at once to come out as a Radical reformer, with the wise intention of demanding only slow and gradual changes. He begins by going to court, and preaching before the king against the dancing and singing of his countrymen as useless waste of time. It was, he thought, the happiness of the community that was the chief good, not that of the individual, and the community might be very happy, wealthy, and powerful, even if every member of it were wretched, dependent, and in debt. Utility was the object of human life; wants, however, were the motives for progress, and unfortunately for his countrymen, they had none. They spent their lives in a condition of purely useless well-being; if, instead of this, they would begin to take advantage of the situation and natural wealth of the island, its mineral treasures and extensive harbours, there was good reason to hope that the inhabitants would soon be a terror to all other countries, and in a condition to disturb and plague every nation of importance.

When the king of the Isle of Fantaisie begins to smile, Popanilla tells him, in Bentham's formula, that a king is only the first magistrate of the country, and that His Majesty has no more right to laugh at him than the village politician. The king takes the reprimand quietly; but when Popanilla by degrees fills the island with loud-talking schoolboys, the reforms go too far for him, and he takes the spirited revenge of declaring himself a convert to the new doctrines, and, as a proof of it, appoints Popanilla captain of his mail-packet. "As the axiom of your school seems to be that everything can be made perfect at once, without time, without experience, without practice, and without preparation, I have no doubt, with the aid of a treatise or two, you will make a consummate naval commander, although you have never been at sea in the whole course of your life. Farewell, Captain Popanilla!" * And in the twinkling of an eye the Radical reformer is at sea in a canoe, with water and provisions for a few days.

The purpose of this rather mild joke about utilitarianism is to show the fundamental discrepancy between progress in civilization and the greatest happiness of the greatest number, which are combined in the utilitarian theory, and, thus combined, are declared to be its aims. Disraeli implies that there is a contradiction in them, and that a choice of one or the other must be made, since the advance of civilization brings disaster and misery to individuals, while the greatest happiness may be found on the lowest stage of civilization, or without any at all. The utilitarians used to mourn over the scanty wants of a people; he makes game of this by making Popanilla mention it as the misfortune of his people that they are so happy without civilization.† For the sake of the jest, he had to

---

* "Popanilla," p. 384.

† The same paradox has been pointed out by Eduard von Hartmann, in a speech of Lassalle's to German artisans. ("Phänomenologie des Sittlichen Bewusstseins," p. 637.)

presuppose an original paradisaical state of nature à la Rousseau, which has scarcely ever been found by any one else; he certainly did not find it himself in Cyprus, when, in 1878, it fell to his lot as Prime Minister to have Popanilla's speech made to the natives. In my opinion, this assault does not really hit the utilitarians. True civilization must in the end increase the happiness of the masses; the happiness of the child or the savage is not the highest happiness. John Stuart Mill says, in his "Theory of Utilitarianism:" "It is better to be a human being dissatisfied than a pig satisfied, better to be Socrates dissatisfied than a fool satisfied." And he is right; greater sensitiveness, even to pain, is not too dear a price to pay for increase of the value of life.

The banished reformer lands in the empire of Braibleusia, "the freest country in the world," where freedom consists in every one's being at liberty to do exactly like everybody else—a country precisely like Great Britain. From the moment of his reaching this country, it is all satire on the social condition, manners, and constitution of England. Everything that in the public opinion of that day was above criticism—the doctrine that England was the home of civil and religious liberty, and that free trade was the only true principle of political economy—is made the subject of satire. Blind English Conservatism is hit by a satire on the anti-quated constitution of courts of justice. An attack on the Corn Laws shows, as some passages in "Vivian Grey" do also, that Disraeli little then foresaw the part he was to play in future as their advocate. Things turn out very badly for Popanilla in Braibleusia; after being fêted for a while, he is unjustly banished, and on meditating on his fate, he comes to the conclusion that, if a state of nature is not very admirable, a country like that he had just visited was too artificial, might have too many assumed principles, a civili-zation too unnatural. With this moral the story ends, just as the reader begins to weary of the long-drawn allegory—and Popanilla sets out on his long voyage.

VII

TRAVELS ABROAD

❧ Disraeli soon followed his example. From 1829–31 he was
on his travels. It is, so to speak, the correct thing for young men
of the higher classes in England to finish their student years with
a grand tour, which introduces them to active life. All young
men have a desire to see the world, and no one more so than he
who does not feel himself altogether in harmony with his native
land. There are many indications in Disraeli's writings that a
certain discontent immediately preceded his travels. The first
embarrassment in which we find ourselves generally leads to our
first travels, he says somewhere; and the heroes in both his earliest
romances set forth at a juncture when staying at home had grown
painful to them. Perhaps various unfavourable notices of his first
works might have contributed to the desire for a long residence
abroad, or it may have been that he was merely actuated by love
of travel and knowledge. Formerly, young Englishmen went on
the Continent to see what, according to Lord Bacon, "especially
deserves to be seen and observed," the courts of sovereigns; at
that time, however, they travelled, as some one in "Vivian Grey"
remarks, "to look at mountains, and catch cold in spouting trash on
lakes by moonlight." *

As a politician and novelist, the objects of travel of the
seventeenth century had as much attraction for Disraeli as those
of the nineteenth. Courts had an attraction for him, and he was no
less fascinated by the romance of certain cities and neighbourhoods.
He had made a short tour before, as is shown by "Vivian Grey."
Now it was not the countries and cities mostly visited by everyday
European travellers, nor any of the larger centres of civilization

* "Vivian Grey," p. 209.

which attracted him. No, totally different names had rung in his ears from childhood—Syria, Jerusalem, Spain, Venice.

Everybody has, besides his accidental home on earth, some other cognate one which he dreams of and longs for. With his double nationality, and from dwelling on the memories of the race and his forefathers, Disraeli had from his earliest youth an ardent longing for the East. He longed to see the spots on which the eyes of his forefathers had rested, to tread the soil trodden by their feet; in these spots he felt that his prematurely hardened spirit would be softened, his oppressed soul would expand with devotion. Yes, it was just this; for a pilgrimage to those lands was to him not only a longing desire, but a religion. He wanted to behold that glowing land which was the cradle of the race; the holy city which his people had built, lost, rebuilt, and lost again; the sacred mount whence their religion, which had conquered Europe, had gone forth. Still, as every man only belongs to his nation through family ties, the spots connected with the family are dearer to him than those belonging to the race. He wanted to see the countries on the Mediterranean, where his fathers had dwelt for five hundred years; Spain, where, under the protection of their Moorish brethren, they had made progress in civilization, and produced poetry in the ancient language of the race; and he sought among the names of the distinguished families of Spain for the one which his fathers might have borne before they changed it, and lingered dreamily over the proud and fine-sounding name of Sidonia, which, years afterwards, he gave to one of his heroes in "Alarcos" and "Coningsby;" but, above all, he longed to behold the wonderful city on the Adriatic, whose patron, St. Mark, himself a child of Israel, had been so kind a lord to the banished race. When, as a boy on his grandfather's knee, he had heard of the city of the doges, with its floating palaces, and learnt that the city was no longer free, he had in his early dreams fancied himself the liberator and doge of the restored republic. Now, as a young man, he longed to see Venice as he longed to see Jerusalem. It seemed to him as if he must go there, as if he were expected, had been expected for centuries—he, the inheritor of all these memories. Distant voices seemed to call him, and the blood in his veins answered, and his heart beat high for this fantastic calling, until the day came for him to bid farewell to his father, and to address to England the parting words which, some years later, he made Contarini Fleming address to his Scandinavian home: "And thou, too, Scandinavia, stern soil in which I have too long lingered, think of me hereafter as of some exotic bird, which for a moment lost its way in thy cold heaven, but now has regained its course, and wings its flight to a more brilliant earth and a brighter sky!" *

Disraeli has not written anything about the journey itself. But we find from his writings that he visited all the countries bordering on the Mediterranean, that he was in Rome and Constantinople in 1829, Albania in 1830, Egypt, Syria, and Jerusalem in 1831. The tour has left traces in all his works, and whole works owe their origin to it.

Various feelings agitated the mind of the young traveller as, for the first time, he approached Venice. When Contarini Fleming was nearing the Italian frontier, he dreamed one night at a village at the foot of the Simplon that he was in a large apartment in a palace, where richly clad and honourable men were sitting in council, and that the president, on seeing him, held out his hand to him, and said with a smile, "You have been long expected." The council is at an end, and the president, as *cicerone*, conducts Contarini into a smaller apartment, hung with pictures, where, on one side of the door, there was a portrait of Julius Cæsar, and on the other of Contarini. His guide points to the portrait and says, "You have been long expected. There is a great resemblance between you and your uncle."† A third time he hears it confirmed in his dream that he has been expected in these halls; and suddenly he beholds a splendid city, whose marble palaces gleam in the sunlight along a broad canal, where multitudes of long boats pass to and fro on the blue waters, and then he knows where he is. No sooner is he awake than he proceeds to Venice. The first thing he

* "Contarini Fleming," p. 190.   † "Contarini Fleming," p. 197.

meets in the street is a procession of chanting priests with their saint, and when he hears the words of the hymn, it seems to him that these words are applicable to himself—"Wave your banners! Sound, sound your voices! for he has come, he has come! our saint and our Lord! He has come in pride and in glory, to meet with love his Adrian bride." *

In such a frame of mind as this Disraeli first took boat on the canals of Venice, and set foot on the Piazza. Some have loved the beautiful city, without dust or noise, for its peculiarity; others for its art treasures; others, yet again, for its historical associations; but Disraeli's love was not so impersonal. He had no enthusiasm for the Venetian school of art, nor for its aristocratic republican constitution, whose introduction into England he began, a few years later, to mourn over and attack. The city moved him so deeply because it had been the asylum of his fathers; he loved it for the sake of his kin, his race. It is chiefly personal reasons like these that call forth his love.

But Venice only stills his first thirst for seeing. No country or city of Europe could turn his mind from the East. He visited Egypt, saw the Pyramids, for which his people of old had had to drag the materials, stone by stone. He succeeded in getting several audiences of the reigning pasha, and, having attracted the notice of Mehemet Ali by his ready and thoughtful answers, Mehemet seems to have even asked his advice as to the system of government best adapted to the country. He has mentioned this, not without pride, in his "Vindication of the English Constitution," where the travelled young Englishman is, of course, the author himself. It was in the year 1829 that an assembly had been convened by the reform-loving Egyptian despot at Cairo, which might, according to Turkish notions, be called a representation of the people, and the pasha asked the intelligent young Englishman what he thought of an Egyptian representative constitution after the English pattern.

"The surprise of our countryman, when he received the com-munication of the pasha, was not inconsiderable; but he was one of

* "Contarini Fleming," p. 207.

those who had seen sufficient of the world never to be astonished; not altogether untinctured with political knowledge, and gifted with that philosophical exemption from prejudice which is one of the most certain and most valuable results of extensive travel. Our countryman communicated to the Egyptian ruler, with calmness and with precision, the immediate difficulties that occurred to him, explained to the successor of the Pharaohs and the Ptolemies that the political institutions of England had been the gradual growth of ages, and that there is no political function which demands a finer discipline or a more regulated preparation than the exercise of popular franchise." *

Disraeli with Mehemet Ali is a sort of historical parallel to Byron with Ali Pasha. Byron's vanity is flattered because Ali discerns the aristocrat in his outward appearance; Disraeli's because Mehemet discovers his political sagacity.

It is plain that it was not clear to Disraeli at that time whether poetry or politics was his true vocation. His self-esteem inclined him to overrate his abilities, and while wandering in Byron's footsteps in the East, he often fancied that English poetry would find compensation in him for what it had lost. Self-criticism was never his strong point, especially in his youth. Perhaps nothing in his life has given plainer proof of this than what he tells us of a poetical idea which he conceived soon after setting foot on Asiatic soil. In a high-flown and theatrical preface, he tells us how, as he wandered over the plains of Troy, with his head full of the Homeric poems, he cursed his fate in having been born in an age which boasted of being unpoetic; and how, just as the lightning flashed over Mount Ida, the idea flashed into his mind that all the great epic poems in the world had embraced the spirit of a complete age, and that he, in order to be a true poet, had only to give poetic expression to his own. He goes on to say that the heroic epic, the "Iliad," originated in the greatest heroic deed of a heroic age; the political epic, the "Æneid," in the establishment of the Roman Empire of the world; the national epic of Dante, in the first dawn of the Renaissance; the

* "Vindication of the English Constitution," p. 102.

religious epic of Milton in the Reformation and its results; and he then asks himself whether the spirit of his own age is to remain unsung. "How," I exclaimed, "is the French Revolution an event of less importance than the siege of Troy? Is Napoleon a less interesting character than Achilles? The revolutionary epic has been reserved for me."

I will not now dwell on the grotesque coupling of the names of Homer, Virgil, Dante, and Milton, with that of Disraeli, nor on the parallel between the most famous poems in the world and an epic of which but an unhappy fragment ever saw the light, only to retreat into the dark womb of obscurity, scared by the ridicule with which it was assailed; but I wish to call attention to the fact that Disraeli, whom we find warning Mehemet Ali against radical attempts at reform, was in his youth attracted to the French Revolution as the most important and interesting subject of the age. He was never adverse in principle to modern political ideas. When he has opposed them, it has been from interested motives or on some incidental ground. There is a great difference in this respect between him and theoretical Conservatives, like his present colleague in the Ministry, Lord Salisbury. He has even a curious sympathy with decidedly revolutionary phenomena. In his writings he has portrayed men like Byron, Shelley, and Mazzini in a remarkably favourable light. He has, in his old age, described with absolute enthusiasm the character of a goddess of liberty, the very ideal of revolutionary freedom, Theodora in "Lothair." Many will have queried, in reading his books, whether there was not a touch of the revolutionist in the bosom of the old Tory leader. The question, What is the inmost or deepest sentiment in a man? is always difficult to answer, especially in the case of very composite characters.

In reviewing the whole of Disraeli's literary productions, and the whole of his political action, there will always be found beneath the Conservative groundwork a layer of Radicalism, and at the same time a firm Conservative basis beneath any surface Radicalism. On the religious question, he has from the first been on the liberal side, but the desire to assert the absolute superiority of his race has compelled him to make the very most of the religious benefits which it has conferred on mankind, and of the gratitude which mankind owes it. He began his career as a novelist with "Vivian Grey," without any particular principle, and his first political *brochure* was ultra-Radical; I have already referred to the political reactionary impressions he had received from his father. Did they at first excite his opposition? A youth so much inclined to make himself the standard of all things, without regard to any external authority, must inevitably have a strong tendency to opposition; but who can say whether what appears uppermost is also the deepest down in a man's heart? Besides, all such expressions are but metaphors.

"The Revolutionary Epic," which, although conceived when on his travels, was not published till 1834, and may have undergone several Conservative retouches in the interval, was intended to depict the struggle between the feudal and the federative principle, and the transition from the one to the other. The fragment which appeared began with strange, supernatural machinery. Magros, the genius of feudalism, and Lyridon, the genius of federalism, plead in turn for their cause, and it ends by Napoleon—Lyridon(!) giving his word as a pledge of faith; the third canto accompanies him through the whole Italian campaign to the conquest of Lombardy, and closes with the planting of the Tree of Liberty. In the preface, the author made the continuation of the work dependent on the verdict of the public, and said that if it were unfavourable, he would, without regret, hurl his lyre into the nether regions.

There were far deeper impressions and stronger excitements in store for Disraeli on his tour than those which he experienced on the plains of Troy, and the deepest of all was on the day when, after a ride of several hours among wild and barren rocks, he ascended a hill, and was told that it was the Mount of Olives, and beheld before him a city on the steep and lofty precipice, surrounded by an old wall, which, with its towers, pinnacles, and gates, rose and fell, wavelike, with the undulating ground. His eye lingered on the splendid mosque which towered above the city, on the beautiful gardens in front of it, and the numberless cupolas which rose above the light-coloured stone houses, and he felt that he was gazing on Jerusalem. One of the old Crusaders could scarcely have been more deeply moved than he was, though his feelings might have been different. They loved the city for heaven's sake, for the salvation which the conquest of it was to procure for them; he loved it for the sake of the race which had built it. He mentally compared the city of the many hills before him with the city of seven hills in Europe, and remembered with pride that Moriah, Zion, and Calvary were far more famous than the Aventine and the Capitol; for not Asia alone, but Christian Europe knew their names, while in Mohammedan Asia the others were but empty sounds. The old Crusaders considered the Saracens unworthy to possess the Holy City and the Holy Sepulchre; he considered them far more worthy than any of the European hosts; for not only did they venerate the city and the sepulchre, these sons of the desert were far more nearly allied to Him who had lain in the grave than any Teuton or Gaul. The Crusaders held faith to be all in all; he knew, as he oft repeated to himself, that "all is race; there in no other truth."*

He felt himself at home in this country where there were caravans of turban-wearing men; where the sheikh, as thousands of years before, was the patriarch of his tribe, and opened his tent to him as in the olden time. He loved these palms, these cedars and olive groves. And when Jerusalem lay before him in the glow of a summer day, like a city of stone in a land of iron under a fiery heaven; and when the burning glare of the surrounding landscape made the spectator afraid of being blinded; when everything was so awfully and brilliantly clear, that the pilgrim

* Sidonia in "Tancred." Compare his expressions in "Coningsby" and Disraeli's own in the "Life of Lord George Bentinck," and in the "General Preface." In "Tancred" the author calls this dogma "the great truth into which all truths merge."

stood like the shadowless man in the fairy tale, with a shadowless world around him—he felt his brilliant mind and his fiery imagination to be akin to this arid and glowing land. There was no shady spot in his soul, there was no place there for rest or repose; he had always despised and shunned the shady aspects of life. He was happy in this land, where every inch of ground reminded him of Israel's greatness; at the foot of Sinai, from which the law of Moses was proclaimed, to be learned even now by every civilized child; among the ruins of the Temple, which recalled to mind the great king, whose wisdom still lives in the Proverbs; at Gethsemane, where the martyr had suffered, whose pure and simple teaching has conquered the Western world. He did not in his reflections separate Jesus from the other lights of the Hebrew nation. He did not doubt that Jesus was descended from the royal house of David; Biblical criticism did not then exist, and even when it was introduced it did not fit in with Disraeli's system to degrade the genealogy of Jesus in the New Testament into a mere invention with a special purpose; Jesus must and should be a prince. It is deeply characteristic of Disraeli's mental habit, that in the numerous passages in his works where Jesus is mentioned, he never speaks of Him otherwise than as a Hebrew prince, a Hebrew ruler. His estimate of Him is increased because He comes of the aristocratic blood of the race; the instinctive attraction which he had always felt for the highest aristocracy compelled him in this case to lay most stress on that which best comported with his ideal; hence it is that the royal blood, the princely descent, is much more to him than the supernatural origin; and so much the more because the latter made the former impossible, as it is Joseph, not Mary, who is shown to be the descendant of David. That Disraeli, nevertheless, from the moment when he appeared as a Conservative statesman, was not afraid of the paradox of maintaining extreme orthodoxy, is to be explained by the fact that, in the nineteenth century, a statesman, especially in England, and especially a Conservative, must, above all things, offer orthodox guarantees; but it was also to be attributed to the fear that, if he dropped the supernatural origin of Jesus, he would be depriving his race of the nimbus which encircled it, as the people among whom God Himself, as Redeemer of the race, was born. But his own private ideas respecting Jesus were different when on the soil of Palestine. He compared Him, in his reveries, with Cæsar and Alexander, who were both deified after death, and he found new proof of the superiority of his race by comparing the duration of their influence as deities, with that of Jesus considered as God. Both were called gods, but who burnt incense to them now? Not even their own nations worshipped them, while they and scores of others bend the knee before the altars erected to the descendant of David. Could there be a greater triumph for the race which he felt to be personified in himself? What was this New Testament? According to its own testimony, it was only a supplement. Jesus came to fulfil the law and the prophets. It was, therefore, by no means enough to say that Christianity was unintelligible without Judaism. If Christianity was not Judaism completed, it was nothing. What was the fundamental difference between Jesus and His predecessors? It was that through Him "God's Word" was diffused among the Gentiles, and not among the Jews only. And Disraeli summed up his conception in this concise and Jewish-aristocratic phrase, "Christianity is Judaism for the multitude."*

But different as his sentimentality was from that of the Crusaders, he had poetic dreams which were akin to their poetic religious projects. He, too, dreamed of a liberation of this country, inasmuch as in his imagination he pictured former attempts to do it; the peculiarity of them was that the liberation was to restore the country to the original race.

It was at the burial-place, north of Jerusalem, called the Tombs of the Kings—and of its very uncertain title to the name he, in his romantic mood, entertained no doubt—that the memory of a figure of the twelfth century occurred to him, which had interested him even in his boyish years, and whose character and fate he had early begun to weave into a fiction. This was the Jewish prince, and afterwards legendary hero, Alroy.

* "Sybil," p. 130. "Tancred," p. 427.

He lived at a time when the Caliphate was weakened, and four Seljuk sultans had divided the inheritance of the Prophet between them; but they, in their turn, had begun to languish from luxurious living, and therefore saw with concern the increasing power of the kings of Karasme. Although the Jewish nation after the conquest of Jerusalem had acknowledged the supremacy of its conquerors, the Jews of the East still retained self-government within certain limits. They had their own courts of justice under a governor of their own race, who bore the title of the "Prince of the Captivity." The power of this prince always rose and fell in inverse proportion to that of the Caliphate, and the annals of the people tell of periods when the Prince of the Captivity enjoyed power and dignity scarcely less than those of the ancient kings of Judah. David Alroy was one of these princes, the memory of whom was recalled to Disraeli's mind by the Tombs of the Kings, and he pictured to himself his inner life. What a painful paradox, even in the title! A prince without territory or independence, a tributary prince, the ruler of a captive people! Disraeli knew what he must have had to suffer who was born to be a ruler of this sort; he could readily imagine Alroy's humiliation and grief when the first yearly tribute-money was demanded by his powerful oppressors; and even though he found his people not only despised and scorned, and still worse, so degraded that they no longer cared, but doggedly put up with it all, even though they were so enslaved and dishonoured that their state by the rivers of Babylon was a paradise compared with it! . . . See the chief of the Seljuks now defies David Alroy himself; he even dares to lay hands on his sister! Now the measure is filled up; Alroy slays the tyrant, flies the country, and resolves to become Israel's deliverer. Why should he not succeed? The greatest of the ancient kings, the first David, had raised himself to the throne from being the outlawed captain of freebooters; why should not he be able to do what his fathers had done? Solomon had built the Temple, and made the kingdom famous; he would rebuild the Temple, and make the kingdom more famous than ever. He would wield the sceptre which Solomon had wielded; he would make the times, which lay buried in the Tombs of the Kings, rise up again from the dead.

And Disraeli gazed across the great forecourt hewn in the rock, to the Tombs of the Kings—on the western side of them a vestibule opened, once supported by pillars, the stone pediment of which was still decorated with a carved frieze of uncommon beauty—and he dreamed that the fugitive Alroy approached this place by magic, where the departed kings of Israel were sitting on their thrones, and the realities around him resolved themselves into a splendid imaginative picture. David Alroy had to pass through long alleys of colossal lions of red granite till he came to an enormous portal in the rock, several hundred feet high, supported by immense caryatides. Alroy presses his signet-ring against this gigantic door; it opens with a rumbling noise, like that of an earthquake, and, pale and trembling, the Prince of the Captivity enters the vast hall, which is lighted with hanging globes of glowing metal. On either side are seated, on thrones of gold, the kings of Israel, and as the pilgrim enters, they all rise, take off their diadems, wave them three times, and three times repeat, in solemn chorus, "All hail, Alroy! Hail to thee, brother king! Thy crown awaits thee!"* As Contarini Fleming was expected at Venice, so David Alroy is expected here.

He stands, trembling, with downcast eyes, leaning against a pillar; but when, having come to himself, he looks up, he finds that the kings are still sitting on their thrones, gazing lifelessly before them, apparently unaware of Alroy's presence. He advances into the hall till he comes to an immense throne, extending all across the room and towering high above the others. A figure with imperial bearing sits enthroned on it, who amazes and dazzles Alroy. Ivory steps, every step guarded by a lion of gold, lead to a jasper throne. Light emanates from the glittering diadem of the figure and from its face, which all at once becomes beautiful as a woman's and majestic as a god's. In one hand he holds a signet-ring, in the other a sceptre.

When Alroy reaches the foot of the throne, he stands still

* "Alroy," p. 91.

for a moment, and feels as if his courage would fail him. But he soon regains self-possession with a silent prayer, and ascends the ivory steps. The Prince of the Captivity stands face to face with the great king of Israel. But Alroy tries in vain to attract his attention. The large dark eyes, which shine with supernatural radiance, and look capable of seeing through and revealing everything, are blind to Alroy's presence. The pilgrim, pale as death, once more summons up all his courage for the sake of the people of Israel. With deep emotion he stretches out his arm, and with gentle firmness, without meeting with any resistance, he wrests the sceptre of Solomon from his great ancestor's hand.

Just as he grasps it the whole scene vanishes from his view, and at the same moment it vanishes from that of the dreaming Disraeli. He stood again in the great rocky forecourt of the little vestibule from which the steps led down to the subterranean space hewn in the rock, in the midst of the miserable realities which had called up these glowing visions.

But it was while still in Palestine that he began to write his romance of the singular destinies of Alroy. He became for Disraeli, so to speak, what the Aladdin of his day was for Oelenschläger, an Oriental fabulous or mythic personage, in whom he could conveniently embody some of his boldest youthful fancies, and his greatest idiosyncrasies. The romance "Alroy" did not meet with success; it was not appreciated. But Alroy has never altogether deserted Disraeli; it was not one of those ideas of which a poet delivers himself by carrying it out. Alroy has certainly accompanied him through life, and I should not be surprised if the passage in which he seizes the sceptre occurred to Lord Beaconsfield, when, at the Congress of Berlin (in full accord with his definition of England as an Asiatic power), he snatched the British supremacy over Asiatic Turkey which brought those countries, over which David Alroy acquired dominion, under the sovereignty of Benjámin Disraeli.

"Alroy" is a work with great faults. The style is, in many parts, an intolerable "poetic prose;" especially in the beginning the rhythm is affected. The supernatural apparatus derived from the

Cabbala and the Talmud is superfluous, and recalls Southey's unfortunate poem, "Thalaba." The narrative is something between historical romance and legend; it is only in the dialogue that you see Disraeli's extraordinary superiority to Southey, for he has the true Oriental temperament, which supplies him with the colouring; but, with the exception of the dialogue, all is unreal, and a great deal childish; the descriptions of Alroy's combats with the caliph's armies, for example, remind one of troops of leaden soldiers moved hither and thither. The chief performs marvels of valor, and slays the sultan's standard-bearer, but, unfortunately, 10,000 soldiers are killed; the centre is broken by Midianitish cavalry, whom the Caucassian soldiers put to flight with the loss of so many men, etc. The romancer can narrate what he likes, slay at his pleasure, but you find yourself in an unreal world, and amidst child's play, which has no psychological interest.

The psychological interest of the romance consists almost exclusively in the development of Alroy's character. He has scarcely come off victorious, and achieved his first task of liberating Israel, than the task itself seems insignificant to him, and he seeks for some greater object, for no one has been able to withstand him, and Western Asia lies at his feet. He will not be content with rebuilding Solomon's Temple; his ambition is not to be so easily satisfied; he wants to found a great Asiatic empire. "The sceptre of Solomon!" he seems to hear re-echo around him, but those who thus speak begin to seem to him narrow and bigoted. Is not the sceptre of Alroy greater than Solomon's? Shall it be recorded in his annals that he conquered Asia, and employed his power in rebuilding a Temple? Shall the ruler of Asia sink into the governor of an insignificant province like Palestine, the virtuous patriarch of a pastoral tribe? No, Bagdad shall be his Zion, victorious Israel must and shall be reconciled to vanquished Ishmael, and they must, in spite of the protests of Jewish fanatics, be placed on an equal footing. "Universal empire must not be founded on sectarian prejudices and exclusive rights."*

* "Alroy," p. 141.

This ambition occasions Alroy's fall. The Israelitish religious fanaticism, which raised him to victory, now turns against him with embitterment, at the time when he is himself forgetting the projects and resolves of his youth by the side of a Mohammedan Sultana in luxurious Bagdad. The King of Karasme assassinates him, and succeeds to his empire and his bride.

It appears as if Disraeli, when at Jerusalem, had for a moment indulged the idea that his powers were equal to the task of restoring the Holy Land to the chosen people, but had come to the conclusion, on thinking it over, that his ambition for statesmanship on a grand scale could never be realized if allowed to spend itself in a contest for power of extent and importance so limited. He perceived that, even if he were permitted to arrange everything according to his will, abilities like his could never find a fitting arena, but on the soil of a great Power in Europe. Much had taken place there during his absence, and while he was dreaming in the East of the deeds of mythic heroes.

In France, the July revolution had overturned a monarchy, and placed a wandering Ulysses on the throne. In England, a revolution, no less complete, was projected, which was to be carried out amidst general agitation—that revolution in the British Constitution called the Reform Bill.

VIII

LIFE IN LONDON

⋘§ At that time there were still *salons* in London, and one of the most frequented was that of the well-known Lady Blessington, a great beauty, who was inseparable from her son-in-law, Count d'Orsay. Her house had a certain character of distinguished Bohemianism. The countess had long been separated from her second husband; Count d'Orsay's wife had left him after two years of marriage, and made way for her stepmother. The *salon* was only frequented by gentlemen; but all the men, so to speak, assembled there, who had inherited a distinguished name or made a name for themselves. In 1847, H. C. Andersen met there such men as Dickens, Bulwer, and the eldest son of the Duke of Wellington. When Disraeli returned from the East in 1831, Lady Blessington's house was one of those he most frequented.

In a literary aspect, the bias of the house was to admire Byron, and do homage to his memory. Lady Blessington and Count d'Orsay had made Byron's acquaintance in Italy, and had won his regard; Count d'Orsay especially, as shown by the poet's notes, made a very favourable impression on him. Lady Blessington had for some time taken upon herself to defend Byron's memory from unjust attacks, and did it without any ideal exaggeration. This tendency could not fail to suit an ardent admirer of Byron like Disraeli. In Lady Blessington's house, as it appears, he made the acquaintance of the influential statesman, Lord Lyndhurst, afterwards Lord Chancellor, to whom, several years later, he dedicated his romance, "Venetia," a sort of Byron memorial.

Politically, Lady Blessington's *salon* was decidedly opposed to the Whigs. Count d'Orsay was a celebrated caricaturist, and all his caricatures were intended to make the Whig policy ridiculous. In this also, the tone of the house suited Disraeli.

On the one hand, he was sufficiently aristocratic in his tendencies to feel himself attracted by the Tory party, and on the other, he was sufficiently revolutionary to sympathize with the masses and the Radicals; but from the first, the Whigs were repulsive to him, and in nothing, throughout his life, has he been so persistent as in his antagonism to them. In " Popanilla," when describing the British Constitution, under the form of an image of gold, silver, and iron, he remarks that the race of iron, namely, the populace, if they cannot exactly have their own way, would far rather vote for gold than silver, if it were a question of repairing the statue. So early as this is the alliance indicated between the Tories and the masses.

Lady Blessington was, besides, an intimate friend of the Bonaparte family; fifteen years later, Hans Andersen found a portrait of Napoleon I in every one of her rooms. At that time, she frequently saw at her house the exiled members of the family, and thus Disraeli was brought, by a curious chance, at the beginning of his career, into contact with two other ambitious men who were destined to play a great part in politics, Louis Napoleon and Count de Morny. The latter was at that time far from having acquired the brilliant polish which made him the personification of the Second Empire, and the model after which Feuillet drew his Monsieur de Camors, and Daudet his Duke of Mora. He wrote little French love songs, which he sang to his guitar. It is interesting to think of Napoleon III and Lord Beaconsfield meeting, as young men, in the same room. What similarity, yet what a contrast! Both, when they were nobodies, dreamers of wild dreams of grasping the highest power; both were of imperialist-democratic tendencies; both had fantastic notions that they were the chosen scions of a chosen race. But at the same time, what a contrast between the son of Hortense, born, as Sainte-Beuve satirically remarks, "near the purple," growing up in the shadow of Cæsar, and never giving up the idea of returning to the splendours in which his childhood had been passed; and the plebeian son of Isaac d'Israeli, by whose cradle it was never sung that he would one day be the acknowledged leader of the proudest aristocracy in the world! And, finally, what a contrast between the premature failure of the one and the indomitable energy of the other!

It is scarcely to be doubted that, on his return from his tour, Disraeli was to all appearance as much occupied with society as he was with the studies by which he was preparing himself for his political career. The idea never seems to have occurred to him of choosing a calling; he scarcely ever doubted that he would possess a mine of gold in the future. A young man with so firm a belief in his star, would have little scruple about anticipating some of the money which its ascendancy was to bring him; and Disraeli, it may be conjectured, soon found himself compelled to incur debts. Anyhow, it is indisputable that from the moment when he entered on a political career, he had to contend with great pecuniary difficulties. Election expenses were enormous, the bribery necessary engulfed fabulous sums, and so far as Disraeli was concerned, all these expenses were at first thrown away; whenever he offered himself as a candidate, he was defeated. When he at length succeeded in getting returned for Maidstone, he did not stand next time for the same place, probably because he was unable to meet the demands of the avaricious constituency. He offered himself for Shrewsbury, and a statement, published on this occasion by his opponents, shows that during the years from 1838 to 1841 alone, there were fifteen different claims made upon him for debts, for sums varying from £20 to £700, and amounting altogether to £20,000.

Gold had a great attraction for Disraeli from his earliest youth. From different points of view, it might be said that he had the greatest respect or the greatest contempt for it. He despised it, for he always regarded it as a thing of no importance except in heaps or by the ton—as something that it behoved him to have, and which he must have, as soon as occasion should arise for him to scatter it freely. And he cherishes a repulsive respect for money, because he has such a taste for wealth and luxury that life does not appear to him worth having without it; all his works, without exception, deal with very rich men and women; millions and such nice round sums roll from side to side through his novels; the few poor people who appear in them end inevitably, if they enjoy the author's sympathy, by gaining or inheriting a fabulous fortune. Balzac is a novelist who is considered on paper to be fond of rolling in riches; but in comparison with Disraeli's dukes and lords, his counts and bankers are insignificant people, millionaires with francs instead of pounds sterling; and compared with the London described by Disraeli, Balzac's Paris is a mere decorated workhouse. His descriptions ripple with gold like the waves of a gold river; there is a sound like the rattle of gold pieces when you put his books to your ear.

He must from time to time in his early youth have keenly felt the want of the treasure he so much coveted, and have felt longings for the precious metal. Did he ever play? Both as a novelist and a man of the world he wanted to be acquainted with everything, to have experienced all sorts of mental excitement at least for once.

Even in "Vivian Gray" there is a gambling scene, which betrays early experience; but of far more importance is the great scene, portrayed by a master hand, in "The Young Duke." It is so heartfelt, so evidently the result of experience, so thoroughly true, that Disraeli has never written anything showing equal insight and commanding power. All the stages of agitation through which the hero passes in the two days and nights during which he plays, are described with so much psychological delicacy, that they are no less interesting than the vicissitudes of a love story or of a battle. You feel how at first gambling is a pleasure, raises the spirits, sharpens the appetite, and how by degrees it becomes a passion which deadens every sense except the eye for the cards, so pregnant with destiny, which are brought in fresh every half-hour, while the old ones are thrown on the floor. I quote a passage:—

"Another morning came, and there they sat, ankle-deep in cards. No attempt at breakfast now, no affectation of making a toilet or airing the room. The atmosphere was hot, to be sure, but it well became such a hell. There they sat, in total, in positive forgetfulness of everything but the hot game they were hunting down. There was not a man in the room, except Tom Cogit, who could have told you the name of the town in which they were living. There they sat, almost breathless, watching every turn, with the fell look in their cannibal eyes, which showed their total inability to sympathize with their fellow-beings. All forms of society had been long forgotten. There was no snuff-box handed about now, for courtesy, admiration, or a pinch; no affectation of occasionally making a remark upon any other topic but the all-engrossing one. Lord Castlefort rested with his arms on the table; a false tooth had got unhinged. His Lordship, who, at any other time, would have been most annoyed, coolly put it in his pocket. His cheeks had fallen, and he looked twenty years older. Lord Dice had torn off his cravat, and his hair hung down over his callous, bloodless cheeks, straight as silk. Temple Grace looked as if he were blighted by lightning; and his deep blue eyes gleamed like a hyæna's."*

During the forty-eight hours during which he is at the gaming-table, the young duke loses over £100,000; but his fortune can bear it, and the loss only serves to cure him of his passion for play. Disraeli maintains that not only is this passion one of those most easily overcome, but that play is a habit which frequently gives young men knowledge of themselves, because, when on the brink of ruin, their better self awakens and asserts itself. This last opinion would not seem to have been drawn from the experience of others.

On reading the pathetic words in which, at the beginning of "Henrietta Temple," he warns young men never to accept an offered loan without sure prospect of being able to repay it, one imagines that he must sometimes have felt it a real misfortune to be in debt. "If youth but knew the fatal misery that they are

* "The Young Duke," p. 244.

entailing on themselves the moment they accept a pecuniary credit to which they are not entitled, how they would start in their career! how pale they would turn! how they would tremble, and clasp their hands in agony at the precipice on which they were disporting!"*

This exclamation is not the less sincere because, singularly enough, he dates the year before the one in which actions for debt, mentioned above, began to shower down upon him. But although he really meant it, my idea is that it was rather a momentary outbreak, and a warning for less hardened and more impressible minds, than Disraeli's customary way of regarding debt. In his novels there are many young men in debt, none of whom do any work—their social status is too high for that—but who, in spite of the various difficulties in which their creditors involve them, all escape from them with whole skins, rich and prosperous. Captain Armine, the hero in "Henrietta Temple," is undoubtedly depressed by the pecuniary troubles which he has brought upon himself by his extravagant bachelor life; he has to pay humiliating visits to hard-hearted money-lenders, and to accept services from others; he even makes a short acquaintance with the debtors' prison, described with Dickens-like humour; but his marriage with Miss Temple brings him compensation in the wealth of Golconda. Egremont, the hero in "Sybil," is unable to meet the great expenses of his election, and, like Captain Armine, keeps concealed for a time in a small country house, but when his beloved Sybil comes to glory and honour as heiress of princely estates, his embarrassments are soon forgotten. But I do not imagine that it is in the sentiments of these gentlemen of the fair-skinned race that we find Disraeli's own reflected, but in Fakredeen's, the young emir, described in so masterly a style in "Tancred," who is always over head and ears in debt, but never feels the least inconvenience from it—on the contrary, he pays visits in the utmost good humour to his creditors in the towns along the Syrian coast.

"Fakredeen was fond of his debts; they were the source,

* "Henrietta Temple," p. 62.

indeed, of his only real excitement, and he was grateful to them for their stirring powers. The usurers of Syria are as adroit and callous as those of all other countries; and possess, no doubt, all those repulsive qualities which are the consequence of an habitual control over every generous emotion. But, instead of viewing them with feelings of vengeance or abhorrence, Fakredeen studied them unceasingly with a fine and profound investigation, and found in their society a deep psychological interest. His own rapacious soul delighted to struggle with their rapine, and it charmed him to baffle with his artifice their fraudulent dexterity. He loved to enter their houses with his glittering eye, and face radiant with innocence, and, when things were at the very worst, and they remorseless, to succeed in circumventing them?"*

Does not the reader see Disraeli's own character in this description? Just so one can picture him taming and managing his creditors more like a tiger himself than the tigers around him. "Dear companions of my life, that never desert me!" Fakredeen exclaims of his debts. "All my knowledge of human nature is owing to them."†

Minus the jest and exaggeration, I do not doubt that Disraeli has felt the same, has found pleasure in feeling his capacities develop, and in measuring his craftiness with that of others, when it was necessary to find expedients, to practise patience and diplomacy until—like his heroes—a wealthy marriage with a beloved lady helped him over these fugitive studies in the vestibule of political intrigue.

It is not alone in Fakredeen's relations to his debts that I find a likeness to the character of young Disraeli. There is in the emir's political character the most curious mixture of lofty aims and ambiguous conduct, of faith in an idea, and faith in intrigue; and this is characteristic of Disraeli himself, when he is about to throw himself into active political life. Fakredeen is engrossed with the idea of the reorganization of Western Asia. Sometimes he is animated by Disraeli-like confidence in the power of ideas, or in

* "Tancred," p. 270.   † Ibid., p. 271.

formulæ which appeal to the imagination, but the next moment he looks about him for petty means and artifices; now he fully believes in a policy of magic and spells, such as that "a man might climb Mount Carmel and utter three words which would bring the Arabs again to Grenada, and perhaps further."* Then, again, the idea appears too improbable that any great religious truth can again proceed from the plains of Mesopotamia, and he thinks of nothing but by what intrigues he can obtain a large loan, or arms without paying for them. In a way somewhat analogous to this, Disraeli, on his return to England, was divided between the desire to gain political influence, by proclaiming some great simple truth, that might be of service to the country, and the desire not to frustrate his aims by any ill-judged or irrevocable partisanship. He could not resist the possibility of advancing himself by intrigues. He has indirectly acknowledged this when he says, in a passage in "Coningsby:" "The two years that followed the reform of the House of Commons are full of instruction, on which a young man would do well to ponder. It is hardly possible that he could rise from the study of these annals without a confirmed disgust for political intrigue; a dazzling practice, apt at first to fascinate youth, for it appeals at once to our invention and our courage, but one which really should only be the resource of the second-rate; great minds must trust to great truths and great talents for their rise, and nothing else."†

It did not require this veiled confession to tell us how great was the charm for Disraeli in those days of the game of politics and its labyrinthine and hidden paths. His first political campaigns reveal it plainly enough.

* "Tancred," p. 303.   † "Coningsby," p. 66.

IX

FIRST POLITICAL CAMPAIGNS

⋙ We have now reached the year 1832, the great year of the Reform Bill.

The opposition at first raised by William IV and his Tory Ministry to Parliamentary Reform was, as is well known, overcome in 1830, the first year of his reign, and a Whig administration was formed by Earl Grey. The Bill brought into the House of Commons by Lord John Russell, as a member of this administration, in the following year, by which a number of rotten boroughs were disfranchised, and representation given to twenty-seven large towns, was thrown out and Parliament was dissolved. The new elections gave the Reform party the majority in the Lower House, but the Bill was again thrown out in the Upper. This time, however, its rejection raised such a storm in the country that, when it was brought in again, the Lords gave up their opposition from the dread of seeing their influence annihilated by the creation of a number of new peers, and finally, on the 4th of June, 1832, the Reform Bill was passed, by which the number of British electors was raised from a practically small number to 300,000.

Only a few days after this great event in England's modern political history, and before the first echoes of applause had died away—on the 13th of June, 1832—Benjamin Disraeli made his entry into the little town of High Wycombe, for which, for the first time in his life, he had offered himself as a candidate. True to his principle of attracting attention by his appearance, he drove, elegantly dressed, in an open carriage drawn by four horses, accompanied by a band of music and a troop of admirers with banners. He bowed to the spectators who thronged the windows, and when he reached the Red Lion, sprang from the carriage on to

the porch, and made an animated speech an hour long, in which
he lashed the Whigs with biting sarcasm—not that the Reform
Bill was too liberal for him—it did not go far enough; he came
out as a full-blown Radical.

In the works which he had published up to this time, there was
no definite political creed, but they contained traces throughout
of what may be called the Liberalism of a good fellow. The place
for which he stood had hitherto been represented by Liberals
with a dash of Radicalism; being a very small borough, it was
dependent on the Tory landowners around; but the Conservatives
were in a decided minority, and it might be safely reckoned that,
as they hated the Reform administration, they would sooner vote
for a Radical, who hated it also, than for a Liberal of the
Ministerial stamp. Their organs also supported Disraeli. Politically
unknown as he was, he had tried to add to his dignity by procuring
letters of recommendation from the Radical Parliamentary leaders;
and really had two good letters from Joseph Hume and the famous
Daniel O'Connell. He had them printed and posted up in High
Wycombe. To his great mortification, Hume withdrew his letter at
the last moment, apparently from distrust of Disraeli's political
honesty, but he still had O'Connell's powerful name as a guarantee. In his first election speech he came forward as a democratic
plebeian. The Reform Bill was, in his view, not a definite step,
only a means to a greater end. He hoped that reforms of every
kind would arise out of it; but, above all other progress, he placed
the improvement of the condition of the poor; it was his principle
that the happiness of the many was to be preferred to that of the
few. He was the man of the people, for he had himself sprung
from the people, and had not a drop of the Plantagenets or
Tudors in his veins. He was glad to see the Tories for once on
the side of the people; the Tories must now rely on the people
for support; the people did not need to be supported by them.
He spoke vehemently against long Parliaments, then a standing
topic with the Radicals, who desired triennial elections.

Whether it was that Disraeli was regarded as a dangerous foe in Ministerial circles, or whether it was mere chance, the Prime Minister sent his own son, Colonel Grey, to High Wycombe, accompanied by two high officers of State, and the consequence was that Disraeli suffered his first defeat. The result was scarcely made known when he again ascended the hustings and made a speech, concluding with the following words: "The Whigs have stood in my way, and they shall repent it"—the earliest public expression of the assurance with which Disraeli has always contrived at the moment of defeat to regain the mastery over his fate by a sarcasm, a threat, or a prophecy.

The dissolution of Parliament during the same year occasioned Disraeli to offer himself the second time to the electors of High Wycombe. In a letter he addressed to them he speaks with great bitterness of the aristocratic Whig Ministry; it had sought to gain popularity by the Reform Bill, but it had stood in the way of the rights of the people by not keeping its word about the ballot and triennial Parliaments. But his Radicalism, even here, is mixed with Tory sympathies; he appeals to the fact that Lord Bolingbroke, "the cleverest statesman that ever lived," was in favour of triennial Parliaments, and he defines his own political standpoint by the reasonable but somewhat trite saying that he was "a Conservative to preserve all that is good in our Constitution, a Radical to remove all that is bad." * This cautious position gave him the name, among his opponents, of a Tory-Radical and Radical-Tory, and he was again defeated at the election.

In order to understand Disraeli's first appearance as a politician, it must be borne in mind that the actual difference between the two contending aristocratic parties was very ill defined, and that, in spits of their efforts at reform, the Whigs had really but little claim to be considered a Liberal party on principle. Various circumstances had for a long period caused power to be divided between two Parliamentary parties, who agreed on one point only, that they must be in power by turns. Among these circumstances were the combination of three estates in one empire, religious

* O'Connor's "Life of Lord Beaconsfield," p. 61.

differences, the victory of the nobility over the Crown, and the
peculiarity of the English aristocracy that it is constantly receiving
reinforcements from the people, while, on the other hand, its
younger sons are surrendered to the people again. Besides this, the
opposition between them had taken various forms: sometimes it
was Popery against Protestantism; then Protestantism against
religious liberty; now popular monarchy against oligarchy; now
warlike tendencies against love of peace; national interests against
cosmopolitanism; the policy of letting things alone against reform,
etc. At one time it was said, "The Tories believe in the divine right
of kings, the Whigs in the divine right of the nobility;" later on,
that the Whigs were becoming Liberal in order to regain their lost
power, the Tories in order to keep the power they had gained.
It was after the year 1830 that the Tories first began to call themselves "Conservatives." The word, as the designation of a political
party, is of modern date, and seems to have been first used in State
papers which came from Russia, and preached "the *solidarité* of
Conservative interests." It is not very happily chosen. To the question, Conservative or not Conservative? there is really no rational
answer but that of Disraeli's above quoted; for there is no reasonable man who would not wish to see anything altered in a Constitution, nor any one so ultra-revolutionary that he would not desire permanent institutions as the aim and end of change.

It was at the time of the introduction of the terms "Conservative" and "Liberal," that the word "Radical" also acquired political
significance. It is said to have been introduced for the first time
by Pitt, in 1798, when he reproached the Opposition with desiring
a "Radical" reform of Parliament. A Radical is one who, having
adopted a principle as sound, will not agree to any stipulations respecting it. Radicalism, therefore, could readily unite with the old
party names in England. There were soon Radical-Tories as well
as Radical-Whigs, that is, politicians of both parties who would
agree to no compromise. Besides these, there was, of course, a
Radical-Democratic party, who wished to see English institutions
remodelled after the American pattern, but who at that period
generally contented themselves with such demands as secret voting

and extension of the franchise, demands now nearly all conceded.*
A sense of justice, no less than an aversion to the middle classes,
attracted Disraeli to the Radical group, whose prospects, during
the democratic tendency by which the nation was affected, did not
seem unpromising. O'Connell, especially, was a power which every
party had to take into account.

When, in 1833, a vacancy seemed likely to occur in Marylebone, Disraeli offered himself as a candidate for the third time.
He sent a Radical address to the constituency, in which he called
himself a scion of a family "untainted by the receipt of public
money," and in which he—the future patron of the landed interest
—expressed a wish to see the whole system of taxation revised
by a Parliamentary Committee, with a view to relieve manufactures of the burdens which the land was better fitted to bear. As
the vacancy did not occur, Disraeli, in his eagerness to attract public
attention, brought out his oft-discussed pamphlet, "What is He?"
which is generally, though incorrectly, said to have been his first
step in the career of an author. It contained what he intended to
have said in Marylebone, and appeared in 1833; for a long time
it had disappeared from the world, and only now exists in an
extract from a newspaper, and in a recently acquired copy in the
British Museum.

The title was singular enough. It is explained by the motto on
the title-page, which apologizes for the notion of making your
début in politics by a book about yourself in the following way,
certainly rather dragged in by the hair: "I hear that——is again
in the field. I do not know whether we ought to wish him success.
What is he?—(Extract from a letter to an eminent personage)."
The "eminent personage" was understood to be Lord Grey.†

The pamphlet contains Disraeli's confession of faith as a
Radical. He says that before the passing of the Reform Bill, the
Government had, at any rate, the advantage of being based on a

* Respecting the names and position of parties in England about the time
of the Reform Bill, see Lothar Bucher's instructive work, "Der Parlamentaris-
mus, wie er est."

† O'Connor's "Life of Lord Beaconsfield," p. 67.

definite aristocratic principle; but now it was based on none at all. A Tory and a Radical he could understand; a Whig—a democratic aristocrat—he could not understand. The aristocratic principle had been overturned for the present, not by the Reform Bill, but by the means by which it was carried; if the Tories, indeed, despaired of restoring it, and if their assertion that the State cannot be governed by the existing machinery be sincere, it was their duty to coalesce with the Radicals, and to let these two political nicknames be merged into the common, intelligible, and only dignified name of the national party. In conclusion, he must observe that there was yet a reason which induced him to believe that the restoration of the aristocratic principle in the Government of the country was utterly impracticable. For Europe was in a transition period from the feudal to the federative principle of government. The revolt of the Netherlands against Spain had hastened, if it had not provoked, the revolution in England under Charles I; the revolt of the American colonies had hastened, if not provoked, the French Revolution; the movement could not be checked. The question which now arises, is therefore: Which is the easiest and most natural method "by which the democratic principle may be made predominant?" * and the answer would be this: "Immediate abolition of septennial Parliaments, introduction of secret voting, and immediate dissolution of Parliament." The condition of England was a melancholy one; it would sometimes appear that the loss of our great colonial empire must be the consequence of our prolonged domestic discussions. Meanwhile we must place our hope and confidence in the national character, and in great men: "Let us not," he concludes, with his usual self-esteem, "forget also an influence, too much underrated in this age of bustling mediocrity —the influence of individual character. Great spirits may yet arise to guide the groaning helm through the world of troubled waters; spirits whose proud destiny it may still be at the same time to maintain the glory of the empire, and to secure the happiness of the people!" †

* O'Connor's "Life of Lord Beaconsfield," p. 68.
† "Benjamin Disraeli, Earl of Beaconsfield: A Biography," vol. i. p. 102.

The reader will recognize the doctrine of the transition from the feudal to the federative principle in "The Revolutionary Epic;" he, perhaps, notes with surprise that Disraeli, the leader of the Tory aristocracy, began his career by declaring the period of government on the aristocratic principle to be at an end; but in the uneasy glance cast upon England's colonies, in his hatred of the Whigs, and the doctrine of the significance of great spirits, he will recognize fixed characteristics of the man.

The political character of the following years was marked by the circumstance that the distress which had long prevailed among the farmers, reached such a height that the agriculturists appealed to the Government to take some measures for their relief, although they were beginning to despair of getting anything from the lethargic Whig Government. The Reform Ministry, once so popular, had become inert; its members had one by one retired; even the Prime Minister, Lord Grey, had been succeeded by Lord Melbourne, and he, too, had become an object of contempt. The Tory star was in the ascendant; their leader, Sir Robert Peel, was daily becoming more influential, and they took no further account of the Radicals, whom they no longer wanted. Meanwhile the landed interest was without a leader, or, to speak more correctly, they had only the Marquis of Chandos for their leader, a man destitute of ability. The result of this state of things was, as far as it concerned Disraeli, that he turned sharp round. He dropped his Radical demands, made approaches to the land party, drew up a petition to Parliament for them, and, finally, when the Whigs went out at the end of the year, he made a great advance towards the Tory side. In December, 1835, he took part in a meeting at Aylesbury, where he, who had said not long before that the manufacturing interest was thrust aside in favour of land, said that "He had long been of opinion that a conspiracy existed among certain orders in the country against what was styled the agricultural interest." *

He spoke of the Marquis of Chandos with a warmth which strongly reminds one of Vivian Grey's enthusiasm for the Marquis

* O'Connor's "Life of Lord Beaconsfield," p. 75.

of Carabas, and made use of expressions such as the following, in praise of his new party, which were certainly very much out of taste: that while no nation could prosper without agriculturists, for they, as bound to the land, are the special and born patriots, "the manufacturers of Birmingham and Manchester would, if it suited them at any time, migrate to Belgium, France, or Egypt."*

The broad, open-air style of the speech is the usual one for platform eloquence in the country, and prevails at the present day with English politicians of all parties, but the tone of it will excite surprise.

That same month Disraeli again came forward as a candidate for High Wycombe, with a long speech, which appeared in print under the title of "The Crisis Examined." It treats of the inevitable necessity of reforms, financial, ecclesiastical, etc.; but tries especially to gain over the constituency for the new Tory Government. He eagerly tries to refute the opinion that no reforms must be accepted from the hands of those who opposed the Reform Bill; he even defends the party beforehand from the accusation of apostasy, if, after having opposed Reform, they should now favour it.

"The truth is, gentlemen," said he, "a statesman is the creature of his age, the child of circumstances, the creation of his times. A statesman is essentially a practical character; and when he is called upon to take office, he is not to inquire what his opinions might or might not have been upon this or that subject—he is only to ascertain the needful, and the beneficial, and the most feasible manner in which affairs are to be carried on. . . . I laugh, therefore, at the objections against a man, that, at a former period of his career, he advocated a policy different to his present one; all I seek to ascertain is, whether his present policy be just, necessary, expedient; whether he is at the present moment prepared to serve his country according to its present necessities."†

It does not concern me to discuss the abstract correctness of this candid avowal, but it is interesting from a psychological point

* Ibid.   † O'Connor's "Life of Lord Beaconsfield," p. 80.

of view; for you may be sure that a man who speaks thus is contemplating a political change of front.

After the apologetic introduction in favour of the Tories, the pamphlet makes an attack on the late Ministry, of which a fragment deserves to be quoted, as a specimen of the political eloquence of young Disraeli:—

"The Reform Ministry! I dare say now, some of you have heard of Mr. Ducrow, that celebrated gentleman who rides on six horses. What a prodigious achievement! It seems impossible, but you have confidence in Ducrow! You fly to witness it. Unfortunately, one of the horses is ill, and a donkey is substituted in its place. But Ducrow is still admirable: there he is, bounding along in spangled jacket and cork slippers! The whole town is mad to see Ducrow riding at the same time on six horses. But now two more of the steeds are seized with the staggers, and lo! three jackasses in their stead! Still Ducrow persists, and still announces to the public that he will ride round his circus every night on his six steeds. At last all the horses are knocked up, and now there are half a dozen donkeys. What a change! Behold the hero in the amphitheatre, the spangled jacket thrown on one side, the cork slippers on the other. Puffing, panting, and perspiring, he pokes one sullen brute, thwacks another, cuffs a third, and curses a fourth, while one brays to the audience, and another rolls in the sawdust. Behold the late Prime Minister and the Reform Ministry! The spirited and snow-white steeds have gradually changed into an equal number of sullen and obstinate donkeys, while Mr. Merryman, who, like the Lord Chancellor, was once the very life of the ring, now lies his despairing length in the middle of the stage, with his jokes exhausted, and his bottles empty." *

The speech has that sweeping, vehement, and entirely popular character which is expected on such occasions in England; and yet one perceives in it the elaboration of the born author. Disraeli conducted his whole electioneering campaign with the same wit and spirit which appeared in this instance; and yet he was again de-

* O'Connor's "Life of Lord Beaconsfield," p. 81.

feated for the third time. The consummate coolness with which he
has always taken disasters of the kind did not desert him on this
occasion. In a speech which he made a fortnight later, at a political
dinner given in his honour, he said, with his usual *sang-froid:* "I am
not at all disheartened. I don't in any way feel like a beaten man.
Perhaps it is because I am used to it. I can say almost with the
famous Italian general, who, being asked in his old age why he was
always victorious, replied it was because he had always been
beaten in youth." *

This confidence in himself, which, in the midst of defeat, enables him to look forward to the laurels of future victories, is all
the more interesting, because the year 1834, which was, politically,
so unfortunate for Disraeli, also brought him ridicule and disaster
in his literary character. It was in this year that the unlucky
fragment of "The Revolutionary Epic" appeared; it turned out to
be a *fiasco*, and was even ridiculed in Parliament. However little
poetical value may be attributed to the fragment, its fate is a
striking instance of the cruel severity with which men who have
contrived to make many enemies are judged if they once commit
an unlucky mistake. Only fifty copies were first printed, and it was
not until thirty years afterwards that the author allowed it to be
republished, in order to put an end to foolish discussions about its
contents, and yet in the mean time, this poem, which could scarcely
be considered as a publication, had played an important part in his
life, and served, mostly to those who had never seen it, as an
unfailing point of attack on the author. The reflections in "The
Revolutionary Epic" were destitute of all simplicity and freshness,
and certainly could not attract any one; the pathos was of that
affected kind which sometimes makes Disraeli's fine writing so
repulsive; and the versification was but mediocre. It is characteristic
of the ambiguous political position of the author that the two first
cantos are in direct opposition to each other, and sum up the re-
spective merits of the feudal and federative systems.

I mention a few characteristic features. In the first canto, the

* "Benjamin Disraeli, Earl of Beaconsfield," vol. i. p. 124.

abstract idea of equality of the French Revolution is attacked on
the ground that the character of a people is not manufactured, but
slowly developed during a long course of time, the natural consequence of which is inequality. If the human race consisted of
philosophers, equality would perhaps be possible; but men, as they
are, are governed rather by imagination than by reason. In the
second canto, the fearful consequences of tyranny and superstition
are described; knowledge, which is power, glorified; and the praises
sung of public opinion as the daughter of Lyridon, namely, of the
federative principle.

The fragment has no distinct ground idea; it was undoubtedly
intended to glorify the spirit of the modern era; nevertheless, in
spite of the revolutionary title, it contains, as appears from the plan
of it, many passages in favour of tradition, of hereditary aristocracy
and monarchical power in true Tory style, and they almost seem
like the forerunners of the lyrical effusions with which "Young
England," Disraeli's subsequent noble body-guard, astonished the
world. When he is reckoning up, for example, what constitutes a
nation in contrast to a tribe, besides honour, justice, and patriotism,
he says:—

> *In multitudes thus formed—*
> *A throne majestic yielding, and a band*
> *Of nobles dignified, and gentry pure,*
> *And holy priests, and reverend magistrates;*
> *In multitudes thus formed and highly trained*
> *Of laws and arts, and truthful prejudice*
> *And holy faith, the soul-inspired race,*
> *I recognize a People.*

Disraeli's many defeats were partly caused by the fact that
nobody could find out exactly from "What is He?" what the
author was, whether Radical or Tory, and he daily felt the necessity
of decidedly taking one side or the other. So he passed the Rubicon,
and went straight over into the Tory camp. He had previously
put down his name for the Westminster Reform Club; he now

withdrew it. He had spoken in favour of secret voting, but, as this was opposed to the Tory programme, because the landowners would lose the power of tyrannizing over the small boroughs at the elections, he not only dropped it, but spoke against it. He had written against the tyranny of the State Church in Ireland; he now demanded that it be retained. He had sought O'Connell's protection; he now tried to win his spurs at his expense.

In April, 1835, Peel was defeated in the House of Commons, and a Whig administration was again formed by Lord Melbourne. When a member of the new Ministry offered himself for re-election at Taunton, he was opposed by the indefatigable Disraeli, who in his speech on the occasion, tried to smooth over the change in his politics by an apparently ingenuous candour. He boasted of his political steadfastness, because of his unchanged opposition to the Whigs. If he no longer advocated certain measures, it was because, since the Tory party had recovered itself, they were no longer necessary. He had, for example, advocated secret voting in order to secure to the towns liberty to vote for members of the land party(!). They now no longer needed this protection. He spoke in favour of the Protestant Church in Ireland; the outcry against it was very much exaggerated; if this Church really was such an intolerable pest, why had it only just been discovered? He accused the Whigs, who supported the Irish demands, of encouraging Ireland to "annihilate the Protestants." He bitterly reproached them with not having been ashamed to grasp O'Connell's bloody hand in order to enter into a league against the State Church, and when the expression, "bloody hand," was objected to, he explained that he did not accuse Mr. O'Connell of entering parliament with bloody hands, but only maintained that his policy threatened the country with disruption, and could not be carried out without civil war. Now, it must be told that just four months before, in his published speech called "The Crisis Examined," Disraeli had said that "Twelve months must not be allowed to pass before even the word 'tithe' in that country (Ireland) must be abolished." He had, indeed, then, as always afterwards, spoken against the entire abolition of the Irish Church, because the plunder of a Church was always a benefit only to the aristocracy, but he would have had large concessions of all sorts made to the Dissenters; but now, when the Irish were in desperation, and the refusal to pay tithes had led to fearful massacres of men, women, and children, he took the side of the State Church out of opposition to the Whigs.

When it is remembered that Disraeli made his first public appearance as O'Connell's *protégé*, the amazement and indignation of the great agitator will be readily imagined when, a few days after the election, he read Disraeli's expression about his "bloody hand" in a paper, in which the subsequent softening down of it was not even mentioned. At a meeting of the Irish Trade Union at Dublin, he answered it. In a speech, brimming over with humour and contempt, O'Connell mentioned that this man had personally sought him out, and called himself a Radical; as such had asked and obtained a letter of recommendation from him, and had so highly valued his autograph that he had had it printed and posted up as a placard; and now he showed his gratitude by calling him a murderer and an incendiary.

"Having been twice defeated on the Radical interest, he was just the fellow for the Conservatives. . . . How is he now engaged? Why, in abusing the Radicals, and eulogizing the King and the Church like a true Conservative. . . . His life, I say again, is a living lie. . . . He is Conservatism personified. His name shows he is by descent a Jew. His father became a convert. He is the better for that in this world; and I hope, of course, he will be the better for it in the next. There is a habit of underrating that great and oppressed nation, the Jews. They are cruelly persecuted by persons calling themselves Christians; but no person ever yet was a Christian who persecuted. The cruelest persecution they suffer is upon their character, by the foul names which their calumniators bestowed upon them before they carried their atrocities into effect. They feel the persecution of calumny severer on them than the persecution of actual force and the tyranny of actual torture. I have the happiness to be acquainted with some Jewish families in

London, and amongst them, more accomplished ladies, or more humane, cordial, highminded, or better-educated gentlemen, I have never met. It will not be supposed, therefore, that when I speak of Disraeli as the descendant of a Jew, I mean to tarnish him on that account. They were once the chosen people of God. There were miscreants amongst them, however, also, and it must have certainly been from one of those that Disraeli descended. He possesses just the qualities of the impenitent thief who died upon the cross, whose name, I verily believe, must have been Disraeli." *

Just about the time when this speech was made, Morgan O'Connell had fought a duel for his father in London. A Lord Alvanley, thinking himself insulted by the agitator, had sent him a challenge; and, as he had had the misfortune in his youth to kill an adversary in a duel, and had made a vow never to fight another, the son took up the challenge given to his father.

A few days after this duel, which terminated without injury to young O'Connell, Disraeli sent him a challenge on account of his father's speech in Dublin, as the only means of obtaining satisfaction. The challenge was refused, and on the very same day, Disraeli seized the pen and sent to the *Times* a letter to O'Connell, which, from its fierce indignation and vigour of style, takes a high place among his political utterances. He begins by saying that, although his adversary had long placed himself beyond the pale of civilization, he (Disraeli) was determined not to suffer insult, even from a barbarian, to go unpunished. The expression applied to O'Connell had been misunderstood and incorrectly reported. If it had been possible for O'Connell to act like a gentleman, he would have delayed his attack until he had ascertained with certainty what really had been said about him. O'Connell, not he, was the renegade, for he was now an ally of the Whigs, while he was, as before, their opponent on principle. He had never sought out O'Connell with any other programme but that the Whigs must be got rid of at any price, and to this programme he firmly adhered. The letter concludes with the following sneer at O'Connell's Irish pension, and

* "Benjamin Disraeli, M.P.: A Literary and Political Biography," p. 611.

with a vigorous threat:—"With regard to your taunts as to my want of success in my election contests, permit me to remind you that I had nothing to appeal to but the good sense of the people. No threatening skeletons canvassed for me; a Death's head and cross-bones were not blazoned on my banners. My pecuniary resources, too, were limited. I am not one of those public beggars that we see swarming with their obtrusive boxes in the chapels of your creed, nor am I in possession of a princely revenue arising from a starving race of fanatical slaves. Nevertheless, I have a deep conviction that the hour is at hand when I shall be more successful, and take my place in that proud assembly of which Mr. O'Connell avows his wish no longer to be a member. I expect to be a representative of the people before the Repeal of the Union. We shall meet again at Philippi; and rest assured that, confident in a good cause, and in some energies which have not been altogether unimproved, I will seize the first opportunity of inflicting upon you a castigation which will make you at the same time remember and repent the insults that you have lavished upon

BENJAMIN DISRAELI*

* "Benjamin Disraeli, M.P.: A Literary and Political Biography," p. 167.

X

THE "VINDICATION OF THE ENGLISH CONSTITUTION"

᪥ When Disraeli, in the summer of 1835, looked back on his three years' political campaign, he had little reason to feel satisfaction in it. He had achieved but little more than to attract attention as a political aspirant, and he had suffered many humiliations, losses, and defeats. It was not easy to work in the political coal-mine without soiling your fingers, but when he looked at his hands, he could not but discover that they were very much soiled in a very short time, and even his face was not free from spots. He did not feel guilty about O'Connell, for when he sought his support, O'Connell had not come out with his most thoroughgoing intentions—he had not advocated the Repeal of the Union, the abolition of the State Church, or of the House of Lords; still, he felt the necessity of clearing himself in his own eyes and those of his fellows, of making the political system which he meant to advocate in the future, plain to himself and others; and after solitary reflections, and interviews with Lord Lyndhurst and other eminent Tory leaders, he began to put down his thoughts in the form of a letter to that statesman, and gave it the rather pompous title of "Vindication of the English Constitution, in a Letter to a Noble and Learned Lord, by Disraeli the Younger."

Various elements combined to give rise to the production of this political sketch; annoyance at his own mistakes, and the need of giving guarantees by an open confession, hastened the project; youthful sympathies, and early imbibed antipathies, with recent experiences, combined to furnish the contents. With all the passionate energy of his nature, Disraeli was deeply chagrined at the political vacillation of which he had been guilty. He had imagined it possible to assume an independent position outside the two old aristocratic parties; this had not proved to be possible, and he now desired, with all the vigour and persistency of which he was capable, to join the Tories, to take a side in such a way as to leave no doubt as to which side he had taken. But at the same time, it was his decided wish to reserve his political liberty, and he was, therefore, by no means disposed to accept the existing Tory policy as a dogma. Having found it impossible to make his way as a Radical, he desired, as far as possible, to carry over the Radical tendencies with him to the Tory camp, and he asserted that the greater part of what were considered the essentials of the Tory cause, were in reality only excrescences of it. Now that the prospect was at an end of forming a great national party out of Radicals and Tories combined, which he had advocated at High Wycombe, his object was to prove that the Tory party, if Toryism were taken in its true sense, was this liberal and national party. His task, therefore, in the future, must be to lead the party back to its principles.*

The "Vindication of the English Constitution" begins, as might be expected from the author of "Popanilla," with a fierce attack on Bentham and his school. Disraeli teaches that legislation cannot possibly be based upon utilitarianism, and ridicules the cognate principle of the greatest happiness of the greatest number as a criterion by which to judge it; not like the Pessimist of to-day, for he does not believe in the possibility of happiness at all—men like Disraeli are born ultra-Optimists—but he adopted the usual arguments of the historic school. Institutions must grow up by degrees and be altered by degrees; they are the outcome of the national character as a whole, and as such cannot be transformed in a day; the system which suits one country does not suit another, etc.— truths which were by no means overlooked by Bentham, when he placed the rights of the public good above those of ancient usage.

---

* An opponent of Disraeli's has epigrammatically said: "We all know that Mr. Disraeli has never believed that the function of Conservatism is to conserve."

The "Vindication of the English Constitution" is a defense of its traditional aristocratic principle. Disraeli's first object is to repel the attacks on the House of Lords common at that time. He attempts, therefore, to point out the harmony between the principles on which both Houses are based, so as to defend the Lords from the charge of being an anomaly. He tries to prove, first, that the Upper House is not less representative than the elective Lower House; and, secondly, that the latter, though not to the same extent, is based on the hereditary principle like the other.

He declares that it is untrue to say that the representative and aristocratic principles are opposed to each other; it is untrue to speak of the Commons as the popular House, as opposed to the Lords as aristocratic. For both Houses are composed, so long as universal suffrage is not a part of the Constitution, of the privileged classes; both are at once popular and representative. The proof is adduced, premising that the chain of reasoning is condensed, in the following bold style:—Representation is not dependent on elections; a chamber may be representative without being elective (as, for example, the Press represents interests and ideas, although journalists are not elected). In the House of Lords, for instance, the bishops represent the Church, and they having often (?) risen from the lowest ranks of the people, "form the most democratic element among the many popular elements in the Upper House." The whole difference, then, between the two Houses consists in the great difference between the number of members in the two political classes from which they spring. The one is a privileged class of 300,000 persons, who are represented by delegates, because they are too numerous to appear in person, the other is a privileged class of 300 nobles, who attend in person.

Having demonstrated the popular character of the Upper House in this remarkable manner, Disraeli proceeds to discover the hereditary principle in the composition of the Lower. He is of opinion that this principle of hereditary legislature is the principle on which the English Constitution has been upreared, and to which it owes its strength in comparison with the impracticable paper constitution of the Continent, particularly of France. Everybody knows that the Upper House is an assembly where the right to make laws is hereditary, but it is overlooked that in the Lower House the right to elect legislators is scarcely less hereditary, that practically, if not nominally, the heredity of the legislative office is the rule; the representative of a county is invariably chosen from one of the first families of the county, and ten years after his election he, as invariably, leads his son to the hustings, and commends him to the confidence of the constituency, so that he succeeds to his father—he enters on his inheritance.

Thus, then, it is demonstrated that the Lower House is the House of a privileged class, based upon inheritance, and that the Upper House is not an aristocratic, but a representative, and in many respects democratic, assembly; and next Disraeli passes on, with a light heart, to his favourite theme, the mischief done by the Whig party. He seeks to prove that the Venetian Republic has for a long period served the Whigs as a model, and that since the English Revolution they have persistently carried out their plan of robbing the King of his rights, and reducing him from an English sovereign to the position of a Doge of Venice. Their aim has ever been to establish an oligarchy which should absolutely govern the Crown and people. Their watchward, it is true, is civil and religious liberty, but by civil liberty they mean that the sovereign shall be a doge, and by religious liberty that the State Church shall be abolished for the benefit of the fanatical Puritanism with which it has allied itself. The Tories, on the contrary, who felt compelled to adopt the unpopular watchword, "the kingdom by the grace of God," were originally the really Liberal party, who wished to secure their rights to the people by upholding the power of the sovereign. The watchwords had quickly become antiquated, the Tory party held more, the Whigs less, popular and liberal views than would be supposed from their party cries, and thus it had been rendered possible, even at the beginning of the eighteenth century, for the Tory party to undergo a regeneration similar to that which was now taking place. The portraiture of the statesman to whom it owed this reorganization, Henry St. John, Lord Bolingbroke, Disraeli's extolled political ideal, is highly interesting, for it obviously contains confessions as well as promises, and an attempt at a description of himself:—

"In the season of which I am treating, arose a man remarkable in an illustrious age, who, with the splendour of an organizing genius, settled the confused and discordant materials of English faction, and reduced them into a clear and systematic order. This was Lord Bolingbroke. Gifted with that fiery imagination, the teeming fertility of whose inventive resources is as necessary to a great statesman or a great general as to a great poet," he was "the ablest writer and the most accomplished orator of his age, that rare union that, in a country of free Parliaments and a free Press, ensures to its possessor the privilege of exercising a constant influence over the mind of his country. . . . Opposed to the Whigs from principle, for an oligarchy is hostile to genius, . . . it is probable that in the earlier years of his career he meditated over the formation of a new party—that dream of youthful ambition in a perplexed and discordant age, but destined in English politics to be never more substantial than a vision. More experienced in political life, he became aware that he had only to choose between the Whigs and the Tories, and his sagacious intellect, not satisfied with the superficial character of these celebrated divisions, penetrated their interior and essential qualities, and discovered, in spite of all affectation of popular sympathy on one side, and of admiration of arbitrary power on the other, that this choice was in fact a choice between oligarchy and democracy. From the moment that Lord Bolingbroke, in becoming a Tory, embraced the national cause, he devoted himself absolutely to his party: all the energies of his Protean mind were lavished in their service. . . . It was his inspiring pen . . . that eradicated from Toryism all those absurd and odious doctrines which Toryism had adventitiously adopted, and clearly developed its essential and permanent character." *

* Hitchman's "Public Life of the Earl of Beaconsfield," vol. i. p. 113.

Bolingbroke wrote a work called "A Patriot King," in which he suggests that the king and the Tory aristocracy should unite with the masses, in order to suppress the Whigs and the middle classes. Disraeli's pamphlet suggests something very similar. He was, by nature, half popular tribune, half courtier. His sympathies went with the poverty of the people, and the splendour of the throne. A less bourgeois, or bourgeois-aristocratic, character can scarcely be conceived. As his dæmonic ambition now compelled him to make choice between the Tories and Whigs, he decided for the Tories, and at the moment of choice turned it into an advocacy of an alliance between the Crown and the masses, so that it thus became an expression of his own native sympathies.

XI

"VENETIA" AND
"HENRIETTA TEMPLE"

ᴇᶳ Disraeli was now over thirty, and the years between thirty and forty are generally the most productive for creative minds, in every sphere of action. The sun of passion is then in the sign of the Lion, and the mind is comprehensive enough to embrace thirst for action as well as visionary fancies. Before the age of thirty, much time is lost in frivolity and indecision—you fancy that there is time enough and to spare. After forty, imagination is often quenched by active life, which calls all the powers into requisition. But in these early years of mature manhood, the mind is both young and old enough to exercise the creative and practical faculties at the same time.

While Disraeli was keeping the political public in a state of constant excitement by a series of anonymous articles in favour of and against English statesmen, which were published in the *Times* under the title of "Letters from Runnymede," and while he was involved in a fierce controversy with the *Globe* newspaper, in consequence of numerous accusations of political treachery, he withdrew into the more peaceful arena of fiction, and wrote the only two of his novels in which there is but a faint trace of politics, "Venetia" and "Henrietta Temple."

"Venetia" is a very peculiar book, a mixture of imagination and reality, to which even Disraeli's novels offer no parallel; it is an attempt to treat of characters and circumstances in the form of a romance, with whom and with which the whole first generation of readers were contemporary, and they are still so well known that the reader always feels put out and confused when historical truth ceases and fiction begins.

Considering how deep an impression Byron had made upon Disraeli, it will be readily understood that he took the misunderstanding of the great poet much to heart. He saw with regret that, long after Byron's death, the old narrow-minded and bigoted condemnation of him still prevailed in English good society, so called, and he made up his mind to do away with it. That his private life had not been so blameless and brilliant as his public career, was a circumstance which, in Disraeli's eyes, need not lessen his reputation in the eyes of posterity. It is even characteristic of Disraeli that, with a freedom from prejudice very rare in England, he has always pronounced those men to be great or eminent whose distinguished qualities the crowd, with their petty bourgeois moralizings, were disposed to overlook, on account of failings in their private life, as, for instance, Lord Bolingbroke, Lord Byron, and Count d'Orsay. The study of Byron seems to have led Disraeli to the study of Shelley, from which it is inseparable; and although Shelley's ethereal nature was less congenial to him than Byron's tempestuous power, his deep occupation with these contemporaneous spirits led him to embrace both in his creative enthusiasm. He wanted to write a book which should gain the admiration of their countrymen for their two great sons, which should regain for Byron the hearts which he had lost, and open people's eyes to what they had possessed in Shelley, and had, with cruel folly, thrown away. In the centre of the book he places a young girl, a beautiful character, from her innocence and latent energy, modest and high-minded; she is a link between the two great men, for she is Shelley's daughter and Byron's *fiancée*. He divides Byron's life into two halves; the greater part of the incidents of his career—his gloomy childhood, his relations with his unwise mother, his first success as a poet in London and his deification there, his relations with Lady Caroline Lamb, and the fall from being a lion to a scapegoat—he attributes to Plantagenet Cadurcis, a young man whom he endowed with all the essentials of Byron's character and tendencies.*

* Compare G. Brandes, "Die Hauptströmungen in der Literatur des 19 Jahrhunderts," vol. iv. p. 395.

Other equally well-known incidents of Byron's fate—the unfortunate marriage, the separation soon after the birth of a daugher —he attributed to the elder poet and hero, who is ideally handsome, and enthusiastic for reform, Marmion Herbert, to whom he gave Shelley's character and genius. Lady Byron, very much idealized, is Shelley's deserted wife, which is confusing, and the young lady whose position agrees with that of Byron's daughter Ada, is Byron's playfellow and Shelley's daughter—you have to pay close attention in reading the book to keep the relationships clear. And yet it was a success. In spite of its violation of all æsthetic rules, it is a beautiful, impassioned, and spirited book; a good genius presides over it, and a waft of liberty flutters through its pages.

Venetia is the name given by Disraeli to the heroine, in honour of the city in Europe dearest to his heart, and of which both Byron and Shelley were very fond. She is brought up, without knowing her history, by a mother who lives in retirement, and without venturing to ask the name of her unknown father, though she conjectures that he is still living. She one day enters a room which had always been kept locked, sees Marmion Herbert's life-sized portrait, is struck by its supernatural beauty, finds verses which he had written in his joy at her birth, and begins secretly to idealize her unknown father. The playmate of her childhood, Lord Cadurcis, Byron's *alter ego*, who had been brought up in the narrowest and most rigid Tory notions of that day, offers her his hand; and Venetia, although she likes him, replies to his proposals by expressing her desire above all things to live for her father. His wounded pride causes him to heap reproaches on Herbert's name; he calls Herbert, that is, Shelley, "a man whose name is synonymous with infamy;" in short, he gives vent to his feelings against free-thinkers, republicans, and immoral people in general. Venetia's anger is roused, and she answers: "Passionate and ill-mannered boy! words cannot express the disgust and the contempt with which you inspire me."*

* "Venetia," p. 201.

Years go by; the young lord comes to London, sees life with the eye of genius, and all his foolish prejudices and theological absurdities fall from his eyes like scales. He finds Marmion Herbert's poems, reads them with amazement, enthusiasm, and admiration, becomes his sworn disciple, and would sooner outdo him than shrink from the consequences which the great exile has brought upon himself.

When himself compelled to turn his back upon England, he meets with Herbert in Italy, wins his affection and Venetia's love. Herbert and his wife are reconciled. The paradisaical happiness, which seems to be dawning for everybody, is destroyed by the catastrophe of the book; the fate of Shelley befalls both the great poets. They go to the bottom, with their yacht, in a voyage near the coast of Tuscany.

It is interesting to note that this is the first subject which charms our new Tory convert. Is it not perfectly clear that he wished, after his fierce political struggles, to plunge into the pure waters of poesy, and to convince the world and himself that, by going over to the Tories, he had in no wise pledged himself to the narrowness and hypocrisy of the "stupid party"? He reserved his right to contemn Byron's notorious Tories as much as he contemned them, to extol the unselfish philanthropy and world-embracing poetic mind of the Pantheistic Shelley, though he was still looked upon by the Whig champions of religious liberty as a hybrid between a madman and a criminal. Was it also a satisfaction to him, just as he had made, for political reasons, the transition from Radicalism to Toryism, to describe how a richly endowed genius had made the transition from the narrowest and early imbibed Toryism to the most large-hearted and advanced Radicalism? I have an idea that he felt that it tended to restore his mental equilibrium; an equilibrium which, perhaps, with men of passionate natures, is easily disturbed, but which every one involuntarily seeks to preserve.

The romance of "Venetia" is a masterpiece of tact: it conducts the case of the two unjustly exiled men, without coming into too close quarters with any living person; it transfigures Lady Byron into a highly poetic being, though it fervently advocates Byron's cause; it does not condemn a single one of the enemies of the two poets, only the "despicable coterie," which had taken upon itself to represent England, and had driven Byron into exile in England's name, and had thus misled him into hurling his darts at his country, instead of at this miserable coterie alone; it is only on Lord Melbourne, husband of Lady Caroline, that a somewhat comical light is thrown, but he was purposely selected as a victim, being then the Whig Prime Minister.

Further, "Venetia" is a poetical work: it was a fine idea to allot to a woman, a young, pure, strong-hearted girl, the part of mediator, first between Byron and Shelley, and then between them both and the English people. With her brightness and golden hair, she comes before us as the dauntless genius of love, understanding all, forgiving all, and blotting out with her finger the stains in the lives of the two men of splendid genius, whom she adores and admires as daughter and *fiancée*. "Venetia" is the only one of Disraeli's romances in which he has introduced lyrics of no small value, for his verses generally leave much to be desired. The poem which Marmion Herbert writes on the night when Venetia was born, is particularly successful; it is not altogether unworthy of Shelley—certainly very high praise.

Finally, "Venetia" is a fine piece of psychological criticism. The portraiture of the two poets is, on the whole, as spirited as it is correct; even their less conspicuous works, as, for example, Shelley's Essays, are introduced with great skill, and Shelley's influence on Byron is demonstrated with much penetration. There is a charming and truly Byronic humour in the passages where Byron acknowledges his plagiarism from Shelley, and laughingly confesses that he did not always quite understand what yet appeared to him so beautiful that he appropriated it. At the same time, it cannot be denied that we have only a sketch of Shelley, and not the finer physiognomical features. Byron is a spirit with whom Disraeli feels on the same level; Shelley was too ethereal for him;

and his portraits were naturally successful in proportion as he comprehended his subjects. There is a conversation in "Venetia" in which a good old Tory bishop compares the two men: "He [Cadurcis] is of the world, worldly. All his works, all his conduct, tend only to astonish mankind." *

There is some truth in this, only that a bit of Byron is cut out and made into a whole, the bit which Disraeli has in common with him. When Lady Herbert fears that Cadurcis, who is also cast out from society, will end like Herbert, the bishop answers: "He is not prompted by any visionary ideas of ameliorating his species. The instinct of self-preservation will serve him as ballast."†

In these words, which are only given by the author as a bishop's narrow conception of Byron, we perceive, with a little alteration, a characteristic of Disraeli himself. He unites in himself the qualities which are divided between his heroes—the visionary ideas and the making an idol of self. When writing this book, he was inspired by the great humanitarian visions which had pursued him from West to East and back. These visions enabled him to understand Shelley; on the other hand, he was animated by ardent personal ambition and desire for political power, and through these qualities he felt himself akin to Byron. But there was a third element in him, an element which cannot be said to have belonged to either of the great men with whose destinies he was occupied; this was the instinct of self-preservation, which is incorrectly ascribed to Cadurcis by the bishop, for Byron was far from possessing this trait; it has certainly always served to prevent Disraeli from making shipwreck on his way to port with his day's work half done, long and stormy as the voyage may have been.

"Henrietta Temple," the other novel written at this time, has for its second title, "A Love Story," and it is an appropriate one. In this book the author has for once given the reins to this passion as he knew and felt it. He had, of course, treated of it in all his novels, for a romance without love is like a goblet without wine; but he had not, before writing "Henrietta Temple," made it the

* "Venetia," p. 269.   † "Venetia," p. 269.

main topic. In Disraeli's manner of writing about women and love, three stages may be noticed. In his early youth, in "The Young Duke," he shows keen observation and freshness, much insight and surpassing irony; in his manhood, he depicts the ardent, admiring love of two young creatures, and, strongly affected by it himself, breaks forth into a song of praise in honour of Eros; in the third stage, woman is to him a higher, more representative being than man—she is the symbol of a great idea, and he describes her, and love for her, in the appropriate spirit, that of reverent tenderness. Thus Sybil represents the people and the Church; Eva, in "Tancred," Judaism and the East; Theodora, in "Lothair," Italy and national liberty. But through all these stages, there runs, as the most essential feature, a growing, thoroughly English idealism. There is in this idealism obviously something inborn—the home of his soul was rather the inspired East of the Arab than the luxurious East of Hafiz—but there was still more that was acquired by adaptation to his surroundings. He was not originally wanting in sensuous fancy; he had a keen eye for colour, betrayed equally in delight in the contrast between the hue of the lobster and the whiteness of the flounder at a fishmonger's, or the play of the diamonds on a lady's neck at a ball; but he had not enough of nature in him, he lived too perpetually in abstract plans and schemes, to be able to distil a beautiful or poetic side from sensuous life. He does not once describe sensuous attraction as an element in love, not even as an idealist might describe it, with unimpassioned truthfulness, far less with poetical appreciation of this force of nature. For he desires, above all things, to be read by the general public; to be a drawing-room author, recommended by a mother to her daughter. He therefore allows the great naturalistic movement in English poetry to rush past him without learning anything essential from it. He appropriates nothing of Wordsworth's feeling for nature, nothing of the sensuous richness of Keats, nothing of Byron's original native force, which cast propriety to the winds. The stages which I have indicated in Disraeli's treatment of love, are stages in the progress of a drawing-room author, and show rather his tendency to bring himself into accord with the spirit of the age and English taste, than the development of talent independent of the external world. This is one of the many instances of his adroitness in conforming to English manners and English notions of propriety, notwithstanding that he is, to a certain extent, un-English.

Under George IV frivolity was the mode; consequently, in "The Young Duke," Disraeli touches with a bolder and freer hand than he ever did afterwards the various mental and other conditions which result from frivolous or illegitimate love. The delineation of it is clever and in extremely good taste; the critical passages are passed over in jest or in a tragi-comic style. Still, erotic indiscretions have a place here, and are not, as afterwards, systematically excluded from the life of the hero. By his subsequent strictness, he has injured himself as a fictitious writer. He had a tone of delicate and indulgent irony in treating of such phenomena, which, occasionally introduced, would have had a good effect in the somewhat overstrained pathos of his later love stories. I give a few lines from the scene in which Lady Aphrodite, the duke's beloved, breaks to him her fears that he is tired of his relations with her.

"Out dashed all those arguments, all those appeals, all those assertions, which they say are usual under these circumstances. She was a woman; he was a man. She had staked her happiness on this venture; he had a thousand cards to play. Love, and first love, with her, as with all women, was everything; he and all men, at the worst, had a thousand resources. He might plunge into politics, he might game, he might fight, he might ruin himself in innumerable ways, but she could only ruin herself in one. Miserable woman! Miserable sex! She had given him her all. She knew it was little; would she had more! She knew she was unworthy of him; would she were not! She did not ask him to sacrifice himself to her; she could not expect it; she did not even desire it. Only, she thought he ought to know exactly the state of affairs and of consequences, and that certainly if they were parted, which assuredly they would be, most decidedly she would droop and fade and die." *

There is a good bit of psychology concealed beneath the irony of this description.

In "Henrietta Temple," love is treated in a totally different style. The praises of love are sung, its omnipotence is gravely described, and it is young, innocent love, sure of itself. All the difficulties with which it has to contend come from without, and do not finally separate the lovers. Captain Armine, the only son of a noble but poor family, is leading the reckless life of a man of fashion in Malta, and discovers one fine day that he is disinherited, and that his beautiful young cousin is heiress of all the wealth on which he had reckoned, and with which he meant to pay his debts. He comes to England, sees his cousin, finds her amiable, and has only to show himself, handsome and manly as he is, to become the object of her warm affections, for she is a girl who has not seen much of the world. His parents and those around him urge him on; the thought of debt and dishonour is a still stronger motive, and Armine engages himself, without a spark of love for her, to Katherine Grandison. No sooner is he engaged than he meets with Henrietta Temple, a young girl without fortune, whose beauty and charms captivate him at first sight, and his sole desire is, if possible, to win her hand. In this Disraeli illustrates the theory he has always held about the origin of love, and it entirely concurs with his deeply rooted prejudice in favour of sudden surprises and striking effects. He says: "There is no love but love at first sight. . . . All other is the illegitimate result of observation, of reflection, of compromise, of comparison, of expediency."

In this kind of love he tells us we "feel our flaunty ambition fade away like a shrivelled gourd before her vision;" fame seems to us "a juggle, and posterity a lie."†

How striking are these words in a psychological aspect! In order to give an idea of the strength of the erotic sentiment, Disraeli compares it with the strongest passion with which he is

* "Young Duke," p. 176.   † "Henrietta Temple," p. 78.

acquainted—ambition, and allows love for a moment to triumph over it. And he continually applies this standard to it. In another passage in "Henrietta Temple" he says, for example: "Revolutions, earthquakes, the change of governments, the fall of empires, are to him but childish games, distasteful to a manly spirit."*

The repeated assertion that the heart, when in love, does not beat for politics, betrays that Disraeli is here speaking from personal experience. And "Henrietta Temple" is altogether a book that speaks from the heart. It may be that sighs and groans, superlatives and *fortissimos*, are rather superabundant. It becomes the author well, who is so fond of representing temporary political party questions as the great questions for the human race, to condescend to the common interests of mankind, and not to be above stenographing for us the talk of two lovers, or showing us their tenderly affectionate letters. It is in the courage exhibited in stenographing the language of love precisely as it is, without any dressing up by the author, that the originality of the novel consists. It might have been supposed that in a "book of love," by a writer like Disraeli, we might have been treated with a mere love of the head, with pure admiration on the part of the young lady for the intellect of her lover; but Disraeli knows human nature too well to fill his book with such counterfeits. It has warmth and soul, and the intrigue is touched with the light, firm hand of a politician.

Still, although it is said to be the strongest evidence of true love when it makes a man forget his ambitious schemes, this first symptom is never described as permanent. The lasting effect of love upon the mind of a man is, as he represents it, and as was to be expected from him, just the contrary—to inspire him and spur him on to action. He says somewhere in "Henrietta Temple:"—

"Few great men have flourished, who, were they candid, would not acknowledge the vast advantages they have experienced in the earlier years of their career from the spirit and sympathy of woman. It is woman whose prescient admiration strings the lyre of the desponding poet whose genius is afterwards to be recognized

* Ibid., p. 137.

by his race, and which often embalms the memory of the gentle
mistress whose kindness solaced him in less glorious hours. How
many an official portfolio would never have been carried, had it
not been for her sanguine spirit and assiduous love! How many a
depressed and despairing advocate has clutched the Great Seal,
and taken his precedence before princes, borne onward by the
breeze of her inspiring hope, and illumined by the sunshine of her
prophetic smile! A female friend, amiable, clever, and devoted, is
a possession more valuable than parks and palaces; and, without
such a Muse, few men can succeed in life, few be content." *

It is entirely in agreement with this that, in Disraeli's novels,
the heroine has generally some keen political interest, a cause in
which she has faith, for which she lives, which fires her with
ardour, and which her lover is to advocate in Parliament. If the
question is asked in Disraeli's novels: "Which is the happiest and
proudest moment in a man's life?" the answer will be: "It is the
moment when he surprises his lady love while reading the speech
he made the day before amidst general applause in Parliament."
It is in this situation that the young duke surprises May Dacre, and
Charles Egremont the enthusiastic Sybil; and this situation may well
be said to be the happiest moment for Disraeli himself.

How ardently he must have looked forward to the moment
when this bliss, or at least the possibility of it, should be granted
him! How near it had often seemed, and then had again eluded
his grasp! One more attempt must be made, one more, to cross
that inhospitable threshold, on the other side of which lay the
path to happiness and power.

* "Henrietta Temple," p. 173.

XII

THE MAIDEN SPEECH

&c§ In the year 1837 Disraeli published both "Venetia" and "Henrietta Temple," and in July of the same year he offered himself as a candidate for Maidstone, with Mr. Wyndham Lewis, who was of the same party; Lewis was not a man of any talent, but was very wealthy, and had contributed £600 to Disraeli's expenses when he last offered himself as a candidate. His address to the electors is in the purest Tory style, but it is characteristic that, together with the old Conservative expressions about the glory of the State Church, etc., there is the most vehement condemnation of the Whigs' new Poor Law; it is called a crime against morality as well as a political folly; indeed, these violent outbreaks have almost a socialistic character. Disraeli gives as the reason of his opposition that the law was based upon an erroneous conception of the rights of the people. The Whig legislators have acted on the principle that the support of the poor is a matter of charity. He and the democratic Tory party are of opinion that the poor have a right to support. The land which once belonged to monasteries was practically, if not in name, the property of the poor; after the great families had divided it among themselves it had become the duty of those families to support the poor, and, before the new Poor Law, it was looked at in this light. The new law had occasioned a justifiable desperation among the poor, for poverty was now punished by compulsory labour, even on Sundays.

The speaker's argument is, as will be seen, directed against the Manchester conception of the State, yet it is not founded on pure socialism. The right of a man out of work to support is based not on an abstract right to work, but on his right to share in the former property of the Catholic Church. But while Disraeli took up the cause of the lowest classes in its social aspect, he left them politically entirely in the lurch. He was opposed at the election by one of the best and most honourable men of the Radical party, Colonel Thompson, a friend of Bentham; he adhered to the demands which Disraeli formerly urged, namely, secret voting (to protect the political independence of the poor and dependent), and the right of the working man to the suffrage—claims which could not be denied, and which have since been granted. Thompson was defeated, and Wyndham Lewis and Disraeli were elected.

His ardent desire was at length attained—attained after full five years' effort, after five futile attempts and four direct defeats; the end was reached—he was a member of England's House of Commons.

The object now was to maintain the position gained after so many fruitless assaults.

William IV had died in June, 1837. On the 20th of November, the new Parliament elected on the accession of Queen Victoria met for a short session, the main purpose of which was to vote a civil list for the young sovereign. It will be seen, therefore, that Disraeli's Parliamentary career coincides exactly with the reign of the Queen whose personal confidence he has so largely succeeded in gaining, and who was to raise him to every post of honour and grant him every distinction that heart could wish.

Disraeli did not allow many weeks to pass before his voice was heard for the first time in Parliament. He had promised O'Connell that they should meet at Philippi, and O'Connell was then one of the most influential members of the House. The importance of the "maiden speech," as it is called in England, is well known. From the impression made by it the horoscope of the new member is cast: he may, by its means, become all at once a political magnate; while, on the other hand, it has sometimes happened that speakers who have shone out of Parliament, and of whom great expectations have been entertained, have met with so poor a *succès d'estime*, that they have not for a long time, if ever, recovered themselves. The moment, therefore, was a most critical one for Disraeli; it was one of those in which a man feels that he must succeed, that a defeat this time would count for ten on any other occasion.

It was on the evening of the 7th of December. The subject of discussion was the "Spottiswoode Subscription," so called. It was an appeal for subscriptions, issued by the Queen's printer, to support the Protestant, and oppose the Catholic, elections in Ireland. Several members of Parliament had subscribed, without considering that, as future judges of the validity of the elections, they would be at once partisans and judges. Whigs and Radicals combined in a vehement attack on the subscription, as a conspiracy against the religious and political liberties of Ireland. The Tories defended it no less vehemently as a weapon against the encroachments of Catholicism, and one of their speakers attacked O'Connell as the man who drove, "in conjunction with a set of priests, Irish voters to the poll, to vote for their god."*

O'Connell replied in a vigorous and cutting speech.

When he sat down, Disraeli rose. His costume was so unusual, that even this attracted all eyes: a green coat, a waistcoat covered with gold chains, a black tie without a collar. His personal appearance was equally un-English: a face pale as death, coal black eyes, and long black hair in curls. People had heard of him as a charlatan, and before he opened his lips they were disposed to ridicule and laughter. He began:

"I hope—I will even venture to believe—that the House will deign to extend to me that generous indulgence rarely refused to one who solicits their attention for the first time, and for which, I can say, without the slightest affectation, that I have already had sufficient experience of the critical spirit which pervades this assembly, to feel that I stand much in need of it."

The introduction, even, was not successful. Here, for the first time, there were mocking cries of "Hear! hear!" He continued:

"The honourable and learned member for Dublin has taunted

* O'Connor's "Life of Lord Beaconsfield," p. 165.

the honourable baronet the member for North Wilts, with having made a long, rambling, feeble, wandering, jumbling speech. I can assure the honourable and learned gentleman that I have paid the utmost attention to the remarks which have fallen from him, and I must say, without intending to make any reflections upon the honourable baronet by any invidious comparison, it seems that the honourable and learned member has taken a hint of the style and manner from the honourable baronet, in the oration which he has just addressed to the House; for it appears to me that there was scarcely a subject connected with Ireland that could possibly engage the attention of Parliament, that he has not introduced into his oratorical rhetoric."*

Renewed and louder laughter followed. This dandified up-start, then, of ambiguous antecedents, wanted, in the very first words he stammered out, to pick a quarrel with the Irish national hero, who, with his Herculean frame, and his hat over one ear, was sitting opposite to his opponent, and, with the broadest laughter, was looking straight into his face. From this moment all the Irish brigade in the House, constituting O'Connell's not over well-behaved body-guard, resolved to leave no method untried of putting the speaker out of countenance—hissing, whistling, laughing, crowing, loud talking, stamping, etc. Disraeli went on. He argued that the object of the subscription was not an attack on the Catholic Church, but a defence against the political agitation of that Church, protection for the Protestant electors and landowners of Ireland; things had gone so far in Ireland that the tenants of a landowner had told him they could not give him their votes because their priests had forbidden it from the altar. In the speech itself there was nothing ridiculous; but his voice had an unusual ring, his action was more violent than happy, and his hearers were prejudiced against him. He could not conclude a single sentence without being interrupted by laughter. He paused in the midst of his speech, and said: "I shall not trouble the House at any length. (Hear, hear, and

* "Benjamin Disraeli, Earl of Beaconsfield: A Biography," vol. i. p. 11.

laughter.) I do not affect to be insensible to the difficulty of my position. (Renewed laughter.) I am sure I shall receive the indulgence of honourable gentlemen—(continued laughter, and cries of "Question!")—but I can assure them, that if they do not wish to hear me, I, without a murmur, will sit down."

He continued again for a quarter of an hour, the noise constantly increasing. When the tumult seemed the wildest, he said: "I wish I really could induce the House to give me five minutes more;" and at the same moment was interrupted by such roars of laughter that he was obliged to pause for a few minutes; but he took up the thread again, without losing his self-command. He had, unfortunately, made a mistake; he had described himself as the representative of the younger members of the House; and now said, after the peals of laughter which followed: "Then why laugh? Why not let me enjoy this distinction, at least for one night?"

The laughter became so loud and so general that he was obliged to pause again. He continued. He pointed out that the Whigs, who had threatened to gain an overwhelming majority at the new election, had lost in numbers; that the Tory party, which they had said was dead and buried so deep that there was no danger of its resurrection, had now raised its head as boldly as ever—when the interruptions again overpowered him.

"If honourable members think it is fair to interrupt me, I will submit. I would not act so towards any one, that is all I can say (laughter). Nothing is so easy as to laugh." He continued, and in a different tone, with bold metaphors and cutting sarcasms, about a Whig Minister and a Whig member, whom he characterized respectively as, "The Tityrus of the Treasury Bench, and the learned Daphne of Liskeard." He reproached the Minister with wishing to free Ireland in order to enslave England, that, standing "secure on the pedestal of power, he may wield in one hand the keys of St. Peter, and——"*

He could not get further; so loud and incessant were the

* O'Connor's "Life of Lord Beaconsfield," p. 166.

noise and laughter around him that it was impossible to finish the sentence. Every time he tried, there was a storm of bellowing, noise, and cries from every bench and corner of the House, and some face glared at him distorted with scornful laughter. At last he lost the self-possession which he had hitherto so remarkably retained, and, looking straight into the faces of some of his jeering opponents, according to the testimony of an eye-witness, he lifted up his hands, and said, with an unusually loud and almost terrific voice: "I am not at all surprised, sir, at the reception I have met with. (Continued laughter.) I have begun several times, many things—(laughter)—and have often succeeded at last. ("Question!") Ay, sir, I will sit down now, but the time will come when you will hear me."

He sat down, and the waves of ridicule closed over him.

XIII

FIRST ATTEMPTS IN
PARLIAMENT

Væ ridentibus! Ay, woe to those who laugh! They are destined to be forgotten and to be trodden underfoot of those they laugh at. Woe to the laughers! that is, to those to whom power, when of a novel sort, is always an object of ridicule, which they think to put down by the rudest of all methods, making grimaces at it. These are they whom the new power most easily disposes of; for among them, among the prejudiced and little-minded, every power, when it has risen, finds its most obsequious body-guard. Those who laugh are the same as those who cry, "Hurrah!" —the crowd of followers, who begin by understanding nothing, and end by admiring everything, having no judgment of their own.

Only a week after his *fiasco*, Disraeli spoke the second time on a subject connected with literature, the rights of authors and publishers, concisely, clearly, and without interruption. A few months later, he spoke again, shortly, simply, and with the same result. By degrees, and by his persistent firmness, he gained a hearing. He spoke on questions of minor importance, always as accurately and concisely as possible, never laid himself open to attack, and threw down no challenges. This went on for a year. In 1839 he began to change his tactics. He spoke on the most important measures, made long speeches, spoke often, and often provoked reply, but no one laughed. The House had grown accustomed to his appearance, and perceived that he was not to be put down by inarticulate brutality.

Among his speeches there are two that seem to me to be noteworthy, as having a psychological interest, and they are on important questions—his speech on Lord John Russell's Education Bill, and the one on the so-called National Petition.

The first measure was a small affair, and I only refer to it because Disraeli, by his opposition to it, for the first time took up a position in Parliament on one of the great fundamental questions of modern times—the relations between the Church, the State, and education. There were at that time in England two educational societies—the one in strict connection with the Church, the other of a more liberal character; the teachers employed by the latter might be of any religious profession, and the children were instructed in other creeds than that of the State Church. This society was accustomed to receive, as an annual Government grant, the sum of £20,000, and Lord John Russell proposed to grant it once for all. The Tory leaders raised a violent opposition, on religious grounds, to this innocent and natural proposition. Gladstone, who was then still a Tory, spoke strongly against it, and said that the State had no right to leave the one true religion in the lurch, and to allow true and false in education to stand on the same footing. The other Tory leaders were still more absurd and narrow-minded. Disraeli opposed the Bill; as a good Tory he could hardly do otherwise. But it is noteworthy that at this stage of his political progress, he neglected to avail himself of the opportunity of taking a side for or against religious liberty as a political principle. He spoke against the measure, on the not very serious ground that it was opposed to the English principle of self-government to establish a sort of State education. The reason was all the less appropriate because it came from an opponent on principle of the Manchester theory, but it was obviously only employed to cover indecision. Disraeli appears to have felt himself embarrassed at that time with some Radical reminiscences about the duty of the State to secure absolute liberty of conscience, and had not yet definitely formulated his doctrine of the State Church as the great guardian of the Semitic principle, which in this capacity must have the education of the people in her hands. Born a dissenter, and having been formerly an advocate of the rights of the dissenters, he could not possibly favour religious intolerance as a political doctrine; nor could he sanction the principle that the State was of no creed, without joining the ranks of those who destroyed faith in the absolute superiority of his race by opposing the ideas and doctrines which have emanated from it, and by which it still rules Europe. There was but one way out of this dilemma, and he was not slow to take it. He continued to advocate the political equality of certain dissenters, but not in virtue of what he afterwards called the "ambiguous principle of religious liberty," but in virtue of his own peculiar conception of Christianity. The Catholics were already emancipated, the Jews only were left, and in order to demand for them equal rights with other bodies it was not necessary to take refuge in the doctrine that the State was of no creed; he argued from the fact that the Jews, as worshippers of the Semitic principle, the English representative of which was the Anglican Church, essentially belong to this Church. Christianity, according to his convictions, was only extended Judaism—Judaism for the multitude. One other class of dissenters was certainly excluded, those who dissented on scientific grounds. But he never interested himself much on their behalf; the scientific free-thinkers were idealists, and must take the consequences. So far as he understood them, they represented the Aryan principle, and therefore they were decidedly opposed to him. It was impossible to entrust education to them, or even to give them an equal share in it. The people must have a religion, and if they were deprived of the higher Asiatic religion which had been introduced, they would doubtless return all over Europe to their ancient heathen worship. *Summa summarum*, the Church should keep education in her hands, and the professors of various creeds should have equal political rights, on a principle which excluded religious liberty.

The second matter of importance on which Disraeli made himself heard in the early part of his Parliamentary career was the National Petition of the Chartists. It is usual to speak of the Chartists as the earliest English Socialists, and the expression is partly correct, in so far as the Chartist rising was based upon a movement of a purely social character; but what makes the term less appropriate is that, first, the Chartists desired only purely political reforms, and secondly, their demands were not in any degree founded on abstract rational ideas, such as the rights of man, and the like, but in true English style they demanded changes in the franchise, and in the organization of the legislative body, as ancient constitutional rights, or rather, they demanded the restoration of these rights.

Since the great impetus given to manufactures by machinery had altogether altered the relations of the workman to his craft, to his master and his customers, the working classes in England felt a profound dissatisfaction with the state of dependence in which they found themselves in relation to capital; and out of this arose an impulse to association in great unions, which were to uphold their common interests. The sufferings of the work-people were all the more severe because there had not yet been any change in the rule of *laisser-aller* in legislation. No Act of Parliament had then fixed a maximum of the hours of labour in factories; the labour of women and children was drawn into the vortex of open competition, without any limitation imposed in the interests of humanity; and wages were, besides this, curtailed by the truck system, the price of goods being arbitrarily fixed by the middleman. About the same time, the agitation for the Reform Bill, which promised to confer new rights on the classes hitherto excluded from political life, set the minds of the working classes in a ferment; but the actual Reform Bill, like the *bourgeois* monarchy in France, greatly disappointed the fourth estate, and, as was natural, the social discontent took the form of a political movement, whose first object was a share in the political privileges of the favoured classes. The new Poor Law soon proved to be the only fruit of the Whig victory for the lower classes, and this fruit was a bitter one. The previous method of caring for the poor was on a patriarchal, unsystematic plan; their education was indeed but poorly provided for, but help was not sparingly given to those in want, and unfortunately often to the idle and to beggars. The new order of things was economical and systematic, but cold and hard. It would have been just if extreme poverty were always the well-deserved punishment of idleness, and this almost appeared to have been the idea of the legislators, for the justifiable and well-meaning war waged against poverty was almost, under the new law, a war against the poor themselves. Relief was given by taking them into workhouses, where husbands and wives, children and parents, were separated from each other. Even old married couples were separated, and only saw each other on Sundays from opposite sides of the chapel, and every attempt at communication was punished as a breach of discipline. Daily labour was hard and unmitigated, space and diet were all carefully measured out, and imprisonment was frequent, although the workhouse itself was very like a prison. Under these circumstances, it was not to be wondered at that disturbances often took place among the working classes about the country—the agricultural labourers revenged themselves more and more frequently by setting fire to their masters' stacks, and almost every day in the year 1839 there were reports of the destruction of agricultural and other machines. The agitation resulted in the drawing up of a Radical project of legislation (the People's Charter), in which universal suffrage, vote by ballot, new electoral districts, annual Parliaments, payment of members, so that men of the working class might also have seats in the councils of the nation, were demanded—all things which would certainly only have indirectly remedied the oppression under which the masses were suffering, but which, nevertheless, appeared to them the best means of alleviating their distress.

The leaders drew up a petition to Parliament, and collected in a short time no less than 1,200,000 signatures. The original proposition of the chief leader of the movement, Feargus O'Connor, was that the petition should be handed in "by a deputation of 500,000 men proceeding in peaceful and orderly procession, each with a musket over his arm."* Instead of this, however, the petition was taken to Westminster on the 14th of June, 1839, in a less

* Hitchman's "Public Life of the Earl of Beaconsfield," p. 156.

tumultuous, if in a less impressive, manner, on a triumphal car, accompanied by the representatives of the Trades Unions in solemn procession. It was found necessary to construct a special machine to convey the enormous mass of parchment into the House. It was taken in, and remained lying on the floor of the House, the silent representative of the voice of 1,200,000 men, during the debate on the cause of the working people. The people had no hope of seeing all their demands immediately granted; but what they did hope, and what the Radical leaders, who found it every day more difficult to withhold the people from violence, had held out a prospect of, was at all events a thorough and searching discussion of the wishes of the working men—a recognition of the existence of this great class interest, a recognition of the social question, as it was soon afterwards called, as a problem the solution of which must inevitably be sought. What actually took place had not been thought possible by any of the delegates or leaders of the party. The National Petition made not the slightest impression. It was laid before an empty House. But a very few of the haughty members of Parliament had thought it worth while to go to Westminster to reject the petition. It excited less interest than the most insignificant party debate; it was thrown into the shade by the passionate interest excited in those days by a discussion about the Constitution of Jamaica. There was not a single member of the Lower House absent from this debate, and the strangers' gallery was crowded to the ceiling. While the discussion of the interests of a few wealthy, half-foreign planters in a distant colony occupied universal attention for weeks, the demands of the great Anglo-Saxon nation, their petition signed by hundreds of thousands, and, so to speak, with the blood of the people, occupied but a few hours, and, after a debate without any depth or seriousness, it was rejected. While the tropical labour question, the subject of the emancipation of the slaves in Jamaica, was warmly discussed, the domestic labour question, the grievances of the white slaves, who were but little better off, excited no interest.

One member only spoke with the sympathy and earnestness appropriate to the occasion, and this was Disraeli. He attributed the agitating attitude of the party of the working men to the agitation of the Whigs when they were working their propaganda for the Reform Bill. The Chartists had only learnt a lesson from the Whigs, and it was therefore most unjust of the Liberals so vehemently to condemn the conduct of the Radicals. Had not a Whig orator in his day, who was afterwards a member of the Cabinet (Lord Brougham), advised that 100,000 men should go from Birmingham to London to demand Reform? He traced the general discontent to the Reform Bill itself; he again took occasion to show that the Constitution of the country had formerly been based on a more aristocratic principle; to a few privileged persons it granted large rights, and therefore laid upon them large obligations; in undertaking the government of the masses, they also undertook to care for their welfare. By the Reform Bill, power had been conferred on a new grade of society, and this class, from its character and traditions, felt no obligation to exercise social duties. What the Chartists complained of, without exactly knowing it, was the government of the middle class—that middle class by which the Government was chiefly supported, and among whom the opposition to the agricultural interests had its chief camp. The Chartists were not inimical to the aristocracy and the Corn Laws. He was not ashamed to say, however much he disapproved of the Charter, that he sympathized with the Chartists.

At that period it required considerable personal and Parliamentary courage to make such a speech as this, although a sort of aristocratic turn was given to it. Disraeli knew how it would be taken and turned to account—it was something like it would be to avow that you sympathized with the Internationalists nowadays —but with these words he clearly referred the *proletariat* to the Tories. Attempts have been made to show that Disraeli was not sincere in the certainly very Platonic sympathy he expressed with the Chartists, from the circumstance that, during the same year, he voted against the ballot and the shortening of Parliaments; this implies that, personally, he did not see a way out of their social difficulties for the working classes by the attainment of political rights, while he professed the contrary opinion; and it was for this reason that he spoke of sympathy with the Chartists, though he disapproved of the Charter. He explained clearly enough in "Sybil," six years afterwards, how he meant his words to be understood. The sum and substance of his opinions was this: The common people are right in calling themselves oppressed and overreached, but they are wrong in the assumption that Toryism is their enemy and approves their present distress; in order to obtain relief, they must learn that they will get nothing from the present leaders, and that no one but the heads of the aristocracy can or will help them. The correctness of this conviction of Disraeli's may well be doubted, but not that it really was his conviction.

Immediately after the rejection of the National Petition, violent popular outbreaks took place in Birmingham and other places. Disraeli voted against the consent demanded of, and granted by, Government, to suppress them by force of arms.

XIV

"YOUNG ENGLAND"
AND "CONINGSBY"

&§ A few months after Disraeli took part in the Chartist debate, he entered the married state. In his thirty-fifth year he married the widow of his colleague, Wyndham Lewis, member for Maidstone. Mrs. Lewis was more than ten years his senior, and had a large fortune. This apparently singular union was well known to be an unusually happy one. They appear to have adored each other. Disraeli's wife took an enthusiastic interest in all her husband's efforts, intellectual and political. Her devotion and strength of mind have been illustrated by a well-known anecdote. One day, when setting off to drive to the House of Commons, two of her fingers were crushed by the door of the carriage, but in spite of intense pain, she concealed it from her husband as he sat by her side, in order that he might not be disturbed in an important speech which he had to make. She kept up, so it is said, till the moment when he alighted, and then fell fainting on the cushions. She seems not to have been a woman who had had much courtly training, but was very enthusiastic, and had great goodness of heart. When, in the year 1868, Disraeli declined a peerage for himself, he prayed the Queen to make his wife Countess of Beaconsfield, and she bore the title until her death in 1873. The present Lord Beaconsfield accepted the rank and title three years afterwards.

The first steps towards Disraeli's Parliamentary career were taken; his social position was secured by his marriage; he now looked around him for some who shared his views, for a party in a more restricted sense, namely, for a group of aristocrats within the great Tory party who were disposed to accept Toryism according to his definition of it. A distinguished man seldom finds those who share his opinions among men of his own age. As the views he proclaims are for the future, he necessarily finds quite different opinions prevailing among his contemporaries; even at the best, it takes a long time to convert men who have once formed their opinions, and it is seldom of much use to try, as the mature man is shy of a party in process of formation. He who wants to make a fresh start must train his followers himself; while, therefore, in his youth, he generally prefers the society of those older than himself, he must now seek those who are much younger. They are more ready to receive impressions, take an idea more quickly, and are sometimes ready to make personal sacrifices for the views they have adopted.

Now, just at that time there was a little band of young aristocrats fresh from the universities, who were born enthusiasts, romantic dreamers, who dreamed of reviving the spirit of the old *noblesse* of England and France, and were deeply impressed with the sentiment that *noblesse oblige*. These young men abhorred the superficial and brutal methods by which the Reformation, in its day, had been carried out. It ought to have been a mental and moral regeneration. All that it had achieved was to despoil the Church of the treasures which had been entrusted to her, and which, in her best days, she had expended in the education of the people and given to the poor, and to give the booty to the Whigs! And they were told by Disraeli's speeches and pamphlets that the sole object of the Whigs had always been to set up an aristocratic republic in England on the Venetian model, in which the Whigs could turn to their own advantage the power of the Crown and the property of the people. These young nobles had that hankering for Roman Catholicism which in every country of Europe has been a result of romanticism. The present, with its absence of ceremonial, was hateful to them, and they longed for the forms and ceremonies and artistic pomp of the earlier Church. They mourned over the coldness and indifference which had arisen between the noble landowner and his tenants; over the disappearance of national costume and the old, simple, rural manners. They were incensed when they saw the old Gothic abbeys in ruins, from which stone after stone had been dragged away to build barrack-like factories. They looked back mournfully to the time when, instead of the wretched race of labourers they saw around them, there was still a yeomanry, a class of free cultivators of the soil, as old as the nobility, and holding a position of equal legal security. Being born at old castles, as heirs of large estates and property, they resolved, as far as in them lay, to change all this, and to give the Church and people their due; their cause was one and the same: there was a time when the priests of God were the born tribunes of the people, and when the nobleman was born to be the protector and father of his peasantry.

This little group of young men, about twenty-two years of age, who, shortly after 1840, acknowledged Disraeli as their leader, adopted the name of "Young England"—a name, of course, which has nothing in common with similar names in the present day. This little aristocratic clique does not recall Mazzini's "Young Europe," nor "Young Poland," nor "Young Germany," nor yet the group of disciples of Victor Hugo, consisting of artists and poets, *"Les Jeunes France;"* for it was neither revolutionary in politics, like the former associations, nor eager for artistic changes, like the latter; it was simply reactionary, with all the enthusiasm of youth. Yet even this "Young England," with its not very numerous members, had, so to speak, its Right and Left. The Right was represented by Lord John Manners, of Belvoir Castle, son of the Duke of Rutland, who gave poetic form to the doctrines of the new school, in an extremely juvenile, not to say childish, collection of poems, called "England's Trust." Lord John Manners raves about the time when the power of the Church was equal to her importance, when haughty monarchs were compelled to crave pardon from some poor man of God, and when the people saw in the king who bore the sceptre the anointed of the Lord. He hopes that a time will come when Catholics and Protestants will reunite to form one Church; he glorifies Charles I as a royal martyr; considers that the nobility alone can save the country, and that England's trade is her curse and misfortune; and with a turn so harsh that it is still sometimes quoted satirically, he exclaims:—

> *In many a hamlet, yet uncursed by trade,*
> *Bloom Faith and Love all lightly in the shade:*
> *Let wealth and commerce, laws and learning die,*
> *But leave us still our old nobility!*

The Left of the group was represented by George Sydney Smythe, a highly gifted young man, son of the diplomatist, Lord Strangford. He also dreamed of a powerful aristocracy, and a Church which should shower down alms on the poor; he also looked upon the Stuarts as noble martyrs, and was both amazed and incensed that, with the example of the Stuarts before their eyes, the great ones of the earth did not see their natural allies in the masses, and their natural enemies in the rapacious minority. But his tendencies were far more liberal than those of his friend above mentioned; he was continually in a state of development, had no ambition to prevent him from acknowledging a change in his views, and soon gave up his enthusiasm for authority as such, in favour of the principle of personal and independent research. He was a zealous Free Trader, and afterwards parted company with Manners and Disraeli. He possessed considerable literary talent, and has left writings of value, both poetical and journalistic.

Such were the noble and high-minded young men who met Disraeli half-way, and formed the centre of the little group who united with him. For the mockers, the whole party, who never had any influence on the history of England, was but "a clique of young gentlemen in white waistcoats, who wrote bad verses." The definition, however, was not appropriate, for the little band comprised missionaries and martyrs to be (Whytehead), and poets, including Tennyson. "Young England" had vast enthusiasm for "Old England," but to the two old political parties it was in the highest degree obnoxious. It wanted to change the whole policy of the country, and cherished the juvenile belief that England was to be saved by its youth—"saved" was the term, no lesser word would suffice.

It will be seen that it was precisely such followers as these that Disraeli wanted. He either overlooked their romantic absurdities or made allowance for them; romance in itself struck an answering chord in his own mind, and their enthusiasm for the Church and the people, their conception of the obligations of the nobility, he could turn to account. He was attracted to these high-minded young men, and felt himself young with them, for the span of years that he was in advance of them had not in the least diminished his vigour. He had always felt that he had a far larger fund of youthful strength than the average of men. It was part of his pride in his race and family. He mentions with satisfaction, somewhere in his writings, that his grandfather attained the age of ninety, and though obliged to confess that his father only lived to be eighty-two, he softens down the fact by stating that this comparatively early death was not caused by decay, but was due to an attack of a virulent epidemic, which desolated the neighbourhood, and snapped the thread of the old man's life. I remember also that Disraeli said (during the controversy with the *Globe* about his political consistency), when thirty-one years of age: "My letter to Lord Lyndhurst, just published, to which you allude, contains the opinions with which I entered political life four years ago; opinions which I adopted when the party I opposed appeared likely to enjoy power for half a century; opinions which, I hope, half a century hence, I may still profess." *

No one says such things unless he looks forward to prolonged youth and long life. According to his ideas, therefore, he was not guilty of any anachronism in placing himself at the head of "Young England" when nearly forty years of age.

The ascendancy which the clever *parvenu* gained over the scions of ancient noble families was by no means agreeable to their parents and friends. A letter from Lord John Manners's

* "Benjamin Disraeli: A Literary and Political Biography," p. 631.

father to the father of George Smythe, in De Fonblanque's "Memoirs of the Strangford Family," bears eloquent testimony to this. The Duke of Rutland wrote to Lord Strangford as follows:—

"I lament as much as you can do the influence which Mr. Disraeli has acquired over several young British senators, and over your son and mine especially. I do not know Mr. Disraeli by sight, but I have respect only for his talents, which I think he sadly misuses. It is grievous that two young men such as John and Mr. Smythe should be led by one of whose integrity of purpose I have an opinion similar to your own, though I can judge only by his public career. The admirable character of our sons only makes them the more assailable by the arts of a designing person."*

It will be readily understood that the sons saw with very different eyes from their fathers, when it is considered how these young men, just fresh from college, must have been impressed with Disraeli's superiority. He had been eagerly prosecuting historical-political studies for years; he had long been a practical politician; he had poetic faculty enough to follow the highest flights of romance, or, more correctly speaking, to lead them; and he had a ready-made political system to offer them which suited their dreams, as far as dreams and system could anyhow agree. They admired his coolness, his acquired repose, his art of characterizing a man or a cause by some telling phrase, and they listened with devout attention to his mystic talk about the great advantages possessed by the race to which he belonged—the only race to which God had ever spoken or had ever made the mediator between Himself and the world. They heard with astonishment that his pedigree was as good and as old as theirs. These Young Englanders had the beauty, the finished education, the teachableness and enthusiasm of the ancient Hellenic youth, and Disraeli sat in their midst at Belvoir Castle, or strolled with them in the park at Deepdene, and expounded to them the significance of race,

* O'Connor's "Life of Lord Beaconsfield," p. 222.

the origin of religions, the long-distorted truths of history, and the only principles which could guide politics aright, in the animated and pregnant discourse of which he was master.

It was in these conversations that the work of Disraeli's which had the greatest success originated, and it marked an epoch in his life, for it was from its publication that the estimation of his importance, both political and literary, by the larger public, may be dated. This was "Coningsby, or The New Generation."

The purpose of the novel, which appeared in May, 1844, with a dedication to a member of "Young England," Henry Hope, of Deepdene, was to assert the right of a select Tory party to be both a popular and a national party, as well as to serve as a programme to the clique, who here boldly appeared under the name of the "New Generation." Disraeli's experience with his "Vindication of the English Constitution" had convinced him of the impossibility of making abstract political essays a propaganda for his ideas among general readers; he resolved, therefore, to harness his talents as a novelist to these ideas, in order to open a wider sphere for them. The result was a novel without any artistic form, whose pages were permeated by political discussions. Still, it was a work which, in spite of its medley of politico-historic reflections and fictitious incidents, was interesting without producing excitement, and deserved success from the excellent drawing of the chief characters, no less than from its spirited paradoxes. Three large editions were called for in three months; 50,000 copies were sold in America. Five "Keys," a parody in three volumes, and a large number of critical articles, still further attested the author's great success.

The book at once arrested the reader by its impartiality; Tories and Whigs were assailed by the same merciless satire. *Punch* had a picture of the author as the infant Hercules, who had strangled two venomous serpents in his hands, the one having the word "Tory," the other "Whig," on its belly. The audacity which the sketch caricatured could not fail to excite curiosity. The treatment which the Whigs received in the novel does not need any long description. On the third page we meet with the expressions about the "Venetian" party, with which we are so well acquainted; about the attempts of a rapacious nobility to degrade the sovereign of the people to the position of a doge ruled by magnates; and about the infringement of the ancient Constitution of England since 1832, for the Lower House has been treated officially as the House of the people, instead of as the representative of a third estate, with certain privileges, which is in principle identical with universal suffrage, etc. But the Tory party comes no better off. The author goes back to the Liverpool administration, and accuses it of either acting on no principle at all, or on principles diametrically opposed to those on which the great Tory leaders of former times acted. He asserts that the members of it were utterly destitute of the "divine" faculties which a statesman ought to possess; they were neither orators, thinkers, nor observers; they knew no more of the actual circumstances of the country than a savage does of an approaching eclipse. Ignorant of "every principle of every branch of political science," they extolled themselves as practical men, but in their language a practical man was one "who practised the follies of his predecessors." On Lord Castlereagh, Lord Sidmouth, and the "arch mediocrity" Lord Liverpool, a condemnation is pronounced, not less contemptuous than that of the great poets who passed judgment on them and for ever branded them with contempt.

The turn then comes of the contemporaneous Tory nobility of the old school. They are represented in "Coningsby" by Lord Monmouth, grandfather of the hero, who, tyrannical and epicurean as a little German sovereign of the olden time, lives exclusively for pleasure, surrounded by a court of admiring millionaires and paid parasites. Lord Monmouth is a cautious, hard man, who hates feelings and detests a scene; he does not like to hear of any one being ill or dead; he wants to be amused at all hazards, and, above all, to do just what he pleases, in a quiet way, without objection or remonstrance. His one political aim is to obtain a ducal coronet. He has in his service a factotum of the name of

Rigby, a politician, journalist, and member of Parliament, who obsequiously executes all his lordship's behests, even so far as to inform an Italian princess, who has been his mistress for years and lives in his house, that he intends to dismiss her in order to marry her step-daughter. Nevertheless, with all his severity and wickedness, Lord Monmouth possesses a certain dignity conferred by consciousness of power, and always maintains a faultless bearing in the Louis Quatorze style.

But the novelist's impartiality does not end here. With a surprising sense of justice, he confronts Lord Monmouth with a representative of the aspiring middle class, Millbank, a manufacturer, who resembles the lord only in his resolute will, but in every other respect is his antipodes, upright and downright, industrious and benevolent, and possessed by a glowing hatred of the ruling class of drones. On personal grounds also he is the bitter enemy of Lord Monmouth.

The lord has sent his orphan grandson, and the manufacturer his son, to Eton, the training-ground of the "New Generation." Here we watch them as they are growing up about the time of the Reform Bill, at their lessons, their discussions, and their sports; we see Young England in the bud. They are all but one sons of noble families—Coningsby, perhaps, intended for the young George Smythe; Henry Sydney for Lord John Manners; and several others. Oswald Millbank, the son of the manufacturer, is the only son of a commoner in the school; he has long felt an enthusiastic admiration for the circle of young nobles, and from the day when Coningsby saves him from drowning, at the risk of his own life, he is his sworn friend. By degrees, as the lads grow older, they begin to be politicians, and their natural instincts lead them to some great political truths, which, in the year 1835, "were at the bottom of every (Eton) boy's heart, but nowhere else"—if not in a *brochure* on the British Constitution, which the author's modesty forbids him to name. Coningsby's talents make him the born leader of these boys. When he leaves school we are told, in the description of him, that he is "not a stranger to the stirring impulses of high ambition," but the world has hitherto been a world of books to him. He is attached to his young friends, but as he has himself formed their opinions and guided their thoughts, they cannot be to him what he has been to them; he longs to meet with a mind equal or superior to his own.

While he is in this frame of mind, he seeks shelter one day from the storm in the public room of an inn, and some one comes galloping on his Arab steed through the wind and rain to the same place. It was a stranger, perhaps ten years older than Coningsby, pale, with thoughtful brow and dark eyes beaming with rare intelligence—Sidonia the Jew, with the wealth of a Rothschild, and the reputation of a Montefiore among the brethren in the faith in East and West, a Disraeli in wit, pride of race, coolheadedness, and political insight. He differs only from the author of the novel in that, being still of the Jewish faith, he is excluded from taking part in the public life of England, and is a striking instance of the forces which she fails to avail herself of through her foolish intolerance. Coningsby and Sidonia fall into conversation; the young noble expresses his desire to travel, to visit the classic sites, especially Athens. "The age of ruins is past," says Sidonia, and he directs attention from Athens to Manchester. Sidonia is not one of those who think that young men of genius require experience in order to perform great things. He allows that, as a general rule, "youth is a blunder, manhood a struggle, old age a regret;" but there is another law for genius. He mentions many great men who have attained world-wide fame, although they died between thirty and forty, and concludes with charging Coningsby to nurture his mind with great thoughts, for "to believe in the heroic makes heroes."

In these phrases the author's conviction may be traced, that highly gifted youth has both the right and the power to effect a thorough reform in the public spirit of a nation, and this was obviously the conviction which kept the little band together.

After the meeting with Sidonia, Coningsby feels as we do when we have closed a book from which our minds have received a powerful impulse. He goes to Manchester, makes acquaintance with the condition of the working classes, and sees for the first time, not without interest, Oswald Millbank's beautiful sister. From the elder Millbank he hears opinions about the aristocracy which astonish and instruct him. He appeals to their ancient lineage.

" 'Ancient lineage!" said Mr. Millbank. "I never heard of a peer with an ancient lineage. The real old families of this country are to be found among the peasantry. . . . I know of some Norman gentlemen whose fathers undoubtedly came over with the Conqueror. But a peer with an ancient lineage is to me quite a novelty, . . . the Wars of the Roses freed us from those gentlemen. I take it after the battle of Tewkesbury a Norman baron was almost as rare a being in England as a wolf is now.'

" 'I have always understood,' said Coningsby, 'that our peerage was the finest in Europe.'

" 'From themselves,' said Millbank, 'and the heralds they pay to paint their carriages. But I go to facts. When Henry VII called his first Parliament, there were only twenty-nine temporal peers, . . . and of these not five remain. . . . We owe the English peerage to three sources: the spoliation of the Church; the open and flagrant sale of its honours by the elder Stuarts; and the borough-mongering of our own times.' " *

The family enmity between the houses of Monmouth and Millbank is a bar to Coningsby's union with Miss Millbank. In Paris, where he receives new impressions, he sees her again, but gives up the hope of winning her, believing that she loves Sidonia. When again in England, he discovers his mistake. But now a fresh obstacle arises: he positively refuses to act in political matters according to his grandfather's wishes, and openly avows that he means to act on principle, and on heroic principles too—for this his lordship has no comprehension—and thus Coningsby forfeits forever the favour of the man on whom his future depends. When Lord Monmouth dies, and his will is opened, it is found

* "Coningsby," p. 169.

that he has left his enormous fortune to a poor young girl, his illegitimate child by a French actress, and has only left Coningsby £10,000—a sum which, in the case of Disraeli's heroes, means poverty and utter destitution. Sidonia comforts Coningsby in his distress by representing to him that, with youth, health, and his knowledge and abilities, and his love of pleasure long ago satisfied, he has no reason whatever to give up hope of a successful future. Just like Count Alcibiades de Mirabel in "Henrietta Temple," he expounds the true view of life, that happiness does not consist in certain possessions, but in the conscious enjoyment of one's own personality, and that so long as existence itself is a source of pleasure, nothing is lost. Coningsby rouses himself, sets to work, makes a name, wins Miss Millbank, and moreover—this is inevitable with Disraeli—is the heir of the young French girl, who dies of consumption, and leaves him all her property, for in all humility she has always loved him.

In spite of its nine books, there is no action in the novel. The gist of it all is that Sidonia educates Coningsby, and Coningsby the rising generation. By the end of the book, he is ready to grapple with the older generation, and to enter upon a contest, for which his victory over the political intriguer, Rigby, at an election is the first good omen. The novelist closes his work with the following query:—"They (Coningsby and his friends) stand now on the threshold of public life. What will be their fate? Will they maintain the great truths which in study and solitude they have embraced? Or will their courage exhaust itself in the struggle —their enthusiasm evaporate before hollow-hearted ridicule? Or will they remain brave, single, and true, . . . and restore the happiness of their country by believing in their own energies and daring to be great?"* Of course, the novel is intended to compel the reader to answer the question in the affirmative.

The plot of the book is so unimportant because nothing turns upon it, but as a compensation there is a whole gallery of portraits. Some of them are mere sketches, for in this instance, as in general,

* "Coningsby," p. 477.

Disraeli has a real person in his mind, and hopes that the public will recognize him, and be able to fill up the outline; but the most important characters are drawn with great power and consistency. A vivid idea may be gained, from the perusal of this book, of the lives and opinions of the English nobles between 1830 and 1840. Disraeli is generally considered to flatter the aristocracy, and there is this much of truth in it—he has now and then abused his talents as an author by flattering some individual whose favour he desired to gain; but apart from this, it may be said that few authors have made the political and social immorality of the nobility the subject of keener satire. Old Lord Monmouth is drawn with a distinctness that makes him a permanent type; it is all carried out to his last breath, and with perfect coolness, not with the moral indignation which Dickens and Thackeray scarcely know how to restrain, superior as they may be as novelists to Disraeli.

Sidonia is the chief character in the book, and Disraeli's liking for him has made him into a genuine hero of romance. He knows everybody and everything, can do everything, goes through the world invulnerable as a god, does not reciprocate the sentiments he awakens, is indifferent to praise or blame, and wrapped up in his pride of race like a Spanish grandee in his mantle. The part he plays is to humble and instruct the nobility around him. Sidonia's family comes from Aragon; among his ancestors, who were all secretly Jews, there was an Archbishop of Toledo and a Grand Inquisitor. He has an unparalleled genius for business, and is the head of a gigantic banking concern, makes millions upon millions by his profound insight into political combinations, and establishes branches of his house in every city of importance in Europe. Not that he has any passion for business or money—he is too cool-headed for that, but as he is shut out by his religion from the only career which appears to him worth following, he occupies himself with mercantile transactions, study, and meditation. In the description of him it is said: "He could please; he could do more—he could astonish. He could throw out a careless observation, which would make the oldest diplomatist start; a winged word that gained him the consideration, sometimes the confidence, of sovereigns. When he had fathomed the intelligence which governs Europe, and which can only be done by personal acquaintance, he returned to this country."* As will be perceived, Disraeli's ideal is grafted on a Rothschild.

Sidonia does not trouble himself much about political forms. He regards the political constitution as a machine, the motive power of which is the national character. So long as the health and strength of the national character is maintained, the State may be strong, even with imperfect political institutions; but if it fall into decay, no political institutions can arrest its downfall. But nationality is to him only an intermediate idea; nationality is based upon race, for without the impress of race, nationality is inconceivable and meaningless. His faith in race concurs with his conviction of the overwhelming influence of individual character; for it is only as a personification of the race that the individual appears to him to be great.

This indifference to political forms prepares the way in Sidonia's mind for the transition to religious and political absolutism. "Man is made to adore and to obey" is one of his favourite axioms, and it necessarily implies that there must be personages made to be adored and obeyed.

Sidonia is of opinion that a Parliament does not offer greater guarantees against injustice and arbitrary acts than an absolute king, and that "public opinion"—this abstraction worshipped as a divinity in modern times, which Lothar Bucher once aptly compared with the Nemesis of the ancients—would exercise the same control over the sovereign as over Parliament. His sympathy with enlightened absolutism is summed up in the following words:— "In an enlightened age, the monarch on the throne, free from the vulgar prejudices and the corrupt interests of the subject, becomes again divine!"†

These theories take exceedingly with his young disciples, and we find them repeating them almost word for word. Coningsby

* "Coningsby," p. 220.   † "Coningsby," p. 303.

laments over an evil age, which has turned "anointed kings into chief magistrates;" changed "estates of the realm into Parliaments of virtual representation;" and transformed "holy Church into a national establishment."* He grieves over the power which the Lower House has obtained through the unfavourable times! "The House of Commons is the house of a few; the sovereign is the sovereign of all. The proper leader of the people is the individual who sits upon the throne."†

That very Young England, just fresh from school, should entertain these ultra-romantic notions is not surprising. But it is more remarkable that Sidonia-Disraeli should confess to and sanction them; for even in the "Vindication of the English Constitution," monarchical opinions were not advanced in so repulsive a form as this. The author of "Coningsby" was, however, too ambitious a man not to meet the views of the younger generation on this point. Utterances like these about the power due to a sovereign always reach the right address; a good word finds a good place. The perpetual flattery of crowned heads is a feature which pervades all Disraeli's writings. He began it in "Vivian Grey," by complimenting George IV on his dignity, his perfect and eloquent art of bowing. In "The Young Duke" he again extolled the extraordinary amiability and sparkling wit of this king, whom, after his death, he ridiculed as a "worn-out voluptuary, who desired but one thing of his Ministers, peace and quiet." In "Coningsby" he flatters Louis Philippe, with whom he was obviously personally acquainted, immoderately, though he must have been repugnant to him as a citizen-king; he makes Sidonia speak of the permanence of his government, and say that it is a definitive victory over the republic; it is even in relation to him that he proclaims the doctrine of the restored divinity of kings. Finally, the following year, in "Sybil," Disraeli falls into a perfect ecstasy about the grace and dignity of Queen Victoria at the time of her accession. In these exaggerated theories we must not, of course, forget to separate what is said from policy from

* Ibid., p. 359. † Ibid., p. 345.

real political conviction. The ultra-monarchical sentiments which Disraeli professes accord well with the value he places on imagination as a political motive. He perceives that the mass of the people understand only the monarchical form of government, and comprehend neither the strict Parliamentary nor the republican form. The multitude readily imagine themselves to be ruled by a king or queen, but they cannot connect any ideas with constitutional government. They follow the family affairs of a royal house with far greater interest than an abstract political event. "The women—one-half the human race, at least—care fifty times more," as Bagehot truly observes, "for a marriage than a ministry."* As a dignitary, as leader of society, as the representative of stability amidst all political changes, the constitutional sovereign of England has always maintained his significance. Even authors of the most advanced Liberal opinion have always admitted that it is a great advantage that constitutional royalty "enables our real rulers to change without heedless people knowing it."† But there is a long way between this and the recognition of a divine character in royalty. What appears to be concealed under all Disraeli's mystical expressions is the hope that the Crown might regain the sort of independence that it had, for example, under Frederick the Great in Prussia. It sometimes appears as if he wished to remind the Crown that it must defend itself vigorously against the claims of the favoured classes, and seek its strength in the broad, popular foundation on which it rests; but these democratic ideas in his case, as a stereotyped Tory, never go very far. The glorification of the royal prerogative in "Coningsby" seems to be, in the first place, intended for the possessor of it, in order to gain favour for the author, and next for the delectation of Young England.

There was another point on which it was easier and more natural for Disraeli to sympathize with the retrograde sympathies of his young staff. This was the taste for forms and ceremonies which the members of it had imbibed from the religious ritual

* Bagehot, "The English Constitution," p. 63.   † Ibid., p. 80.

at the universities; and the sentiment was strengthened when they found that all secular ceremonial, national costumes, ancient usages, fêtes, processions, and the like, were vanishing from their noble castles. I have already pointed out that Disraeli has a fantastic taste for the outward and visible sign of a cause or an idea—for free masonic ceremonial; and this taste formed a point of contact with ritualism. His liking for it was not deep, it did not reach the religious heart of the subject; to this Disraeli was entirely a stranger —so much so that it was reserved for him as Prime Minister, in 1874, in spite of the opposition of his colleagues, to carry a Bill intended to put a stop to ritualism in the Church of England. On this point also, therefore, Disraeli to some extent met his young followers by laying great stress on the points on which they were agreed.

In "Coningsby" the following conversation occurs:—

" 'Henry thinks that the people are to be fed by dancing round a May-pole.'

" 'But will the people be more fed by not dancing round a May-pole?'

" 'Obsolete customs!'

" 'And why should dancing round a May-pole be more obsolete than holding a chapter of the Garter?'

" 'The spirit of the age is against such things.'

" 'And what is the spirit of the age?'

" 'The spirit of utility.' "*

As the reader will perceive, hatred of utilitarianism is the element which binds Disraeli and the ritualists together. Other conversations in Disraeli's novels are in the same tone. The young men wish to see more form and ceremony introduced into life; they explain forms and ceremonies as witnesses of the highest instincts of our nature; and the author himself takes occasion to point out that, under the influence of the highest and most earnest feelings, man always takes refuge in forms and ceremonies, for the excited imagination involuntarily appeals to the imagination

* "Coningsby," p. 134.

of others, and seeks to find expression for it beyond the sphere of daily routine. Here, again, we have stress laid on imagination as the beginning, end, and aim of popular movements.

According to the opinion of the author, a new Tory party might be formed on the basis of the Tory sentiments and Tory dreams propounded in this book—a party which was not to be out and out Conservative, but which, when any one appealed to Conservative principles, should promptly ask: "What do you wish to conserve?" The previously existing Conservative party, according to "Coningsby," was chiefly recruited from those whose idea of politics consisted in £1200 a year, paid quarterly. The ideas of these persons are thus described: "To receive £1200 per annum is government; to try to receive £1200 per annum is opposition; to wish to receive £1200 per annum is ambition."* Young England, with its youthful and pathetic enthusiasm, and its political earnestness, was to sweep away all this stupidity, and to place genius and faithfulness to conviction at the helm.

* "Coningsby," p. 261.

XV

"SYBIL"

The question with which "Coningsby" concludes contains the political problem of the hour. Just a year after its publication, Disraeli had another novel ready, quite as important, which, as a contrast to the other, turned on the social problem. "Coningsby" had treated of two generations, the new work was "Sybil, or The Two Nations."

What were these two nations? Not the English and any other of the rival nations of Europe, but the two nations into which the English people and all others are divided—the nations of the poor and the rich. For the first and only time, Disraeli departed from his custom of seeking his heroes in the most wealthy circles, and interested himself in the cares and opinions of those who work for their bread. "Sybil" is the fulfilment of the promise contained in the speech on the Chartist cause, by its confession of sympathy with the Chartists; it is an attempt to open the eyes of England to the miserable condition of its lowest population, and to bespeak indulgence for the political errors which have resulted from it. Through the mediation of a friend, Disraeli had got sight of the whole correspondence between Feargus O'Connor, leader of the Chartists and editor of the *Northern Star*, and the other leaders and agents of the movement. He had also travelled throughout England, and visited the localities in which he intended to lay the scene, and had thus been compelled to study the poverty of the country. He described what he had seen, not only without exaggeration, but, as he states, he softens down the actual facts, for he felt that, if he stated the whole truth, he would scarcely be believed.

He gives a picture of one of those pleasantly situated little

English villages, which look to the traveller like a smiling patch of colour among the surrounding green hills and gardens. He describes the interior of one of these villages: the holes in the roofs through which the rain pours; the stinking manure-heaps around the house, and even close to the door; no fire on the hearths, even in winter; and the space so narrow that the poor mother, even in the pangs of childbirth, is often surrounded by the whole family, from her husband's parents to the children, whose inevitable presence causes her no less pain than childbirth itself.

Eight shillings a week are labourers' wages, and it is impossible for a man with a family to live on eight shillings a week. The wife works as well as the husband. When the poor man returns from his day's work, he finds no home, no fire, no meal prepared; his wife is either not come home, or is so tired out with field labour that she must lie down on the bed, or she is wet through and has no change of clothes. And in contrast to this wretchedness, there is the cold, philosophic nobleman to whom the seat belongs, which has given its name to the village, and whose one idea is how to get rid of this troublesome tenantry; he builds no new cottages, and allows the existing ones to fall into decay; he considers that emigration on a grand scale is probably the only remedy for these evils; and is, of course, indignant when the poor man now and then seeks forgetfulness in the public-house.

Disraeli goes from the country to the town, and presents a picture of the manufacturing towns, in which want and degradation exceed that in the villages. He shows us the famished artisan, whom machinery has reduced to abject poverty, at work at his loom in the early morning in an attic; his grumbling wife embittered by hunger, and almost exasperated with her husband; the starving little ones lying awake in bed. And this man is not ignorant or incapable. They have dared to tell him that the interests of capital and labour are identical, while he and the 600,000 other hand-loom weavers in the country, in spite of manly struggles, are daily sinking deeper in poverty, in proportion as the manufacturer increases his wealth.

"When the class of the nobility were supplanted in France," says this man, "they did not amount in number to one-third of us hand-loom weavers; yet all Europe went to war to avenge their wrongs, every State subscribed to maintain them in their adversity, and when they were restored to their own country, their own land supplied them with an immense indemnity. Who cares for us? Yet we have lost our estates. Who raises a voice for us? Yet we are at least as innocent as the nobility of France. We sink among no sighs except our own. And if they give us sympathy, what then? Sympathy is the solace of the poor; but for the rich there is compensation." *

We are taken into the streets of the manufacturing town, and come to houses where old women take new-born babes for three-pence a week, and give them back every evening to their mothers, when they return from the factories "to the dung-heaps or holes which they call their homes." The nurses thrive on this trade, for their outlay is not great—opium and syrup, mixed into some kind of national elixir. This drink effectually quiets the little ones, and sends them slowly and surely to the grave. "Infanticide is practised as extensively and as legally in England as it is on the banks of the Ganges; a circumstance which apparently has not yet engaged the attention of the Society for the Propagation of the Gospel in Foreign Parts."†

And yet there are children whose vitality survives both starvation and poison, unnatural mothers and Satanic nurses. We are introduced to such a creature under the fine-sounding name of Devilsdust. We learn his previous history. He didn't thrive, but he wouldn't die. When he was two years old, and the nurse had lost sight of the mother and the weekly pay, he was sent out to play in the streets, in the hope that he might be run over. But this hope failed. All his little playfellows disappeared one after the other. "Playing" in the streets for three months was generally sufficient to get rid of the whole half-naked, bare-footed crew between two and five years. Some were run over, others lost; some took fevers,

* "Sybil," p. 134.   † "Sybil," p. 113.

crept into their cellars, had a dram of brandy given them, and died; Devilsdust was the toughest of them all. He had nothing to eat but what he could get for himself, and he shared the street refuse with the dogs; but pale and stunted as he was, he kept alive.

We descend into still lower depths, into the coal-mines. "Bands of stalwart men, broad-chested and muscular, wet with toil, and black as the children of the tropics. Troops of youth, alas! of both sexes, though neither their raiment nor their language indicates the difference—all are clad in male attire; and oaths that men might shudder at, issue from lips born to breathe words of sweetness. Yet these are to be, some are, the mothers of England! But can we wonder at the hideous coarseness of their language, when we remember the savage rudeness of their lives? Naked to the waist, an iron chain fastened to a belt of leather runs between their legs clad in canvas trousers, while on hands and feet an English girl, for twelve, sometimes for sixteen, hours a day, hauls and hurries tubs of coal up subterranean roads, dark, precipitous, and plashy; circumstances that seem to have escaped the notice of the Society for the Abolition of Negro Slavery. Those worthy gentlemen, too, appear to have been singularly unconscious of the sufferings of the little trappers, which was remarkable, as many of them were in their own employ." *

And as a set-off against this state of things, on the one hand there is the Manchester wisdom, which, with an air of importance, gives lectures to the working classes (in districts where, on an average, the working man dies at eighteen), and tells him that now he has a pair of worsted stockings, while Henry VIII had none, and that therefore the condition of the lower classes is gradually improving; and, on the other hand, there is the brutality of the nobles, which is represented in "Sybil" by Lord Marney, whose war-cry is "war against the cottages," and who thinks the levelling tendencies of the age so dangerous that he even rates vehemently against railways, and the frivolity of the young men in good society who lose their money in betting at the Derby, frequent the clubs,

* "Sybil," p. 161.

are young yet *blasé,* handsome yet worn out, wealthy yet in debt.

It might be supposed, from this description, that the prevailing tone of the book is lachrymose, sentimental, and bitter; but so little is this the case, that, to Disraeli's credit, it is pervaded by a happy humour, sometimes pathetic, sometimes sarcastic, but always in good taste and well sustained. It culminates in the description of Wodgate, a town of smithies, where hammer and axe reign supreme, and in which there is no public building of any sort, neither church, school, theatre, nor assembly room. The people of Wodgate spend their lives alternately in exhausting labour, and Saint Monday joviality, which includes Tuesday; they are so ignorant that many of the inhabitants do not know their own names, very few can spell them; so neglected that it is rare to find a person who knows how old he is, still rarer to find a boy who has seen a book, or a girl a flower. As for religion, they have a dim notion that we ought to believe in our Lord and Saviour, Pontius Pilate, who went about the world accompanied by Moses, Goliath, and the other Apostles. They obey, as their self-elected ruler, an old master smith, whom they call "the bishop;" he is hard, but just, rasps the ears of his apprentices with his file when they are unskilful at their work, and marries young couples in the only valid fashion at Wodgate, by sprinkling salt on a joint of roast meat, and reading the Lord's Prayer over it backwards. He is the highest authority at Wodgate, and rules everybody, except his wife, who is far sharper than he is.

It is on this broad and powerfully painted background that the scene of the novel is laid. It is simple, as is generally the case with Disraeli. Charles Egremont, a young man of a noble family, after a youth in which he did not in any way distinguish himself, is, in 1837, elected a member of Parliament; and while staying in the country, meets, near the ruins of an old abbey belonging to his brother, two men, with whom he enters into conversation, and who greatly surprise him by the originality of their views on the social and political condition of England. They are, as it appears, Stephen Morley, a fanatical but very clever self-taught man, editor of a socialist newspaper, and Walter Gerard, a simple working man, but a type of the noble Saxon peasant race, a man of clear head and great energy, born to be a leader of a Radical working men's party. They are only accidentally in the neighbourhood with Gerard's daughter, who wanted to see the abbey. Egremont has just been pondering, with the ruins of the abbey in view, how it is that the people of the district have taken to burning the stacks of his brother, Lord Marney, while hay and corn were threatened with no such danger in the times of the old Catholic abbeys. This naturally turns the conversation between him and Gerard to the subject of the rule of the monks contrasted with the government of the present day. Gerard extols the monks; they did not possess any private property, nor lay by, nor leave money by will; neither were they absent for years, like the present landowners—on the contrary, they never left the abbey, they built and planted for posterity, founded libraries and schools, showed kindness to the poor of the neighbourhood. Gerard is a Catholic, but the question with him is not a religious one, it is one of right. The most conspicuous result of the Reformation, in his opinion, was that the monasteries were attacked, desolated, plundered to an unprecedented extent, and the treasures of the monks were distributed among the plunderers so as to found, in a pecuniary sense, a new aristocracy. Morley agrees with Gerard, but what he most regrets in the destruction of the old abbeys is that with them the last English type of a society with a community of goods disappeared; instead of association, which is the essence of society, England has now nothing but isolation.

"In great cities men are brought together by the desire of gain. They are not in a state of co-operation, but of isolation, as to the making of fortunes; and for all the rest, they are careless of neighbours. Christianity teaches us to love our neighbours as ourselves; modern society acknowledges no neighbour." *

The words of both Gerard and Morley make a great impression on Egremont, and he is still more moved when Gerard's

* "Sybil," p. 76.

daughter Sybil, whose voice, as she sang her evening hymn to the Virgin, had been heard as she sat apart among the ruins, drew near to the men. Like all Disraeli's heroines, she is an ideal of beauty, gentleness, and enthusiasm; the author has not succeeded in endowing her with very distinctive features, but she fills her place as the incarnation of the hopes and nobleness of mind of the lower classes.

Egremont resolves, partly because he longs to be near Sybil, partly to study the life and circumstances of the factory workers, to settle for a time under an assumed name, in the district where Gerard lives. We are now shown the rise and progress of the Chartist movement; we make acquaintance with the ideas of its leaders and the masses; and the novel which, like all Disraeli's, connects itself with actual events not far distant, describes the handing in of the National Petition to Parliament. How it was received has already been told. The impression made by its reception on the personages in the novel may be imagined. What a disappointment for Sybil, who had so firm a belief that that day would have grand results! Sad at heart, she opens the paper next morning, which contains the report of the proceedings of Parliament. It was a heavy task to read it. Then her face suddenly brightens up. "Yes, there was one voice that had sounded in that proud Parliament, that, free from the slang of faction, had dared to express immortal truths; the voice of a noble who, without being a demagogue, had upheld the popular cause; had pronounced his conviction that the rights of labour were as sacred as those of property; that if a difference were to be established, the interests of the living wealth ought to be preferred." *

It was Egremont who made the speech, but it is plain that it was no superfluous modesty which prevented Disraeli from sounding his own praises through the beautiful lips of his heroine. The word "noble" is the sole slender bulwark to prevent the author and hero melting into one.

To those around him Egremont seems to be the advocate of

* "Sybil," p. 337.

Chartism; in reality, however, he considers it to be a movement without a leader, and his principles are laid before the reader in his conversations with Sybil. He reminds her that her knowledge of the upper classes is derived from books, not from experience, and tells her that since these books were written, a great change has taken place. " 'If there be a change,' said Sybil, 'it is because in some degree the people have learnt their strength.' " Egremont gently begs her to dismiss this fancy. " 'The people are not strong; the people never can be strong. Their attempts at self-vindication will end only in their suffering and confusion. It is civilization that has effected, that is effecting, this change. It is that increased knowledge of themselves that teaches the educated their social duties. There is a dayspring in the history of this nation, which perhaps those only who are on the mountain-tops can as yet recognize. You deem you are in darkness, and I see a dawn. The new generation of the aristocracy of England are not tyrants, not oppressors, Sybil, as you persist in believing. Their intelligence, better than that, their hearts, are open to the responsibility of their position. . . . They are the natural leaders of the people, Sybil; believe me, they are the only ones.' " *

These words, in accordance with Disraeli's peculiarity as an author, contain the gist of the book reduced to a formula. They occur about the middle of the novel, and the latter half is intended to prove their truth. The Trades Unionists, who have seen their hopes of constitutional reforms annihilated, enter into a sort of conspiracy throughout the country; the moderate leaders are carried away by the more violent, and soon disturbances take place. The band to which Gerard belongs is imprisoned, and Egremont succeeds with difficulty in releasing Sybil. In the country, the "bishop" and his flock have risen; this wild mob assassinates Egremont's wicked brother, Lord Marney, and so the hero succeeds to the title; they storm a castle, in which proofs are discovered of Gerard's title to large estates, and thus they help the heroine to an immense dowry; all the bad and ill-conducted persons

* "Sybil," p. 319.

die violent deaths, the Socialist editor among them; the good ones are happily united. The childish and conventional optimism with which Disraeli's novels finish up is almost irritating to the reader, but it is a feature to which he has to accustom himself.

The strong point of the book, as a work of fiction, is the series of well-drawn characters: the high aristocratic society, the young factory workers of both sexes, in whose rough *naïveté* there is a marked individuality, finally the "bishop" and his brother, a London attorney, who supports him without choosing to acknowledge the relationship; all these various groups are well conceived and truthfully drawn. In the pair last mentioned, especially, Disraeli is very successful in depicting lawless violence and worldly wisdom, and in throwing light on each by the contrast. There is the same contrast in "Alroy," between the relentless fanaticism of the Rabbi Jabaster, and the sage epicurean philosophy of his brother Honan; and in both cases it produces great dramatic effect. The character of Morley, the Socialist, is altogether a failure. In the first place, he is sacrificed to the special tendency of the book; for in order to prove the necessity that the people should be led by the aristocracy, the plebeian leader has to be made wicked, and makes an attempt to assassinate Egremont out of jealousy in a love affair. In the second place, Morley is spoiled by Disraeli's taste for the melodramatic and bombastic. In his dying moments, with a bullet in his breast, he make a long theatrical speech to Egremont which ends thus: "Your star has controlled mine: and now I feel I have sacrificed life and fame—dying men prophesy—for your profit and honour." *

An author who was intending to train himself for a Parliamentary speaker, had better have been on his guard against the rhetoric ever ready to flow from his pen, even at the most inappropriate places.

Politically, this novel follows in the track of "Coningsby," but with more steam on. The two old parties are still more plainly told that their day is over, and that there is no essential difference be-

* "Sybil," p. 482.

tween them. The Chartists, it is said, had long ceased to distinguish between the two parties who formerly and at the present time were contending for power. What is the principle that makes the difference between the noble lord who resigns his portfolio, and the right honourable gentleman who accepts it? Here, as in "Coningsby," the British Parliamentary system is vehemently attacked, its government by majority is characterized as power in the hands of a few dozen "unknown and anonymous blockheads," who form the difference in numbers between parties, and whose favour is gained by the promise of a peerage, or a baronetcy, or an invitation to a court ball for their wives. "Such a system may suit the balanced interests and the periodical and alternate command of rival oligarchical connections; but it can subsist only by the subordination of the sovereign and the degradation of the multitude, and cannot accord with an age whose genius will soon confess that power and the people are both divine." *

It is also prophesied again and again that Toryism will rise from the grave in which it has lain since the death of Bolingbroke, in order to proclaim to the world with a mighty voice "that power has but one duty—to secure the welfare of the masses."

There are passages in this book which remind one of Lassalle.

---

* "Sybil," p. 44.

XVI

THE CORN LAWS AND THE
CONTEST WITH PEEL

&§ The fourth decade of the present century opened stormily
in Great Britain. A general discontent and restlessness had taken
possession of the people. Bad harvests, hard winters, the rigid Poor
Law, the Chartist movement, with the burning of stacks that followed, disturbances, and riots, kept the lower classes in a perpetual
fever. Chartist petitions were continually being presented to Parliament; the one handed in in May, 1842, had over 3,300,000 signatures, and as they shared the fate of the National Petition, two
attempts on the life of the Queen were made in three months. High
prices and distress excited a rebellion in Wales; a secret society,
called "Rebecca and her Daughters," insolently bade defiance to
the authorities; and the state of things in the autumn of 1843 was
officially described as "utterly lawless." But nothing equalled the
distress and the spirit of rebellion in Ireland. The population of
that country, destitute of trade or manufactures, was exclusively
devoted to agriculture, and the peasantry of the over-populous
island had sunk into the most abject wretchedness through high
rents and great competition for land. The people's diet consisted
exclusively of potatoes, and in most districts, begging seemed to
be their chief source of gain. The desperation of the famishing
people was so great that the landowners seldom ventured to live
amongst their tenantry, and, of course, the existing evils were only
increased by absenteeism. To all this social ferment, political agitation must be added, for just at this period O'Connell was straining
every nerve in a crusade for the Repeal of the Union, and holding
meetings, attended by an ever-increasing number of people—once

300,000 were present, and on another occasion 1,200,000, while in every chapel enthusiastic and fanatical priests made collections for the purposes of agitation. He was indicted as a conspirator, and in the two first instances, sentenced with unjust severity; he was, therefore, of course, more passionately revered by the people than ever; on the last occasion he was fully acquitted, a circumstance but little adapted to increase respect for the Government.

The agitation, however, which pervaded the country was not confined to these movements of the revolutionary and Radical party. A far more important agitation had been stirred up among the educated and mercantile middle classes against the Corn Laws by the powerful eloquence of Richard Cobden, and arising out of the Anti-Corn Law League. This league, after an existence of a few years, had a million sterling at its command, and with "cheap bread" for its watchword, sought to incite the people to oppose a system of legislation, the result of which, on an average, was described by the Free Traders to be to make bread dearer by £10,-000,000, for the sole benefit of 16,000 landowners and farmers.

The Chartists were at first very cool, or even hostile, to the Liberal agitation; they openly asserted that "cheap bread" would practically result in an agitation for "cheap labour." But by degrees, distress compelled them to give up their distrust of, and opposition to, the Liberals, and when they and the Irish joined the Free Trade movement, it grew stronger and stronger, and soon became nearly irresistible.

The Tory party had taken the helm in 1841. Sir Robert Peel had succeeded Lord Melbourne as Prime Minister. He was then at the summit of his fame; he was not only the most powerful, but the most popular man in England; he was held to be what Disraeli had called him at his election at Shrewsbury during the same year, "the greatest statesman of his age;" and it was the general impression that he would retain his power until his death.

Party interests alone would have induced Disraeli to support Peel; in the "Runnymede Letters," in which he had loaded most of the other politicians with taunts, he had alluded to Peel in touching words as the hope of the nation. About 1840 also he spoke of him in his speeches and writings with an admiration which not seldom approaches flattery; he seems at first to have regarded him as his trump card. He probably cherished a hope that Peel would offer him a place in his cabinet, if only a subordinate one—an Under-Secretaryship of State, for instance, with which Contarini Fleming began his career; but of course, he was too wise as well as too proud to do anything which might be construed into asking for it. But Peel overlooked his ardent follower; it was not his strong point to discern ability before it had been discovered by all the world, and in this case there seems to have been an antipathy also. Disraeli swallowed his disappointment, continued, with unchanged attitude and faithfulness to party, to support Peel during the two following years, and even glorified him in "Coningsby." It was a bad habit of Peel's to treat his supporters with a repelling coldness, as if they were conquered subjects, and to reserve all the urbanity and winning qualities at his command for his opponents. For some years Disraeli submitted to this treatment with perfect discipline. Yet we can scarcely doubt that even from the beginning, there was on his part also a keen antipathy to the statesman whose follower he was. Not that there was any feeling of rivalry—there scarcely could be this between a young member of Parliament and the first man in the country; what he felt was the aversion of the man of the choleric temperament to the phlegmatic, of the man of quick and keen temper to universal and seldom genuine *bonhommie*, the hatred of an original nature for routine, the contempt of the imaginative politician for the unimaginative. As early as in 1829, Disraeli had given the following characteristic description in "The Young Duke:"—"Mr. Peel is the model of a Minister, and improves as a speaker; though, like most of the rest, he is fluent without the least style. He should not get so often in a passion either, or, if he do, should not get out of one so easily. His sweet apologies are cloying. His candour; he will do well to get rid of that." *

When we find the same estimate of Peel reappearing in 1845,

* "The Young Duke," p. 287.

we may conclude that no essential change had taken place in it during the intervening years.

Disraeli was not made for a partisan who is ready to renounce all independence and criticism, and he was still less inclined to submission when his adhesion was rewarded with thanklessness and outbreaks of haughty superiority from one whom he did not consider in his heart to be his superior either in general talent or political ability. Respect for Sir Robert Peel hung like a yoke round the necks of his followers; his position as Prime Minister, his dignity and his mastery in Parliamentary debate, made it difficult to conceive that any one of them could venture to criticise him. Disraeli resolved to throw off the yoke. The action of the Government had appeared to him, in more than one instance, not very statesmanlike, and feeling himself born to be a leader, he ventured, as such men did in the olden time in Scandinavia, to challenge the strongest giant to single combat for the leadership of the host of his followers. As he could not get forward in company with Peel, he must try to do so as his opponent.

Extraordinary courage was required to enter on the contest. When, in 1843, Disraeli for the first time attacked Sir Robert Peel, under cover of an extra polite question relating to Eastern affairs, the effect produced on members was one of simple astonishment; they looked at one another, and asked each other, so to speak, if they had heard aright. The question was curtly and coldly turned off by Sir Robert Peel. But a few days after, the same irrepressible speaker rose again, and asserted that Sir Robert Peel's policy towards Ireland was precisely that for which he had so strenuously attacked the previous Ministry, and precisely the opposite of that which he had recommended as leader of the Opposition. He did not blame the Minister for this by any means; if he was of opinion that the policy he had previously advocated was not such as a Minister can adopt, he had only acted reasonably and rightly in giving it up as soon as he was at the helm. Only he (Disraeli) must draw the conclusion from it that, in relation to Irish politics, those who supported the right honourable gentleman were now left to themselves. This was the style, a polite and cool sarcastic style, well adapted for the skirmish which generally precedes a collision. As to the matter itself, it may be observed that Disraeli has always recommended forbearance and kindness as the best means of pacifying Ireland, and has always declared it to be in accordance with old Tory tradition, as well as the duty of his party, "to govern Ireland in accordance with the policy of Charles I and not that of Oliver Cromwell."

Not long after, Disraeli renewed his objections to the Eastern policy of the Government. In the question as to who should occupy the throne of Servia, Sir Robert Peel had left Turkey, in respect to Russia, entirely in the lurch, and this proceeding Disraeli attacked. It was of no use to endeavour to conceal from himself the situation of Turkey; her power was broken; not so much from internal decay as because she had had a stab in the back. He reminded the House that he had before put a question on this subject to the Prime Minister, and, as he considered, had put it in Parliamentary language with all due respect. To this question the Minister had replied with "all that explicitness of which he was a master, and all that courtesy which he reserved only for his supporters." *

It was impossible to express bitterness with finer irony, and it was a ricochet shot, for it both hit Peel just where he exposed himself to attack, namely, in his bearing towards his own party, and irritated the Tories where their pride was wounded.

These attacks were only the preliminary skirmishes; they were the beginnings of a conflict which lasted for years, carried on by the attacking party with unparalleled persistency, by force and cunning, by raillery and pathos, with darts and clubs, weapons good and bad, fair and unfair—until the foe succumbed, and in his fall lost both his position and his party. What did it avail Peel that thirty-five years of Parliamentary experience had steeled him, and taught him the art of parrying blows? He never knew when the attack would be made, nor to what point it would be directed.

* O'Connor's "Life of Lord Beaconsfield," p. 251.

He suddenly heard the whizzing of the arrow in the air, and it penetrated wherever there was a joint or a weak point in his armour. Of what avail was it for him to assure the House, with the utmost indifference, that he was not in the least sensitive to the praise or censure of the honourable member for Shrewsbury? All at once he saw a flash in his adversary's eye, and, like a dagger hurled by the hand of an Eastern assassin, some cutting sarcasm struck him in what was just then his most sensitive part; and, owing to his long Parliamentary career, he had many sensitive points. One of those was his relation to the great statesman Canning. When Canning, to whom Peel had always been united by personal friendship, assumed the reins of government after the death of Lord Liverpool, in 1827, and exchanged the previous Metternich-like policy of Great Britain for a new and manly one, which was crowned by the battle of Navarino, and won the applause of enlightened Europe, Peel deserted him, and placed himself at the head of the ignoble opposition against Canning which hastened his death. Even when Disraeli was adopting a decidedly apologetic tone towards the Prime Minister, he was not quite ready to exculpate him on this point. In "Coningsby," in spite of his vindication of Peel, he had confessed that his conduct towards Canning, even if it be capable of justification, "may perhaps always leave this a painful and ambiguous passage in his career."

In the beginning of 1845, a member of the Ministry had placed the Government in an odious light by a mean and impolitic act. As the attention of the Austrian Government was fixed upon Mazzini, then residing in England, and his relations with the Italian revolutionists, particularly with two brothers named Bandiera, living in Corfu, Sir James Graham had had Mazzini's letters opened, and had informed the Austrian Government of the schemes of the brothers; he was thus the cause of the two Italian patriots being enticed by a political agent on to Austrian soil, where they were seized and shot. The English were universally indignant that a British Minister should stoop to perform police services for a foreign despotic Power. When the subject came before Parliament, Sir Robert Peel, in his defence, betrayed unusual irritation. In a longer speech which Disraeli made against Graham, he made the dry remark in reference to the circumstance, that the Prime Minister had far too large a mind, and occupied far too high a position, ever to lose his equanimity, but that in a popular assembly it was occasionally advantageous to play the part of the choleric gentleman. He knew from experience that for novices these exhibitions were always somewhat exciting; he made the remark especially for the sake of the younger members, that they might not be needlessly alarmed. They need not be afraid—the Minister was not going to eat them up. And in this tone he went on. It will be observed that the suspicion as to Peel's candour, which had been expressed in "The Young Duke," is here emphasized with taunting ridicule.

Peel replied with calm superiority. He had heard the honourable member assert that the warmth with which he had spoken was feigned, although he stood there charged with having caused the death of two innocent men. "It is certainly very possible to manifest great vehemence of action, and yet not be in a great passion. On the other hand, it is possible to be exceedingly cold, indifferent, and composed in your manner, and yet to cherish very acrimonious feelings. Notwithstanding the provocation of the honourable gentleman, I will not deal so harshly with him as he has dealt with me. He undertakes to assure the House that my vehemence was all pretended, and warmth all simulated. I, on the contrary, will do him entire justice; I do believe that his bitterness was not simulated, but that it was entirely sincere." * He never complained, he said, of hostile conduct; every one had a right to act as he chose; but he complained of the expression which Disraeli had used in the course of his speech, that he had spoken in a friendly spirit. He was quite ready in debate to meet his adversaries in honourable conflict with open front; but it was certainly most unbecoming, although it might be inevitable, for a man to be stabbed in the back from the benches of his own party when he least expected it, and accom-

* O'Connor's "Life of Lord Beaconsfield," p. 265.

panied, moreover, with the assurance that it was done in a friendly spirit. And with his clear, powerful voice he quoted to the House the well-known lines in which Canning has parodied the old theme, "God, save me from my friends!"

> *Give me the avowed, erect, and manly foe;*
> *Firm I can meet, perhaps can turn the blow;*
> *But of all plagues, good Heaven, Thy wrath can send,*
> *Save me, oh, save me from the candid friend!*

The answer was cutting; it hit the right nail on the head, while it laid bare the animosity concealed beneath Disraeli's affected coolness, at the same time protesting against his misrepresentation in speaking of such a criticism as made in a friendly spirit. But let us compare this skirmish with the vigour of the ironical attack with which Disraeli, a week afterwards, ended a long speech:

"If the right honourable gentleman may find it sometimes convenient to reprove a supporter on his right flank, perhaps we deserve it. I, for one, am quite prepared to bow to the rod; but really, if the right honourable gentleman, instead of having recourse to obloquy, would only stick to quotation, he may rely upon it it would be a safer weapon. It is one he always wields with the hand of a master; and when he does appeal to any authority, in prose or verse, he is sure to be successful, partly because he seldom quotes a passage that has not previously received the meed of Parliamentary approbation, and partly and principally because his quotations are so happy. The right honourable gentleman knows what the introduction of a great name does in debate— how important is its effect, and occasionally how electrical. He never refers to any author who is not great, and sometimes who is not loved—Canning, for example. That is a name never to be mentioned, I am sure, in the House of Commons without emotion. We all admire his genius; we all—at least most of us—deplore his untimely end; and we all sympathize with him in his fierce struggle with supreme prejudice and sublime mediocrity, with inveterate foes, and with 'candid friends.' The right honourable gentleman may be sure that a quotation from such an authority will always tell—some lines, for example, upon friendship, written by Mr. Canning, and quoted by the right honourable gentleman. The theme—the poet—the speaker—what a felicitous combination! Its effect in debate must be overwhelming; and I am sure, were it addressed to me, all that would remain for me would be thus publicly to congratulate the right honourable gentleman, not only on his ready memory, but on his courageous conscience." *

In reading this speech, one hears the tone in which every sentence was uttered, and seems to see the impression it made on the House. At first, according to Disraeli's wont, his manner of speaking was low and monotonous, his countenance impassive, grave as a mask, so that it formed the fitting background to the unconscious irony of his words. The House does not yet know what he is aiming at. The beginning of the speech was in a totally different style, and the details of the altercation with Peel a week before had been forgotten. Why this ironical laudation of upholding party discipline by means of quotations? Then, with a sudden flash, Canning's name is mentioned, carelessly thrown in, with a "for example," but with a somewhat lingering emphasis on the word. The speaker becomes slightly warmer, and when he expresses his admiration for the struggle of the late great statesman with "sublime mediocrity"—these words spoken without any preceding pause, but with a fugitive glance at Peel—a thrill of eager attention passes through the House. This attention is divided between the Prime Minister, who, with quiet dignity, but with a somewhat forced and uncertain smile on his lips, thinks he can despise his adversary, and even wishes it to be thought that he is amused at his harmless mischief, and the speaker, who stands there with a courage that fears no requital, and an icy coldness which the laughter with which his direct ebullitions of feeling are always assailed has long since communicated to him. With one thumb in his armhole, and without moving a finger of the other hand; by the masterly dumb-show that accompanies his words; by a fleeting expression of

* "Benjamin Disraeli, Earl of Beaconsfield: A Biography," vol. i. p. 527.

countenance; by a slight intonation of his voice, which is fully under his control, he contrives to express a contempt which good manners and Parliamentary usage made it impossible to clothe in words, and treats his all-powerful opponent like a helpless victim. With cat-like self-restraint Disraeli had at first declared himself willing to bow beneath the rod, with tiger-like caress he had praised Peel's apt quotation, but from the Mephistophelian tone you seemed to hear the words: "Mediocre man! false friend! who worried the great Canning to death; how darest thou to adopt his words about friends? how canst thou be so dense, so obtuse, as not to perceive that thou standest there with his own branding iron in thy hand, and with ludicrous precision stampest it on thy own brow?" And the House which, instead of this, heard the words: "The theme—the poet— the speaker—what a happy combination!" could not suppress a smile, notwithstanding the nervous quiver on Peel's lips; it rose to loud laughter at the comic attempts of Peel to conceal his annoyance at the offensive hilarity of his party; was increased by the imperturbable gravity of the speaker, and his apparent unconsciousness of the effect he was producing; and finally, by the mixed feelings of the laughers themselves: the curious sense of annoyance that they were laughing at their own stringent leader; the relief, for a variety, of having a good laugh at him; the universal love of mischief, and the pleasure for once of listening to malicious wit. But no sooner was the laughter over, than the calm, clear, monotonous voice was heard again uttering its periods with the cold repose of a machine, as if the speaker were far too sublimely lifted above all human passions to be in the slightest degree influenced by what was going on before his eyes. Other people could not help laughing; he did not move a muscle of his face unless he chose. They could not command either their moods or their countenances, while he stood, slightly swaying the upper part of his body backwards and forwards, hurling forth his sarcasms with lofty indifference; he was lashing the leader of the Lower House, and the first man in the Government, and he was performing the operation amidst the involuntary laughter of that leader's own party. Oh, he was acquainted with this laughter! He had taken his revenge; these hilarious gentlemen were not men of his strength of mind.

The subject of greatest interest in England during those years which chiefly occupied the attention of Parliament, and excited the passions of the people, was the question of Free Trade, or Protection, especially the subject of the maintenance, alteration, or abolition of the Corn Laws. The Tories, who had raised Sir Robert Peel to power, were Protectionists, and Peel had the majority in both Houses. Peel was, in the almost unanimous judgment of those who knew him best, not only a great and able statesman, but one entirely actuated by love of truth and justice. He had had equal experience in the management of English sovereigns and English Parliaments, and had a masterly way of tuning a political assembly, and making it give forth the tones which he desired; under his leadership it was like a violin in the hands of a master. But as a politician, he was wanting in principles and in foresight. It was one of his peculiarities to make obstinate resistance to every new measure, and when, in spite of his opposition, it had become popular, to take it up and carry it out to the utmost. This had been the case with the measures introduced year after year in vain by Sir Samuel Romilly, for the mitigation of the barbarous Penal Laws, which Peel, as leader of the Conservatives, had always opposed as philosophic, sentimental innovations.* The same thing had happened in 1829, when he took the emancipation of the Catholics, to which he had been strongly opposed, into his own hands, and carried it through. He took the same course now. After personally heading the opposition to the Anti-Corn Law League, and having sought and found support in a Tory party who had placed him as their head expressly that he might oppose it to the uttermost, in 1845 he suddenly left his supporters in the lurch, came forward as an advocate from conviction of the principle he had so vehemently assailed, and connected his name with the

* Compare G. Brandes, "Die Hauptströmungen in der Literatur des 19 Jahrhunderts," vol. iv. p. 49.

necessary popular reform. That the abolition of the Corn Laws had at that period become an inevitable necessity, is now the almost universal opinion of those who understand the subject, and, as far as I can judge, European opinion is entirely in Sir Robert Peel's favour. By joining Cobden's party, he shattered at one blow the organized resistance of the Protectionists, and made the triumph of Free Trade inevitable. But it is not difficult to understand that those whose cause he had undertaken did not regard the change in a favourable light. He had called it the sacred cause of Protection; he had declared that he would rather be the leader of the country gentlemen of England than possess the confidence of kings. The men whose confidence he had valued more highly than that of the sovereigns of Europe, and whom he a few years later disappointed, could not possibly pass upon him the lenient judgment of modern political economists. Still, apart from mere party interests, Sir Robert Peel's course of action, considered from an ideal point of view, does not appear to me quite justifiable. That a party leader under a Parliamentary Constitution should be placed at the helm, can only signify that the nation, particularly that portion of it which supports him, desires to afford him the opportunity of carrying out his principles into practice in legislation; if he finds it necessary, as head of the Government, to change his principles, he is in duty bound to resign his office; for power should be the reward of political sagacity, forethought, and success, and he who possesses these qualifications should also taste the sweets of power.

If in this case it had been only the political and not also the pecuniary interests of the Tories that were at stake, Peel would undoubtedly have found it possible, with his great Parliamentary influence, to gain over his followers by degrees to his altered opinions; but as matters stood, he had no hope of getting the Protectionists personally interested in the Corn Laws to come round; he did not even try to prepare them for the change by private communications, for, eminent and eloquent as he was in open debate, he was shy, awkward, and taciturn in personal intercourse with his party.

His Government had begun with some modifications in the protective duties, including some unimportant changes affecting agriculture. Although Disraeli upheld the Corn Laws, he asserted, in the early part of the fourth decade, as a faithful follower of Peel, that Free Trade principles were not a privilege of the Whigs, were not invented by them, but were the good old Tory principles of Pitt. He did, it is true, give the phrase "Free Trade" so wide a scope that even Protectionists became Free Traders, and at the same time he so restricted its meaning that absolute Free Traders were only excrescences of the principle. It must not be forgotten, he added, that the term "Free Trade" was formerly used as opposed to the old colonial system, while it is now used by Cobden and his party in a totally different sense, and means that you shall "contend with open harbours against the hostile customs tariffs of other countries." By the Free Trade that he advocated, he seems at that period to have meant a moderate kind of Protection, or, more correctly speaking, he was tacking about, not quite clear what Sir Robert Peel had in view, but firmly resolved not to betray the cause he had embraced at his election, and which he had promised to advocate. But from the moment when Disraeli felt certain of what Peel's real intentions were, and he foresaw them when no one of his party would give credit to his prognostications—he indicated his suspicions in his speeches in Parliament against Peel, and in the Free Trade debate he took up the cause of the ultra-Conservative Protectionists.

The Tory party soon fell into confusion amidst what was taking place; it split into sections, some of which continued their adhesion to Peel from conviction, and some from habit; while the landowning interest looked about for a new and more trustworthy leader. Disraeli, who had early begun to place his powers at the service of the landowners, and regarded their cause rather as a weapon than merely a cause, now practically became their leader.

The time was come at last when he could gain real importance in Parliament; a speechless, confounded, betrayed, and angry host wanted an organ for their passion, a defender of their interests, a

brain to think and project for them; and there was no other than
he. He presented himself, without directly offering his services, as
mouthpiece of the speechless, as head of those who had lost their
leader. He had hitherto had only a slender aristocratic staff. Young
England was an excellent beginning, but it was only a beginning;
its significance in the first place was not very great, and in the
second it had more of a social, and to some extent literary, than a
political, character. Young England formed, so to speak, a little
court round Disraeli; but in spite of his court, he had been, up
to this time, "a king without land." The party of the landed gentry
and the landowners brought him the "land" for his pretendership
to the crown. It was, as before indicated, not a very intelligent set
which now joined him, but they were members of a numerous
and influential class. The landed gentry, even now, far exceed in
numbers any other class in the Lower House; first, because the
country population sends a number of members for the counties;
secondly, because even now, strange as it may appear, half the
boroughs are represented by eminent landowners, for, according to
British prejudices, the possession of land confers a far higher social
standing than trade, manufactures, or learning. To represent, therefore, the landowning interest, means to represent a very powerful
interest, a political great power. But this great power often requires
to have a leader from beyond its borders, because the landowning
interest has, as has been well set forth by Bagehot, adopted a
political watchword which makes it stupid.

"The counties not only elect landowners, which is natural,
and perhaps wise, but also elect only landowners *of their own
county*, which is absurd. There is no free trade in agricultural
mind; each county prohibits the import of able men from other
counties. This is why eloquent sceptics—Bolingbroke and Disraeli
—have been so apt to lead the unsceptical Tories. They will have
people with a great piece of land in a particular spot, and of course
these people generally cannot speak, and often cannot think. And
so eloquent men who laugh at the party come to lead the party." *

* Bagehot's "English Constitution," p. 201.

At first sight, Disraeli's position at the head of the land-owners strikes one as strange and paradoxical. He, who had inherited no estate, whose ancestors had been legally disqualified from acquiring landed property, who was not even a county member; the man who was once a dandy, and now a drawing-room lion, the romance writer of great cities, figuring as the friend of the agricultural labourer, and promising protection to the burly farmer! But on closer inspection it was perfectly reasonable, and the paradox from Disraeli's point of view was absolutely logical. From the first he had suffered from being half a foreigner in England; he must above all things become thoroughly English, must take deep root in English soil. It is for this reason that in this case, as in every other in his political career, we find him adopting the indigenous English point of view. According to the prevailing opinion, the townspeople, compared with the agricultural labourers, were citizens of the world; this notion was an incentive to Disraeli to take the side of the land party in every conflict between town and county. We have found him saying years before that the manufacturers and industrial classes could emigrate to Egypt if they pleased, while the agriculturists were the true-born patriots without whom no nation could prosper.

It had now become a political rule with Disraeli, in order, so to speak, to efface the stain of his birth, always and everywhere to advocate the national, or rather ultra-national, view; and he was, therefore, predisposed to make that cause his own which bore a national superscription as opposed to the cosmopolitanism of the Free Traders, and whose advocates were simply national egotists, and cared nothing for any nonsense about the brotherhood of nations or doctrines about the common interests of humanity. Although the Protectionists were personally interested in the Corn Laws, the question was one of the protection of *national* produce, and Disraeli, who sprang from a foreign stock, made it a point of honour, on this occasion and ever after, to be, if possible, more English than Englishmen themselves.

In their zeal for a principle which they soon adopted as an

absolute one, and almost a religion, the Free Traders went so far that they sometimes overshot the mark. As, for example, slavery had been abolished at great cost, it could only be considered reasonable to afford the English planters in the West Indies some protection by a duty upon the sugar produced in the slave states of America. But in 1843, Cobden, on theoretic grounds, brought forward a motion for the abolition of the duty. Disraeli took occasion to protest that the interests of the English colonies would be sacrificed to those of the slave states, and to insist that, on the whole question, British interests for British statesmen should have precedence of all others.

He thus became the leader of the Protectionists, but as yet without personally and nominally occupying the vacant post. For this a man of rank was required, and he was soon found in Lord George Bentinck, an energetic young nobleman, not without talents, and the first sportsman of the day. He was personally convinced of the excellence of the protective system, and personally indignant at Peel's defection, so he sacrificed his chivalrous tastes to his convictions of duty. He sold his stud, gave a last longing look at his racers, which always won, and, without any ambitious motive, undertook the post of general of the scattered Tory forces, with Disraeli as chief of his staff.

The point of view from which the present Lord Beaconsfield at that time looked at the subject, seems to me to have been this: he considered it both impolitic and unjust to abolish the duty on corn all at once, although he fully perceived that it was mischievous; he had no faith in the beneficial working of absolute Free Trade; in relation to the philosophical, scientific Free Traders, he considered himself to be the representative of the historical school in politics, of which he had been an adherent from the first; he was not blind to the egotism of the agricultural party, but he perceived a good deal of masked egotism behind the humanitarian watchword of the manufacturers and trading classes, who screamed themselves hoarse about the abolition of the duty on corn for the sake of the poor, while they got as much as possible out of their own workmen; and finally, he hated and despised Sir Robert Peel. If the Corn Laws were to be abolished, it ought to be done by Cobden, not by a Minister like Peel, who was bound by previous pledges. Disraeli would not or could not see that Peel was only sacrificing the lesser duty to his party to the greater duty to the nation, for he was of opinion that he was actuated by the vain motive of wishing to associate his name with this great popular economic movement. There is no part of Disraeli's career which has been so much attacked and censured as this. I have no desire to defend his unenviable position as leader of the guardians of the Corn Laws, distinguished by their broad backs and fat acres. I only wish to indicate that light in which he himself saw his opposition to Peel as advocate of their abolition.

Disraeli may also be impugned for having, in the long series of speeches which from this time forward he made against Peel, always taken the ground of making Peel's conversion ridiculous, and having never argued the essential question of the working of the Corn Laws. "The right honourable gentleman caught the Whigs bathing, and walked away with their clothes. He has left them in the full enjoyment of their Liberal position, and he is himself a strict Conservative of their garments." *

In another place he is no less sarcastic: "I look on the right honourable gentleman as a man who has tamed the Shrew of Liberalism by her own tactics. He is the political Petruchio, who has outbid you all." †

In another passage he ironically reproaches the Protectionists in a similar strain for complaining of Peel's conduct. "There is no doubt," he went on, "a difference in the right honourable gentleman's demeanour as leader of the Opposition, and as Minister of the Crown. But that's the old story; you must not contrast too strongly the hours of courtship with the years of possession."‡

And with an orator's intuitive facility of illustration, in one of his great speeches he paraphrases Peel's position in a parable.

* O'Connor's "Life of Lord Beaconsfield," p. 267. † Ibid.
‡ Ibid., p. 270.

"Sir, there is a difficulty in finding a parallel to the position of the right honourable gentleman in any part of history. The only parallel which I can find is an incident in the late war in the Levant, which was terminated by the policy of the noble lord opposite. I remember when that great struggle was taking place, when the existence of the Turkish Empire was at stake, the late sultan, a man of great energy and fertile in resources, was determined to fit out an immense fleet to maintain his empire. Accordingly a vast armament was collected. It consisted of many of the finest ships that were ever built. The crews were picked men, the officers were the ablest that could be found, and both officers and men were rewarded before they fought. There never was an armament which left the Dardanelles similarly appointed since the day of Solyman the Great.

"The sultan personally witnessed the departure of the fleet; all the muftis here prayed for the success of the last general election. Away went the fleet; but what was the sultan's consternation when the lord high admiral steered at once into the enemy's port! Now, sir, the lord high admiral, on that occasion, was very much misrepresented. He, too, was called a traitor; and he, too, vindicated himself. 'True it is,' said he, 'I did place myself at the head of this valiant armada; true it is that my sovereign embraced me; true it is that all the muftis in the empire offered up prayers for my success; but I have an objection to war. I see no use in prolonging the struggle, and the only reason I had for accepting the command was that I might terminate the contest by betraying my master.' And, sir, these reasons, offered by a man of great plausibility, of vast adroitness, have had their effect, for—you may be surprised at it —but I assure you it is a fact, which by the way the gallant officer opposite (Commodore Napier) can testify, that he is at this moment the First Lord of the Admirality at Constantinople, under the new reign." *

It will be observed that all these caustic and witty sallies move within the same circle. It is Peel's passion for appropriating the ideas

* O'Connor's "Life of Lord Beaconsfield," p. 290.

of others that is ridiculed, his want of originality and principle, his betrayal of the party which had raised him to power, and to which he had pledged his word; but of the essence of the subject, the real question of the right of the aristocratic landowners to tax all England for the benefit of the farmers, there is little or nothing. It is more than probable that Disraeli, even in 1845, foresaw the perils, now coming to the front, which threatened English agriculture from competition with America, but in the Parliamentary debates he dealt exclusively with the formal aspect of the question, the renegade conduct of Sir Robert Peel.

Meanwhile, the real question was becoming more urgent. Simultaneously with the failure of the harvest in 1845 in England and Scotland, the potato disease broke out in Ireland, and threatened the wretched population with famine. Under these circumstances, the measure first proposed of admitting corn free from the colonies was insufficient; the Anti-Corn Law League agitated the question to the utmost; the Whig leaders, who had previously advocated a moderate Corn Law, openly declared for absolute and immediate abolition; a large assembly in Dublin declared the adhesion of the Irish to the Free Trade programme; and finally, civil war was at the doors. Sir Robert Peel then, in January, 1846, laid a Bill before the Lower House for the total abolition of the duty on corn, which, after vehement debates for months in both Houses, passed into law.

Peel still maintained his position, but his power was shattered. The details relating to his situation and that of his opponents may be seen in Lord Beaconsfield's "Life of Lord George Bentinck." His opponents had hoped to the last moment that the Bill would be thrown out in the Lords; but as this hope was frustrated, in great measure by the conversion of the Duke of Wellington, hope, as Lord Beaconsfield confesses with the candour of Contarini Fleming, was succeeded by revenge. "The battle itself was lost, but he who by his treachery had caused the defeat should at all events suffer for it."

A whole Parliamentary recess was, as is stated in the "Life of

Bentinck," spent in devising plans to turn Peel out, and in that life the bold intrigues may be traced by which his fall was at last effected by the author of "Vivian Grey," through the instrumentality of the fanatical and unscrupulous Lord George Bentinck, on whom he could fully rely. The final plan adopted was as shabby as it was effectual; it consisted in inducing Lord George Bentinck, as leader of the Tories, and Lord John Russell, as leader of the Whigs, to join in opposing Peel's Bill in the interests of public safety in Ireland, on the second reading, both Lords having, on the first reading, promised their "sincere and hearty support." This desperate measure was effectual. In June, 1846, Sir Robert Peel was in a minority, and laid down his portfolio.

A man who, like Lord George Bentinck, only assumed leadership of the Tories against his will and for a time, was not likely to take Peel's place with his former followers. He was, both by birth and family connection, as brother-in-law of Canning, no less than from his liberal religious opinions, a Whig, and had only joined the Tories from interest in the corn duties. He had been besides, from his youth upwards, above all things, a sportsman, and when he entered the House late in the evening, his red hunting-coat was carelessly concealed by a light grey paletot. Then he was a hesitating and laborious speaker. Through him, and, so to speak, as his mouthpiece, Disraeli now led the Tory party for about a year, until, in 1847, Lord George Bentinck withdrew from the leadership, as it appears from disapproval of Disraeli's arguments about the Bill for the emancipation of the Jews. He argued, as usual, for Semiticism, instead of, as Bentinck wished, in favour of the principle of religious liberty. For a short period, the clique of Tory Protectionists, who had fallen with Peel, were without a leader, for they rebelled against acknowledging as their chief the commoner of Jewish extraction and dubious notoriety when second in command, and who had been formerly a Radical; but by the sudden death of Lord George Bentinck, in 1848, Disraeli became the actual advocate as well as the elected leader of the party, and had thus surmounted the first arduous steps on the path to power.

Up to this time, although leader of the landowners, he had represented the borough of Shrewsbury in Parliament. It was necessary to put an end to this absurd position. At the request of numerous electors, he offered himself as a candidate for Buckinghamshire, in which county he had became a landowner by the purchase of the estate of Hughenden Manor. In 1847 he was elected member for the county, by a large number of votes, and continued to represent it until 1876, when he retired from the House of Commons.

XVII

"TANCRED"

In Lord Beaconsfield's "Life of Bentinck," there is a passage referring to Peel, in penning which he was obviously thinking of himself. "An aristocracy hesitates before it yields its confidence, but it never does so grudgingly. . . . An aristocracy is rather apt to exaggerate the qualities and magnify the importance of a plebeian leader." *

Do these words state a fact or express a wish and a hint? The new leader was evidently followed with reluctance, sometimes almost with aversion. It was his descent that stood most in his way; on every collision with those around him, it had been brought up against him, and so it would surely be in the future. Disraeli's object was, therefore, to attack the prejudice against the Jewish race once for all, and so thoroughly to put an end to it, that, at all events, as a Christian prejudice, it should forever be reduced to an absurdity.

A vigorous attack had been made upon it in "Coningsby." Sidonia had assigned to the Arabian races, as civilized nations, equal rank with the Anglo-Saxon and the Greek races, and had adduced the advantage enjoyed by the Hebrews among the Arab tribes as the oldest race of unmixed blood to be found amongst nations dwelling in towns. He had said: "An unmixed race, with an organization of the first class, is the true aristocracy of nature." And even in "Sybil," the main idea which was always occupying Disraeli's mind had asserted itself. The following peculiar explanation of the author's early sympathies with Catholicism is put into the mouth of a Catholic priest:—"The Church of Rome is to be respected as the only Hebræo-Christian Church extant; all other Churches established by the Hebrew Apostles have disappeared,

* "Life of Lord George Bentinck," p. 318.

but Rome remains; and we must never permit the exaggerated position which it assumed in the middle centuries to make us forget its early and apostolic character, when it was fresh from Palestine, and, as it were, fragrant from paradise." *

It is not, then, for the sake of Rome, but of Palestine, that Disraeli has glorified the Romish Church. And this explains how at last, in "Lothair," he almost made a parody on his own works, for in that work the Catholic clergy, and the religious sentiment which leads people into their arms, are portrayed with penetrating knowledge of men and cutting satire. It was solely the fragrance from Palestine which lingered about the mantles of the first bishops of Rome which made Rome so attractive to him, until this fragrance was overpowered by the odour of incense.

Now, as before, Disraeli hankered for Palestine. It was long since he had beheld the country with his bodily eyes, but in imagination he was ever making pilgrimages to the East. Since he had visited those regions as a young man, the great war between Mehemet Ali and the Porte, in 1840, had caused the Great Powers to interfere in Eastern affairs, and attracted the attention of Europe to them, and about the same time a number of occurrences had taken place which could not fail to affect every one who, like Disraeli, had Jewish blood in his veins, namely, the fearful persecutions of the Jews in Damascus and Rhodes, worse, even, than those of medieval times. At Damascus, the sudden disappearance of an Italian priest had caused the report that he had been murdered by the Jews, and a Jewish barber confessed, under the torture of five hundred blows on the soles of his feet, that the Jews used Christian blood in making their Easter cakes, and had employed him to murder the priest for this purpose. Six respectable Jews were therefore imprisoned on suspicion; they were whipped, and compelled to stand erect for three days following, and when they fell down from exhaustion, were made to get up by thrusts with a bayonet, their beards were set fire to, and lights held under their noses till their faces were singed; even their children were shut up and kept

* "Sybil," p. 129.

on bread and water. In vain they appealed to their Scriptures, in which the shedding of blood was forbidden, and when one of them was daring enough to say that the Christians had probably murdered the priest themselves, he was bastinadoed till he died. Similar horrors were perpetrated about the same time in Rhodes, where a Greek boy disappeared in the same mysterious manner, and the Jews were accused of putting him out of the way; the only difference was, that in this case not the native Christians alone, but the European consuls, including the British consul, gave the reins to their fanaticism against the Jews, who turned out to be entirely innocent.*

As is well known, the reports of these horrors gave rise to Sir Moses Montefiore's first journey to the East, where, with indefatigable persistence, he effected the release of the imprisoned Jews, and obtained from the sultan the remarkable firman in which he stated his full conviction of the innocence of the Jews of the misdeeds they had been accused of, and for which they had suffered. The sultan was more humane than the English consul, who denounced the Jews in Rhodes, or the French consul, who persecuted them at Damascus.

The author of "Alroy" could not hear of these events without being strongly affected by them, and in reading the romance which he now wrote about the East and the Jewish race, the maddening effect of these horrors must be borne in mind. "Coningsby" treated of the political, and "Sybil" of the social, problem, and "Tancred," the last portion of the trilogy, was to treat of the religious question.

"Tancred" is unquestionably one of the most interesting and original of Lord Beaconsfield's works. It is a serio-comic, ironically mystic book; on the first reading, it seems too absurd to be subjected to serious criticism, but one takes it up again, and, although it falls asunder into two large fragments, its wit and brilliant Oriental scenes and conversations dwell in the memory. It comprises, moreover, Disraeli's whole field of vision, and ranges between the veriest frivolities of high life, an amusing gastronomic

* Picciotto, "Sketches of Anglo-Jewish History," p. 347.

disquisition, and the highest religious pathos of which the author is capable, as well as the most far-reaching of his political schemes. To these, however, at this period, 1847, he gave something of a burlesque form, after the manner in which a Hamlet or a Brutus betrays or conceals his plans; but he has unveiled them since 1874, and striven more and more to realize them. It is a book having, Janus-like, two faces—the one expressive of impenetrable irony, the other of almost pure mysticism; and the contrast is not done away with by *diversus respectus*, for the irony hovers over the mysticism, which is the pivot of the book, is to be found in reality in the mysticism itself, and thereby hits the Christian-religious enthusiasm for crusades, the cause of which he apparently advocates. It is usual to speak of Lord Beaconsfield's sphinx-like character, and "Tancred" affords more justification than usual for the term; still, even in this case, it is only mental indolence to take refuge in the assertion that the book is enigmatical, for, if you pay close attention to the meaning, the author says plainly enough to the orthodox:—If you were consistent, and seriously believed what you are always saying that you believe, you would all act as enthusiastically, as simply, as devoutly, as madly as my hero. And if you were sincere, you would acknowledge that it is to the Jews and to Judaism that you are indebted for all your most precious treasures, and instead of contemning and persecuting them, you would hold them in high esteem. But you are neither consistent nor sincere, neither devout nor enthusiastic; you are each and all of you Philistine Rationalists, and as you do not dare to confess it, try your teeth on my book.

Lord Tancred Montacute is brought up at the seat of a ducal family, sole heir of its wealth and honours, and tenderly cherished by affectionate and unworldly parents. He is a young man of the Young England type, earnest, conscientious, and romantically religious. The scene begins with his coming of age. His father wishes him to enter Parliament, and enters into conversation with him on the subject, when he learns with amazement that his son is firmly resolved not to enter Parliament until it has become clear to him on what principles England is or ought to be governed, for he cannot discover that there is any principle in the organization of the State, either monarchical, aristocratic, or popular; everything ancient is destroyed, and with the consent of those who ought to have been the guardians of it; and he could not see whither the new order of things was tending, nor on what principle it was based. He, therefore, did not mean to devote himself to politics; he meant to travel. To Paris? No, not Paris. To Rome? No, nor yet Rome. Where then? He wished, after the example of his great forefathers, to make a pilgrimage to Jerusalem. The duke, who cannot bear the idea of sparing his son, even for a short time, and knows what grief this journey will cause his wife, is equally alarmed and surprised. He cannot imagine what Tancred wants to go to Jerusalem for. But Lord Montacute coolly tells him that he is convinced that the only land in which the Creator has deigned to reveal Himself to man—the land in which He assumed a manly form, and met a human death, must be a country endowed with marvellous and peculiar qualities. It was these qualities that drew Europe to Asia many times during the Middle Ages. Their castle had before this sent a De Montacute to Palestine. He, too, would kneel at the Holy Sepulchre, would lift up his voice to heaven, and ask, What is duty, and what is faith? What ought I to do, and what ought I to believe?

The parents, in their alarm, persuade their friend the bishop to try to bring the young lord to reason; but he is an insignificant, ambitious man, whose sole desire is to make a career for himself, and he cannot find any answers to Tancred's doubts and arguments. Tancred says that society was once regulated by God, and is now regulated by man. He prefers divine to self government, and wishes to know how it is to be attained. The bishop replies that the Church now represents God upon earth; but the young man objects that the Church no longer governs man. The bishop speaks of the progress of the Church in our days: "We shall soon see a bishop at Manchester." "But I want to see an angel at Manchester," answers Tancred. "An angel?" "Why not? Why should there not be heavenly messengers, when heavenly messages are most wanted?" "We have received a heavenly message by one greater than the angels," answers the bishop. "Their visits to man ceased with the mightier advent." "Then why did angels appear to Mary and her companions at the holy tomb?" inquired Tancred.* The bishop leaves him without having effected his object, and with a diminished opinion of the young lord's intelligence.

They succeed in delaying Tancred's departure for a time. A thousand preparations have to be made; a yacht must be bought, choice is difficult, and the vendors are not to be trusted. Various circumstances intervene: the introduction of the young lord to London society, and an innocent love affair with a woman of the world, who affects the greatest interest in the Jerusalem scheme, but is in reality chiefly engrossed in speculations in shares, and she startles Tancred with the exclamation: "If we only had a railway to Jerusalem!" A railway to Jerusalem! The very idea incensed Tancred. He would have been still more incensed had he known that the realization of the project would be advocated in the future by no less a person than Lord Beaconsfield.

In spite of every obstacle, Tancred adheres firmly to his plan, and at length gets off, provided with letters of introduction and letters of credit from Sidonia, the only person who understands why he wants to go to the Holy Land, and sympathizes in his desire to penetrate the "Asian mystery." Accompanied by a Jewish servant, procured for him by Sidonia, who had accompanied him in his travels in the East, and provided with a regular suite from the parental castle, Tancred arrives at Jerusalem.

The first adventure he meets with is a *rencontre* with a young lady in a garden near Jerusalem, whose perfect Oriental beauty dazzles and captivates him, and her conversation appears to him so wise and true that she all at once convinces him that his youth had been passed in a series of delusions about the highest things. It comes out that the young beauty, dressed in the Turkish style,

* "Tancred," p. 74.

and glittering with jewels, is a Jewess, called the Rose of Sharon; her name is Eva, the daughter of the Crœsus of Syria, the noble and wealthy Besso, and granddaughter of a powerful Bedoueen chief, the sheikh of sheikhs, Amalek.

" 'You Franks love Bethany?'

" 'Naturally; a place to us most dear and interesting.'

" 'Pray, are you of those Franks who worship a Jewess; or of those others who revile her, break her images, and blaspheme her pictures?'

" 'I venerate, though I do not adore, the mother of God,' said Tancred, with emotion.

" 'Ah! the mother of Jesus!' said his companion. 'He is your God. He lived much in this village. He was a great man, but He was a Jew; and you worship Him.'

" 'And you do not worship Him?' said Tancred, looking up to her with an inquiring glance, and with a reddening cheek.

" 'It sometimes seems to me that I ought,' said the lady, 'for I am of His race, and you should sympathize with your race.'

" 'You are, then, a Hebrew?'

" 'I am of the same blood as Mary, whom you venerate, but do not adore.' "

Eva has obtained a New Testament to read from the English bishop; she does not find, however, that the Christianity in that agrees with what passes for it in actual life. Tancred suggests that she should seek the guidance of the Christian Church.

" 'Which?' inquired the lady; 'there are so many in Jerusalem;' " and she names the English, the Latin, the Armenian, the Abyssinian, the Greek, the Maronite, and Coptic Churches.

" 'In this perplexity, it may be wise to remain within the pale of a Church older than all of them, the Church in which Jesus was born, and which He never quitted, for He was born a Jew, lived a Jew, and died a Jew; as became a prince of the house of David, which you do and must acknowledge Him to have been.' "

Eva suspects that Tancred thinks the present state of her race penal and miraculous?

"Tancred bowed assent. 'It is the punishment ordained for their rejection and crucifixion of the Messiah.'

" 'Where is it ordained?'

" 'Upon our heads and upon our children be His blood.'

" 'The criminals said that, not the Judge. Is it a principle of your jurisprudence to permit the guilty to assign their own punishment? They might deserve a severer one. Why should they transfer any of the infliction to their posterity? What evidence have you that Omnipotence accepted the offer? It is not so announced in your histories. Your evidence is the reverse. He whom you acknowledge as omnipotent, prayed to Jehovah to forgive them on account of their ignorance. But, admit that the offer was accepted, which in my opinion is blasphemy, is the cry of a rabble at a public execution to bind a nation?' " *

The theological, historical vindication of the Jewish nation, which the author puts into the heroine's mouth, is precisely the same which, a few years afterwards, he tried to impress upon his readers in the "Life of Lord George Bentinck," and almost in the same words, only it is more circumstantial and expressed with more care. As Lord Beaconsfield's own face appears so plainly behind Eva's beautiful mask, it will be worth while to linger a little on the point. He says that the traditional doctrine, that the dispersion of the Jews was a punishment for the crucifixion of Christ, was neither historically true nor dogmatically sound—an assertion altogether superfluous for his and Eva's enlightened readers, but not needless in his own country, especially thirty years ago.

Not historically true. For the Jews were at that time as much scattered in proportion over the then known world, as now over the whole civilized parts of the earth. Many Jews were living at that time, highly respected and well off, in Alexandria, as well as in Jerusalem. Less than two months after the Crucifixion, there came to Jerusalem, as we are expressly told, "devout men, from every nation under heaven, Parthians, and Medes, and Elamites, and the dwellers in Mesopotamia," from Asia and Asia Minor, and

* "Tancred," pp. 188–190.

even from Rome. What had all these to do with the Crucifixion? Besides, as we know, "the Jews were originally a nation of twelve tribes; ten, long before the advent of Jesus, had been carried into captivity, and scattered over the East and the Mediterranean world; they are probably the source of the greater portion of the existing Hebrews." What had they to do with the death of Jesus? Jerusalem has not been conquered oftener than Athens, or treated worse; but its people, unhappily, fought too bravely and rebelled too often, so that at last they were expatriated. Expatriation is a purely Oriental custom. "We will suppose," says Eva, "all the Jews in the cities of the world to be the lineal descendants of the mob who shouted at the Crucifixion. Yet another question! My grandfather is a Bedoueen sheikh, chief of one of the most powerful tribes of the desert. My mother was his daughter. He is a Jew; his whole tribe are Jews; they read and obey the Five Books, live in tents, have thousands of camels, ride horses of the Nedjed breed, and care for nothing except Jehovah, Moses, and their mares. Were they at Jerusalem at the Crucifixion, and does the shout of the rabble touch them? Yet my mother marries a Hebrew of the cities, and a man, too, fit to sit on the throne of King Solomon; and a little Christian yahoo, with a round hat, who sells figs at Smyrna, will cross the street if he see her, lest he should be contaminated by the blood of one who crucified his Saviour; his Saviour being, by his own statement, one of the princes of our royal house. No; I will never become a Christian if I am to eat such sand!" *

The discourse is carried on with short questions and answers, from which it appears that the Armenians, who have not crucified a Redeemer, are still more completely expatriated than the Jews, and that the assumed curse cannot have been so very effective, since in Europe, where nothing is so much honoured and sought after as money, the wealthiest men in all countries are found among the Jews.

The conversation has now reached the point where Disraeli

* "Tancred," p. 191.

brings forward, through Eva, his second objection to the retributive
theory, that it is dogmatically unsound. For the sake of brevity, I
give the statement as he is accustomed to formulate it himself:—
It can by no means be said with truth that even the small section
of the Jewish race living in those remote times in Palestine rejected
Jesus. Were it not for the Jews of Palestine, the Northern and
Western races would know nothing of the gospel now. The first
Apostles were Jews, exclusively Jews; the first evangelists were
Jews, and Jews only. For more than a century none but Jews
believed in the teaching of Jesus. It was not a Roman senator, nor
an Athenian philosopher, but a Jew of Tarsus, who founded the
Seven Churches of Asia; and that more famous Church, which
avenged the conquest of Jerusalem by conquering Rome, and turning all the Grecian and Roman temples into altars to the God of
Sinai and Calvary, was founded by a Galilean Jew. There was no
difference between the morality of the new doctrine and that of
the old.

"They, who, in those somewhat lax effusions, which in these
days are honoured with the holy name of theology, speak of the
morality of the gospel as a thing apart and of novel revelation,
would do well to remember that in promulgating such doctrines
they are treading on very perilous ground. There cannot be two
moralities; and to hold that the Second Person of the Holy Trinity
could teach a different morality from that which had been already
revealed by the First Person of the Holy Trinity, is a dogma so
full of terror that it may perhaps be looked upon as the ineffable
sin against the Holy Spirit. When the lawyer tempted our Lord,
and inquired how he was to inherit eternal life, the great Master of
Galilee referred him to the writings of Moses. There he would
find recorded the whole duty of man." *

If, then, the essence of Christianity does not consist in a new
system of morals, it can only consist in the fore-ordained sacrificial
and atoning death of Christ. Eva attacks Tancred on this point:—
"Suppose the Jews had not prevailed upon the Romans to crucify

* "Life of Lord George Bentinck," p. 48.

Jesus, what would have become of the atonement? Where was the inexpiable crime of those who fulfilled the beneficent intention? The holy race supplied the victim and the immolators. . . . And with such a doctrine, . . . with divine persons for the agents, and the redemption of the whole family of man for the subject; you can mix up the miserable persecution of a single race! . . . Persecute us! Why, if you believed what you profess, you should kneel to us! You raise statues to the hero who saves a country. We have saved the human race, and you persecute us for doing it." *

In thus presenting the substance of these ideas to the reader, the artistic form is marred, and this important dialogue may appear hyper-theological, but in connection with the context it is not at all inartistic; it is in harmony with the surroundings of the speakers, and is well adapted to produce an impression on the young man, who is interested in theology. As far as the relation of the author to its contents is concerned, it seems to me that Disraeli has remained true to his watchword in "Vivian Grey." In order to oppose some of the orthodox formulas which stand in his way, he admits the rest without hesitation; and when he makes Eva speak of these things, the discussion of them is fresh, sincere, and without false pathos or unction, while, when he is speaking in his own name (as in the "Life of Bentinck"), he feels compelled to have regard to his position as Tory leader, and he speaks with tears in his eyes, and in a sanctimonious tone. Those who have a lively recollection of the enlightened views of the leading statesmen of the eighteenth century, and of their liberal way of treating of the scholastic problems here treated of in so narrow a spirit, cannot fail to regret the retrograde step; but, when it is considered that Disraeli was speaking to England before the year 1848, and that his Liberal opponent, Gladstone, still in his most liberal phase ("Juventus Mundi," 1869) showed an entirely different bias on theological topics, and seriously thought he had found the Christian Trinity among the Homeric gods, even in Poseidon's trident, we see Disraeli's doctrines of atonement and predestination in another light, and perceive that,

---

* "Tancred," p. 195.

within the prescribed limits, for a Tory, he is almost an advocate of religious Radicalism.

Poor Tancred is pursued by a certain irony. His theological discussion with Eva leads to his being at least as much in love as he is convinced. His journey from Jerusalem to Sinai results in his being attacked by the Bedoueen horde of her grandfather, who takes him for the brother of the Queen of England, and demands an enormous ransom. After a brave resistance, he is overpowered and taken prisoner. In the camp he makes acquaintance with Arab life and ways of thinking, sheikhs and emirs, wins the heart of the young emir Fakredeen, and soon obtains his liberty. He has now imbibed the impression of the superiority of the Arab race; he has repeatedly heard the Bedoueen chief say: "Men may doubt the existence of unicorns; of one thing there can be no doubt—that God never spoke to a man who was not an Arab." He is already accustomed pathetically to call himself of the religion, though not of the race, of the Arabs; he recalls with shame and regret that he has been brought up from childhood to consider it the noblest pedigree to be descended from a band of Baltic pirates, who never received a revelation; now he is ripe for the pilgrimage to Sinai. At the cypress, half-way up the mount, which, tradition says, is the scene of the revelation, the solitary Tancred falls on his knees, and prays at midnight to Jehovah. He seems to see a mighty luminous form; he calls himself the Angel of Arabia, and speaks consoling and stirring words to him.

This angelic revelation reminds the reader of a similar one in the fantastic "Alroy," and, though treated as purely subjective, it is quite a failure. The angel's long palaver is nothing but a concise résumé of all that the chief personages in "Tancred" are in the habit of saying, and all pretence to style is at an end when such phrases as "the social problem" pass his lips. The Angel of Arabia belongs to that class of sovereigns who have learnt nothing and forgotten nothing, for he proclaims a pure theocracy, the equality of men under the government of God. But this geographical angel is at the same time a very Disraeli-ish potentate, for he concludes by exhorting Tancred to adopt the watchword of his originator: "Fear not, faint not, falter not. Obey the impulse of thine own spirit, and find a ready instrument in every human being."

Unfortunately, the reader is not told to what extent the angel's promises are fulfilled, for the novel ends when the lovely Eva gives her hand to Tancred, and England and the East enter into a symbolic union in their persons, like that between aristocracy and trade by the marriage of Coningsby and Edith Milbank, or the Tories and the people by the marriage of Charles Egremont and Sybil Gerard, in the author's earlier works.

The strong point of the book is the masterly way in which Eastern life in the present day is sketched, especially where the introduction of European ideas and usages is illustrated. The dialogues of the natives are in harmony with the scenery of the desert, and the solitary castles beneath the Syrian hills. With the intuition of mental affinity, Disraeli has divined the Oriental way of looking at things, and imitates the mode of expression to a nicety. Two of Tancred's English servants play the part of fool, in English and Spanish plays, amidst these curious surroundings, and relieve the pathos of the book by introducing a comic element. Technically speaking, Disraeli has scarcely written anything better than the contrasts produced by the *naïve* English arrogance and homely wants of these servants. We hear them complaining, when in imprisonment in the Bedoueen camp, that the "savages" have drunk up all the blacking for cleaning my lord's boots, and find that their wants, during the painful absence from their own country, culminate in a sigh for a little sugar for their coffee.

Among the Orientals, the emir Fakredeen is distinguished for his brilliant and paradoxical qualities. This character is the most original Lord Beaconsfield has ever drawn. Fakredeen is a political genius, wanting in knowledge and firmness of purpose, but he has picked up a few crumbs of European culture; he served the author's purpose in 1847, in enabling him to sketch, in caricature, some of the schemes which were running in his head. Fakredeen, who in his earlier years only aimed at a sort of Syrian sovereignty, now longs for a larger sphere of political action. He wants to astonish Europe instead of the Lebanon, and to checkmate the thrones and powers of the great world instead of the sheikhs and emirs of his own mountains. He sits through the long Eastern days, with his Turkish pipe in his mouth, on Tancred's divan, and pours the wildest political fantasies into his friend's ear.

Among his fugitive projects, there is one as follows:—"You [Englishmen] must perform the Portuguese scheme on a great scale; quit a petty and exhausted position for a vast and prolific empire. Let the Queen of England collect a great fleet, let her stow away all her treasure, bullion, gold plate, and precious arms; be accompanied by all her court and chief people, and transfer the seat of her empire from London to Delhi. There she will find an immense empire ready made, a first-rate army, and a large revenue. . . . I will take care of Syria and Asia Minor. The only way to manage the Afghans is by Persia and by the Arabs. We will acknowledge the Empress of India as our suzerain, and secure for her the Levantine coast. If she like, she shall have Alexandria, as she now has Malta; it could be arranged. Your Queen is young; she has an *avenir*. Aberdeen and Sir Peel will never give her this advice; their habits are formed. They are too old, too *rusés*. But, you see! the greatest empire that ever existed; besides which, she gets rid of the embarrassment of her Chambers! And quite practicable; for the only difficult part, the conquest of India, which baffled Alexander, is all done!" *

It is impossible to read this passage without perceiving that every sentiment in it agrees with some utterance or action of Lord Beaconsfield's. He has since defined England as an Asiatic power. He has not, it is true, removed the seat of government to India, but he has emphatically said that the centre of gravity of British power lies in this colony. He has not asked the Queen to go there, but he has made her Empress of India, and sent the Prince of Wales there, well furnished with "treasure, bullion, and precious arms," and "accompanied by his chief people." He has summoned Indian

* "Tancred," p. 263.

troops to Europe to support England. He has, in literal accordance with Fakredeen's plans, made Asia Minor acknowledge the sway of the Empress of India. His object in buying the Suez Canal shares was to secure the way to India, and if he has not acquired possession of Alexandria, which was, however, once projected, and only given up in order not to offend France, he has taken Cyprus instead. While these lines are being written, he is engaged in subjugating the Afghans, and—to include the last clause in this long passage—he has shown a strong inclination to make short work with both Chambers when he wanted, by decisive action, to steal a march on a powerful adversary who was under no obligation to announce his schemes to any popular assembly.

"Tancred," in its relation to the Eastern politics of Lord Beaconsfield, is a veritable palimpsest; beneath a layer of poetical and grotesque fantasies, the book concealed for thirty years the serious programme of this policy, and not until Time, the greatest of critics, has by degrees, during the last four years, corroded the surface, were other critics enabled to decipher the concealed and instructive original writing.

XVIII

DISRAELI AS TORY LEADER

With "Tancred," Disraeli's work as a novelist ceased for full twenty-three years. The only book which he published during this long period, the "Life of Lord George Bentinck" (1852), is of a political character, an account of the early Parliamentary contests in which the author was engaged; and the rest of the contents, the exhaustive memorial relating to the emancipation of the Jews, is but a variation of the ideas in "Tancred." But, although Lord Beaconsfield's literary activity ceased in 1847 it certainly did not arise from any feeling of exhaustion on his part. He is not one of those men whose energies flag early. It was only because, from the period when he became Tory leader, he no longer had time for literary production. From his earliest years he had, like Contarini Fleming's father, placed action above authorship. He had long been firmly resolved, as he wrote of his ideal, Lord Bolingbroke, "to sacrifice himself absolutely to his party, and to spend in its service all the energy of his Proteus-like mind." He, therefore, made no attempt to serve two masters. He allowed his literary abilities to enter exclusively into the service of politics.

The sudden death of Bentinck, in 1848, left Disraeli the sole leader of the Protectionists; the equally sudden death of Sir Robert Peel, by a fall from his horse, left him the most distinguished man of the two sections of Conservatives. The leader of the Tories in the Lords, Lord Stanley, afterwards Earl of Derby, recognized him as a political ally of equal rank. It was not long before the noble lord, like Lord George Bentinck previously, even drew his political inspiration from Disraeli, and while he contented himself with being nominal head of the party, he smoothed the last bit of the *parvenu's* stony path to power.

Still, there was a long way yet to actual power; the party which followed the Tory leader was in a decided minority. The banner which he had inherited, the white banner of the duty on corn, was so unpopular that it seemed most prudent to furl it up and put it in his pocket; the future offered him no other part to play than that of watchful, but for the present powerless, critic of Lord John Russell's Whig administration, and that of encouraging leader of a totally routed and embittered party, whose impatience he had to control, but whose illusions as to the possibility of a financial political change, having the keen eye of a statesman, he did not for a moment share.

Almost from the day on which the Corn Laws were abolished, Disraeli openly gave out that it was useless to think of reopening the question, or of reintroducing the abolished laws; the voice of the country had decidedly declared against protection, and no statesman could disregard so powerful an opinion, however strongly he might be convinced that it had been produced by artificial, or even unjustifiable, means. All the speeches, therefore, which he made in favour of the landed interest, from 1848 to 1852, drop the old watchword, "Protection against Free Trade," entirely, and turn exclusively to other means of healing the wounds which, by the Whigs' confession, the sudden abolition of the corn duties had inflicted on the landowners and farmers. As a great actor can shine in a small and thankless part, and cause its insignificance to be forgotten by the masterly way in which he plays it, Lord Beaconsfield shines at this period by the care and sagacity with which he brings forward every acknowledgment that a wrong has been done to the agriculturists, which ought to be made good; and no less so by the clearness and force with which he suggests how the difficult position of the British farmer may be mitigated without recurring to the settled question of duties. He showed that the sum of ten millions annually demanded for "local purposes," fell almost exclusively on the landed property, although these purposes concerned the whole country, and not the land only. It was unreasonable to consider such burdens as the care of the poor, the maintenance of roads and bridges, and police expenses, as local, instead of national, and to throw them on the land. The unreasonableness of the present system was so great, that lately, a London Quaker, who had committed a murder in Buckinghamshire, was prosecuted at the expense of the county; they might just as well demand—indeed, better, that the Liverpool merchants should bear the expense of England's interference in La Plata, for it was solely for their benefit. He adroitly quoted Cobden's remark, that no tax on raw material should be tolerated, and defined the soil as the raw material of the necessaries of life; and Cobden sanctioned the definition.

"Do not," cried he, one day in Parliament, "under this system, oppress the land of England with the pharisaical pretence that you are the advocates of a great politico-economical scheme that will not tolerate the taxation of a raw material, and suppose at the same time that we will endure that the whole social existence of England shall be founded on a system which, morning, noon, and night, in every duty of the life of an Englishman, taxes the most important raw material of a nation's industry." *

His efforts were of no avail; his motion was rejected. He then proposed to abolish the duty on malt, as oppressive to the farmers. He appealed to the fact that, two years before, no less a man than Richard Cobden had promised the abolition of this tax, with the acknowledgment: "We owe something to the farmers, and will try to pay our debts." But in vain; the Commons decided, by an overwhelming majority, to retain the Malt Tax. He showed that the celebrated Free Trader, McCulloch, in his treatise on taxation, had stated that the English farmers, in order to be placed on an equal footing with foreign producers, were entitled to a protective duty of six to seven shillings per quarter, and said that the abolition of the Corn Laws had been carried by false statements and misrepresentations of every kind.† But it was all in vain; the victorious Free

* Hitchman's "Public Life of the Earl of Beaconsfield," vol. i. p. 304.
† McCulloch, "A Treatise on the Principles and Practical Influence of Taxation and the Funding System." Second Edition, pp. 195–202.

Traders turned a deaf ear to him; the old statements and promises had long been forgotten, and nobody quite believed in the grievances of the landowners and farmers; they had foretold that all sorts of disasters would follow the abolition of the Corn Laws; they had not followed, and the exchequer revealed that the country was in an unusually flourishing state. The landed interest was like the shepherd boy in the fable: it had so often cried for help against the free trade wolf, that it was not believed when danger really threatened. There was, therefore, nothing left for Disraeli but to warn the Free Traders in general against arrogance and exaggeration, and to threaten them with the Nemesis. They had said that it did not signify whether there was an acre of cultivated land; England should monopolize the trade of the world, and be the workshop of the world. He pointed to the fate of Venice and Tyre, which abundantly showed what became of great mercantile powers, if they were destitute of the stability and firmness of the territorial principle. Perhaps the parallel seemed a little far-fetched to the cool-headed Free Traders.

With more skill, if not with greater success, Disraeli was, during this period, the inexorable critic of the foreign policy of the Liberal administration. It was that policy which has become notorious under the name of the "meddle and muddle policy." After the disastrous commotions of 1848, England interfered in all countries, under the auspices of Lord John Russell, as the friend of the oppressed, as the ally of the Liberals, as adviser and monitor of reactionary Governments, and when her inconvenient counsels were rejected, she left her *protégés* in the lurch. The English Ministers appeared to act on the assumption, without any special study of local circumstances, that it must be the salvation of every country to have an Upper House, a Lower House, and a commercial treaty after the English model. They gave their advice accordingly, and if it was not followed, the cause of the malcontents in the various countries was dropped. There was something appropriate, when viewed in a purely æsthetic light, in the unqualified expression by the Whig Ministers of their sympathy with European Liberalism. Nothing could exceed English pride and the jaunty complaisance of Lord Palmerston, when, as Minister of Foreign Affairs, after Kossuth's flattering reception in England, he graciously received addresses, thanking him for what he had done for the famous exile, in which the Emperors of Russia and Austria were called "detestable and odious assassins, relentless tyrants and despots." He declared himself highly flattered and exceedingly pleased with the addresses, only taking care to guard his position with respect to the friendly powers, Russia and Austria, by the not very large reservation that he must not be supposed to agree with every expression made use of.

This sort of thing certainly looks bolder, more amiable, as well as more liberal, than Disraeli's denunciations, almost at the same time, of the league between the British Ministry, and the un-English Continental Jacobinism, which was even intending to supersede the legitimate sovereigns of Italy; but when we look at the results of this noisy but feeble Ministerial policy, we can but justify Disraeli's polemics against their perpetual interference. In 1848 the Spanish Government had replied to an injudicious admonitory letter of Lord Palmerston's by dismissing the English Ambassador from Madrid, and breaking off diplomatic relations. In the following year, the English Minister sent six confidential agents to no purpose, one after the other, to La Plata, a second-rate rebellious Spanish colony, and it followed the example of the mother country, and gave the British Minister his passport. Interference in the affairs of the King of the two Sicilies had no better result. The first evidences of the disesteem into which England, as a Great Power, was to fall through her feeble foreign policy in the course of the next thirty years of an almost unbroken Whig Ministry were beginning to show themselves. Ministers were even then obliged to tell the Opposition that England must not overrate her influence. Disraeli did not leave this unanswered. The conclusion of a speech in Parliament about this time sounds like a prophecy of the totally different spirit in which he would conduct the foreign policy of the country.

"At all events," he said, "he would rather that his tongue were paralyzed than advise the English people to lower its tone. Yes, he would rather leave that House for ever than tell the English people that it overrated its position. He left these delicate intimations to the glowing patriotism of the gentlemen of the new school. For his part, he deplored their policy, and defied their prophecies, but he did this because he had faith in the people of England, in their genius, and in their destiny."

The measure of the Russell administration was filled up; it had long been weakened by the intrigues of the Prime Minister against Lord Palmerston which drove him from the Foreign Office; an abortive Reform Bill, and a no less abortive Militia Bill, gave the final blow. The discontented Whigs, the Peelites under the leadership of Palmerston, and the Tories under that of Disraeli, brought about the fall of the Ministry in 1852. The Queen charged Lord Derby with the formation of a new administration, and after the office of Chancellor of the Exchequer had been declined by Lord Palmerston, it was accepted by Benjamin Disraeli, and in his suite, so to speak, and as representative of the almost forgotten "Young England," his pupil, Lord John Manners, took office as "First Commissioner of Works and Public Buildings," and he has held office in all Disraeli's subsequent Ministries. Thus Disraeli became for the first time a member of the Government; the once isolated Parliamentary gladiator had become an English Minister.

XIX

FIRST MINISTERIAL OFFICE

❧ Disraeli did not find himself, however, on a bed of roses. The Tory party was in the minority in the Lower House, and was not strong in the Upper. In the Commons, the numbers of the Tories and the Whigs and Radicals allied were about equal, so that it was the party of Peel's old adherents that turned the scale, and it will be readily believed that Disraeli had no fiercer opponents. The administration was no sooner formed than the revival of the Anti-Corn Law League throughout the country was planned, and there was a vehement agitation against the dreaded protective reaction. I have already mentioned that the new Chancellor of the Exchequer was far from having any design of conducting such a reaction; but his followers undoubtedly hoped for it, and, unfortunately, there was so much disagreement on the point in the Cabinet, that while Disraeli, in a programme addressed to his constituents, prudently avoided the word "Protection," and only spoke in general terms of "curative measures," to which the producers were entitled, Lord Derby, in his first speech in the House of Lords, imprudently adopted so challenging an attitude, that in consequence of it, £27,-ooo were subscribed for the league at a meeting at Manchester in the course of ten minutes. Seldom has a witty remark been so completely confirmed as was, on this occasion, Disraeli's designation of Lord Derby two years before, as the Prince Rupert of Parliamentary debate; his attack was always irresistible, but on his return from pursuit he constantly found his camp in the hands of the enemy. The new Chancellor needed much dexterity not to make a false step on the very threshold.

The office of Finance Minister, which had been allotted to Disraeli, could scarcely have been his own choice; it has been said that it was given him because, at that time, probably through the influence of Prince Albert, the Queen was very unfavourable to him, and in this office he would not come into personal contact with her. However that may be, he has since discovered, better than any one else, how to gain the Queen's favour, and in 1852 he performed the task confided to him with such remarkable ability, that even his opponents could not refuse recognition of it. His first budget, which necessarily did not differ essentially from that of his predecessors, was received with applause. In a letter from Lord Palmerston to his brother, of 30th of April, 1852, he says: "Disraeli has this evening made a very good financial estimate. His speech of two hours was excellent, well arranged, clear, and well sustained. . . . He has entirely thrown overboard the idea of an import duty on corn, in other words, the principle of protection." In fact, Disraeli had said, on the very first day of his taking office, in answer to a query on the burning question of the corn duties, that as the Free Traders had succeeded in exciting so much prejudice and hatred, even against the purely fiscal measure of a low-fixed duty, he should consider it to be the most senseless and useless undertaking for a Government to bid defiance to this popular opinion, and in his speech on the budget, he expressed himself to the same effect. This attitude seems to have irritated his chief, Lord Derby, more than any one. Only a week later, in order to do away with the impression of what the Chancellor had said, Lord Derby, with his accustomed impetuosity, dropped hints in an after-dinner speech about the necessity of compromises between the corn-producing and the corn-consuming classes. The consequence was that in the next sitting of the Commons after this speech, the Government found itself in a minority of no less than eighty-six. The unfortunate Tory Ministry, then, only lived by favour of its opponents, and prudence on the Free Trade question was more necessary than ever. Disraeli again rose, with the assurance that he considered the Corn Laws dead and buried. He even spoke with a certain disdain of protection as "an exploded system." "The spirit of the age," he said, "tends to free intercourse, and no statesman can disregard with impunity the genius of the epoch in which he lives." He had never so decidedly cast off the Protectionists. He proposed, in order to relieve the landed interest, a revision of the system of taxation, as he had suggested when leader of the Opposition. But the difficulties which a Tory administration had to surmount under these circumstances were too great. The dissolution of Parliament did not give the Cabinet a majority, scarcely a more favourable position. In a brilliant speech of over five hours, the Chancellor of the Exchequer brought forward his second budget—a well-devised, bold budget, reforming on a large scale; the principle of it was to relieve, by reorganization of taxation, the classes which had suffered from the legislative changes of the last few years; but the most interesting feature in it to my mind is, that Disraeli proposed a large diminution of the tax on tea, by carrying out which Gladstone gained so much credit several years later. But the budget was assailed with vehement criticism from all sides. The Protectionists gave vent to their disappointment at Disraeli's adoption of the principle of Free Trade, the Peelites gave abundant expression to their personal dislike to the foe and successor of Peel, Whigs and Tories demonstrated that all the proposed changes in taxation were bad, and when the division took place, a majority of nineteen against the budget put an end both to it and the Derby Ministry. The Tory Government had only lasted ten months, from February to December, 1852.

Among the Peelite opponents of the budget, one personage played a foremost part, whose shadow was thenceforth to be cast on Disraeli's life, and whose name, as his successful rival for twenty years, has always been coupled with his—William Ewart Gladstone. He was the foe marked out for him by fate for the rest of his life. If it really was the case, as the keys to "Coningsby" assert, that the author had Gladstone in his mind when portraying the manufacturer's son, Oswald Millbank, who was so enchanted with the young Tory aristocrats, Gladstone, whom Macaulay called, not many years later, "the rising hope of the rigid and inflexible Tories," has confounded both his and Disraeli's prognostications.

He has ended with being the hope of the directly opposite party. While Disraeli's career has brought him from an almost Radical starting-point to the leadership of the Tories, Gladstone, on the other hand, has gradually passed from extreme Toryism to an almost Radical policy. And while the careers of the two opponents form a symmetrical contrast, their talents and characters are so decidedly opposed, that this seems the place, where they are first confronted with each other, to allow the character and talents of Gladstone to throw light on the peculiarities of Lord Beaconsfield.

There is that abstract likeness between the rivals which serves to make the contrast the more marked. Both are practical politicians and distinguished Parliamentary speakers; both have made a name as authors outside the sphere of politics. They belong to the same generation (Gladstone was born in 1809), and were, in their youth, not only contemporary with the period of the great political and religious reaction, but experienced it themselves, and, as the result, both statesmen have a bit of the theologian in them. Gladstone became a Puseyite when Disraeli was a ritualistic enthusiast; and, as speculative theologians, they are equally unscientific: Gladstone has his peculiar theory about the Trinity and Homer, and Disraeli has his own private doctrine of preordination about the Crucifixion and the Jewish race. But even within these narrow limits, the likeness does not extend further; for Disraeli's theological narrowness always seems more than half-intentional, while Gladstone's is *naïve*. Gladstone is, above all things, a man of conviction, but this does not preclude changes in his convictions; bit by bit he has entirely changed his political creed, but he has had at each moment a firm belief in the truth of the creed that he professed. Lord Beaconsfield, on the other hand, has plumed himself on his political unchangeableness, and has, on all essential points, been consistent with himself; if, in spite of this, he has taken very various standpoints, the modifications which may be pointed out in his political attitude do not seem to have been determined by altered convictions, but by an intelligible regard for circumstances. Gladstone is a character, a man capable of development and always developing, and of extraordinary gifts, especially of great practical understanding; he has the head of a financial minister, and the heart of a philanthropist; he is a man of figures, with sympathy for the sufferings of humanity; but he is uninteresting and wanting in originality. The character of Lord Beaconsfield, on the contrary, is absolutely original; there is something dæmonic in him. His mind is of the metallic order, while Gladstone's is of the fluid sort. Disraeli became what he is all at once, and could scarcely change; he broke himself in, learnt self-control, acquired great knowledge of human nature, and a flexibility and dexterity which sometimes remind you of a lawyer, but in any deeper and more special sense he has not developed at all; he has only rubbed off his angles on the world around him. While it does not cost Gladstone much to confess that he has been mistaken, Disraeli never allows himself to have been in the wrong, and with a certain justification, for his character appears to him as a whole, over which time has no power; he is the man who cannot err, as he is the man who does not change. This is the point where the real and the theatrical in his character meet; he does not confess any political error, any more than he confesses to a single grey hair. But if you take the word development in the less precise sense of self-culture and self-control, Disraeli is far more capable of development than Gladstone. While Gladstone, up to old age, indeed in an increasing degree as he has advanced in years, has given way to vehemence and temper, has been sensitive and impatient, his rival has been constantly growing quieter and cooler. In his youthful works the superlative reigned supreme, and in "Contarini Fleming," for example, the hot stage of fever only gave way to the cold; but he has grown into the party leader who never loses his composure, who knows better than any one how to keep silence—prefers, indeed, to keep silence; he is imperturbable, impenetrable; he is the Parliamentary sphinx, the personification of patient waiting. Gladstone flung away the leadership of his party in a moment of irritation, and, after the fall of his Ministry, withdrew angrily into his tent. Lord Beaconsfield, after every defeat, has only been cooler than ever.

The two rivals betray the profound difference in their natures as speakers. Gladstone appeals, in order to produce conviction, to the eternal ideas of truth and justice; he speaks in the name of Christianity and humanity; he recognizes philosophic, philanthropic, and cosmopolitan ideas as the highest, even in the sphere of politics. For Lord Beaconsfield, on the contrary, the great statesmen of England are the decisive authorities; he does not appeal to ideas, but to precedents, not to principles, but to Bolingbroke or Shelburne; he does not quote Shakespeare, but Hansard; he desires, above all things, to be national and historical. And as the contents of his speeches differ from those of Gladstone, so does the form. Gladstone is a clear and energetic, but far too discursive speaker; not a single word, not a telling phrase, stands out in the torrent of his eloquence, so as once heard, never to be forgotten. He has himself defined the relations between the speaker and his hearers; he says that the speaker gives them back in the form of a river what he receives from them as vapour. He himself is the speaker thus defined, and it is on the close relation to his hearers here indicated that the great effect of his words depends; they seldom read well. Lord Beaconsfield's speeches, on the contrary, are eminently monologues, the products of an original, paradoxical, and therefore isolated mind, the work of a born author, brilliant and sparkling, excellent in parts, but long passages in them are trivial, a mere tissue of spangles.

Still, it is not as members of Parliament, but as leaders of foreign policy, that these two great statesmen are most strikingly contrasted. It was Gladstone's highest ambition, systematically to diminish the National Debt by extraordinary financial measures; he succeeded in doing so, and in order not to disturb this result, when controller of England's destinies, he sank into an unexampled state of blissful tranquillity and indifference about foreign policy, and carried the principle of non-intervention so far that he lowered the dignity of England in every quarter of the world, nay, made her almost an object of ridicule. The chief strength of his opponent, who is by no means his equal as a financier, consists in his advocating precisely opposite tendencies in foreign policy, and in his having made amends for Gladstone's failures in this respect. The man whom Gladstone not long ago called "a foreigner, with not a drop of English blood in his veins," has kept the colonies, whose continued connection with the mother country Gladstone treated as a matter of indifference, as closely as possible under English rule, and, by an energetic policy in face of England's foes, he has restored the lost prestige to his country's name.

XX

DISRAELI AS LEADER OF THE OPPOSITION, AND HIS SECOND MINISTERIAL OFFICE

∽§ The fall of the Derby Administration in December, 1852, again placed Disraeli in the Opposition camp. For the sake of convenience, I give the particulars of his political position from that time to the present. Out of the twenty-one following years, he was scarcely four at the helm. He was only twice in the Ministry during this time; he was Chancellor of the Exchequer under Lord Derby from March, 1858, to June, 1859, and he entered the Derby Ministry in the same capacity in July, 1866, and became Prime Minister when Derby retired on account of ill health in February, 1868, but he with difficulty retained his position up to December of the same year. It is only since February, 1874, that is, after his seventieth year, that Lord Beaconsfield has attained decisive influence as an English statesman; and in order to judge him justly in the intervening years, it must not be forgotten that he was not in a position, with the short and sporadic possession of power that fell to his lot, to carry out large or matured projects. During these years, the part he played was chiefly that of critic.

Lord Aberdeen's Coalition Ministry united in itself, according to Lord Palmerston's definition, "all the men of talent and experience in the House of Commons, with the exception of Disraeli." Disraeli, therefore, immediately christened it with the nickname of the "Ministry of all the Talents," and it began with a series of indiscretions and mistakes. At a time when the alliance with France was a necessity for England, members of the Cabinet were guilty of using grossly insulting language towards the emperor in public speeches, when almost immediately afterwards, the Government had to sue for his confidence and friendship. Sir Charles Wood told his hearers that "a despotism like the present had not reigned in France, even in the time of Napoleon I;" and in another speech he expressed his conviction that Napoleon III, without carrying on a regular war with England, "would suddenly land various corps of five thousand men on our coasts," and asked the meeting to consider "how their wives and daughters would be treated then." Another member of the Government, Sir James Graham, First Lord of the Admiralty, openly called Napoleon "a despot, who was treading the liberties of forty millions of men under foot." This was fine sport for a leader of the Opposition, and Disraeli closed a speech, brimming over with wit and satire, with the query: Are these utterances indiscretions? Can indiscretions proceed from "all the Talents"? Impossible!

How the Aberdeen Ministry drifted into the war with Russia, without resolve or forethought, is well known; the careless words of the Prime Minister, "We drift into a war," have become historic. Palmerston, whose plan was to act with energy and promptitude, was compelled to tender his resignation; and just at the moment when the Russo-Turkish war began with the defeat at Sinope, Lord John Russell, the most maladroit member of the Government of "all the Talents," brought in a Reform Bill, taking advantage, so to speak, of the interval during which Palmerston, who had a marked aversion to all reform schemes, was out of the Ministry. The decidedly warlike feeling of the country, however, induced Palmerston to withdraw his resignation; and Disraeli had the opportunity, without speaking against reform in the abstract, of preparing an important defeat for the Ministry, by inveighing against Lord John Russell's folly in choosing a moment like this for bringing forward the difficult domestic question of Parliamentary reform, when the nation was rallying its forces for the conflict at hand.

He successfully impugned both the attitude of the Government towards Turkey, and the wretched administration of the army. Disraeli's special tenderness for Turkey has often been ridiculed; but surely no impartial person can fail to see that, from the English standpoint, he was right in upholding Turkey as long as possible. And the members of the Coalition Ministry were as imprudent in the expressions about this ally of England as they had been about the French. One of them said that the sultan "had chiefly himself to blame for his misfortunes, through his senseless policy and reckless misgovernment;" another Minister, Gladstone, made a speech at Manchester, in which he gave the country to understand that the situation of Turkey was hopeless; and these were the assurances with which they called upon the nation to fight for the integrity of the Turkish empire. The beginning of the Crimean war agreed only too well, as we all know, with the vacillating policy which had preceded it. The leader of the Opposition in December, 1854, summed up the results of the Ministerial preparations for the first few months of the campaign in the following words:—"You have chosen a winter campaign, and what have been your preparations for it? In November you gave orders to build huts. You have not yet sent out that winter clothing which is adapted to the climate. . . . You have commenced a winter campaign in a country where it most of all should be avoided. You have commenced such a campaign—a great blunder, without providing for it—the next great blunder. The huts will arrive in January, and the furs probably will meet the sun in May. These are your preparations!" *

It was not necessary to be an eminent politician to lash with severity the gross mistakes of the Government, and no one will attribute any special merit to Disraeli for doing it; what is much more to his credit is the way in which he then, as ever afterwards, at critical periods, put the interests of the country entirely above those of his party—the genuine patriotism with which, from the moment when the Government and the country took up the war in earnest, he offered his support to the Government. Even before the outbreak of the war, when speaking in favour of a peaceful

* Hitchman's "Public Life of the Earl of Beaconsfield," vol. i. p. 422.

solution of the question, at the close of his speech he addressed the following words to the Ministry:—"But, if war should be found inevitable, the Opposition will cordially and sincerely support their sovereign, and maintain the honour and dignity of their country. This I can say—I can answer for myself and my friends, that no future Wellesley on the banks of the Danube will have to make a bitter record of the exertions of an English Opposition that depreciated his efforts and that ridiculed his talents. We shall remember what we believe to be our duty to this country; and however protracted may be the war, however unfortunate your counsels [to the Ministry], at least we shall never despair of the republic." *

This retrospective attack on the conduct of the Whigs towards Wellington cannot be considered unnatural, when we recall the English demonstrations against Turkey during the last Russo-Turkish war. The Whigs, who were then agitating against Lord Beaconsfield, had neither his self-control nor the patriotism which determined his attitude before the Crimean war. And when, after the retirement of Aberdeen, and the futile attempts of Lord Derby and Lord Russell to form a new administration, Palmerston took the conduct of the war in his firmer hand as Prime Minister, Disraeli again declared that her Majesty might firmly rely on her Parliament in the renewed conflict; there was no sum which her Parliament would not joyfully grant, and her people joyfully raise, to protect the honour and interests of the empire.

Only compare Gladstone's noisy demonstrations and fanatical denunciations of Lord Beaconsfield's Oriental policy in the course of 1877!

The Treaty of Peace with Russia resulted in disappointment. A feeling prevailed that the results gained were in no kind of proportion to the sacrifices made, and Palmerston himself did not expect, as Lord John Russell tells us, in his "Recollections and Suggestions," that the Treaty of 1856 would last the fifteen years it did last. And yet the war with Russia was scarcely over, when Palmerston's restless foreign policy involved England in a series of new wars. The unjust and repulsive war with China, a little war

* Hitchman's "Public Life of the Earl of Beaconsfield," vol. i. p. 413.

with Persia, and difficulties with the kingdom of Naples and the United States, followed quickly upon each other. After a cutting speech from Disraeli on the Chinese war, Palmerston found himself in a minority in the Commons, and a dissolution followed. But when the new elections showed his undiminished popularity by a large majority for the Government, and when just at the same time the Indian Mutiny broke out, Disraeli again gave up his opposition. He gave the assurance in the House of Commons, that "it was his intention to support the Sovereign and the Government in all the measures which so grave and critical an event might demand." This loyal behaviour did not, of course, however, preclude a very different opinion of the Mutiny from the Ministerial one. He met with no success with a motion for the appointment of a Committee to inquire into the causes which led the natives to rebel, but long before the Government understood the ominous threats or, at least, would acknowledge the danger, Disraeli foresaw the coming storm. To his first question on Indian matters, he received an answer from the Ministerial benches, that it was altogether an insignificant affair; the discontent was almost entirely confined to the army in Bengal, and any attempt at mutiny would be sure to be nipped in the bud by Lord Canning. Disraeli replied that the disturbances in India did not appear to him at all like a mutiny among the soldiers, but like a revolt of the people. He was not to be put off with the usual explanation of the origin of the mutiny, the introduction of the Enfield rifle, with cartridges greased with beef suet and lard; he allowed that this disregard of the religious prejudices of the Hindoos may have been the immediate occasion, but he ascribed the Mutiny to much more general causes. He showed that all the great Indian statesmen had been in favour of the principle of respecting the rights and privileges, the laws, customs, and religions of the nations to be governed; and brought forward instances to show that, in all these respects, this rule had been violated. There was one passage in the speech which threw light on his subsequent Indian policy. He told the House that it must, no matter whether tidings of victory or defeat reached it, proclaim to the people of India that the relation between them and their true sovereign, Queen Victoria, would be more closely drawn. The House must, in this affair, exert an influence on public opinion in India, and it was only through the imagination that the public opinion of Eastern nations could be worked upon.

Disraeli recognized, better than the statesmen in office, the necessity of not wounding Asiatic prejudices if you wished to be an Asiatic sovereign, and he knew better than any man what vast power Oriental imagination offered the British Government for confirming its supremacy.

During the five years which elapsed between the first time that Disraeli held office, and the second, he trained himself to be a trustworthy and watchful party leader of the first class. He was a master of the art of keeping his followers together, knew how to encourage the younger men, and to gain the elder ones by recognition of their services; above all things, he possessed the gift of never wounding anybody's vanity; as leader of Opposition, he did not thrust any aspiring colleague into the shade; and later on, when Prime Minister, he permitted his colleagues to explain and defend their opinions and actions themselves. In this, also, he was a contrast to Gladstone, who, in the conviction, perhaps not in-correct in itself, that he could best advocate the views of the Ministry in person, has subjected his colleagues to many an unwise humiliation. And while, by these qualities, Disraeli was increasingly gaining the confidence and devotion of the Conservative party, he was one of the two or three Parliamentary orators on whose lips all parties hung. There was soon no one whose words were looked for with greater eagerness, no one who was greeted with more applause. Seldom has the art of compelling an assembly to listen to every word of the speaker been carried to greater perfection.

Towards Palmerston, Disraeli adopted neither the disdainful attitude which he had assumed towards Peel, nor the satirical style which he usually assumed in the Opposition towards Aberdeen and Russell. He used, half ironically, to take Palmerston, whom he once jestingly called the "Tory chief of a Radical Cabinet," under his protection as a distant ally. But when, after Orsini's attack on Napoleon III, in the beginning of 1858, Palmerston took in so unmanly a style Walewski's insulting note calling England the protector of assassins, and the address of the French colonels to the emperor, printed in the *Moniteur*, asking permission to call England to account, "that land of impurity, that infamous nest," and obligingly laid before the House the Bill against conspirators desired by Napoleon, Disraeli helped to overturn his Ministry, and the administration once more fell into the hands of Lord Derby.

It was the misfortune of the new Cabinet that, as previously, it had a majority only in the Commons. It tried to make up by skill what it lacked in power. At first Disraeli's tact succeeded in pacifying the French Government, without any humiliating concession. He spoke of the alliance with France with a warmth that was obviously sincere. "The alliance between England and France," he said, "rests upon a principle, which is wholly independent of forms of government, and even of the personal character of the rulers." Then passing over to his youthful acquaintance of Lady Blessington's *salon*, he lauded the French emperor as an eminently gifted man: "The Emperor Napoleon is not only a ruler, but a statesman. He possesses not only great knowledge of human nature in general, but of the human nature of the Englishman in particular," etc.

With similar firmness he arranged another painful affair which the previous Government had vainly attempted, the release of two Englishmen taken prisoners by the Neapolitan Government, on board the steamer *Cagliari*, and who, though quite innocent, had been languishing for months in horrible prisons, and could not be released because Palmerston, in order to punish the King of the Two Sicilies, had taken the futile step of withdrawing the English Ambassador from Naples.

Two important matters were then decided by legislation. By a compromise between Lord John Russell and Disraeli, India was placed directly under the dominion of the British Crown, a centralizing measure demanded by circumstances, and which is in full accord with the subsequent Imperial policy so called. Further, Lord

John Russell brought in a Bill under the Derby-Disraeli administration, by which the House of Commons was opened to the Jews; and the first Jew admitted to Parliament, Baron Lionel de Rothschild, was introduced by Disraeli.

In 1831 Macaulay wrote his famous essay on the Emancipation of the Jews, in 1833 the law for their emancipation was passed, and in 1847 two Jews were elected members of Parliament. But the law was nugatory, and the elections null and void, so long as the words in the formula of the oath, "on the true faith of a Christian," stood in the way. It was now for the first time made permissible to omit them; and thus by a chance, which seems like intention, it fell to the lot of the chief of the formerly intolerant Tory party, and the creator of Sidonia as representative of the literary and political intelligence of the Jewish race, to introduce the representatives of Jewish commercial enterprise and wealth to the exercise of their political rights as citizens.

Although Disraeli's budget in April, 1858, was well received, the position of the Government was extremely weak. The only possible means of obtaining a majority was to bring in a Reform Bill. It had always been Disraeli's desire to snatch this card from the hands of the Whigs, and he now made the first attempt, which was encompassed with difficulties of all sorts. The Tories regarded every innovation in popular representation with extreme suspicion, and it was necessary for Disraeli, in order to avoid being left in the lurch by his own party, so to prepare the Bill that the Conservatives might hope for an increase of votes from a considerable increase of agricultural voters; on the other hand, it was easy to foresee that the Liberals would think any measure proposed by the Tories inadequate, even if quite as honest in intention and going as far as those which they themselves had in reserve. What an egg-dance Disraeli had to execute is clearly shown by the fact that no sooner was his scheme of reform laid before his colleagues, than two of them resigned—Henley, because he desired to see a much further extension of the franchise among the working people; and Walpole, because he did not wish to see the concessions made to them in 1832 exceeded. The reception the Bill met with in the

Cabinet was ominous of its further fate. It was assailed with fierce criticism on all sides. The whole of the press was opposed to it: the Tory organs, because they saw no reason why they should have a Reform Bill from Disraeli, who had vehemently opposed it when originated by Lord John Russell; the Liberal papers, first, because they did not see why the Tory Ministry should have the merit of solving the great reform question, and next, because they had all concurred for years in calling Disraeli a political mountebank, without any real convictions, and they considered his Reform Bill only fresh evidence how little he was *un homme sérieux*. In Parliament itself, the Bill was opposed by Lord John Russell and the Radicals with vehemence and scorn as nothing but a sham. The scheme was certainly not democratic, although it went further than the Whigs' next Reform Bill; but it is certain that the Chancellor of the Exchequer was even then in favour of a much more Radical change in the franchise; he even proposed household franchise in the Cabinet, but was compelled to abandon it, convinced that it was impossible to pass it at that time. The Bill, being laid before the House in a form which was neither fish nor fowl, soon succumbed to the attacks of its enemies; the Government, which had too often before been in the minority, had in this case a majority of thirty-nine against it. The Liberal press was, of course, triumphant; but it is interesting to find one among the many merely scoffing articles which hits with great subtlety and acumen the peculiarity of Lord Beaconsfield:—"Gone for ever is the opportunity which Mr. Disraeli is supposed to have been aspiring after, since the first doors of office opened to his ambition—that of revealing himself to the people of this country as at heart their friend, as one with them in political sympathy and purpose, though it was his policy to serve, that he might ultimately command, an aristocratic faction." * This sarcastic journalist was only mistaken on one point —the opportunity had by no means gone for ever.

Disraeli did not accept his defeat; as in all such cases, he wished first to appeal to the country; Parliament was dissolved, and the

* Hitchman's "Public Life of the Earl of Beaconsfield," vol. ii. p. 112.

elections took place amidst great excitement. They occurred just as the Franco-Austrian war was breaking out, and, curiously enough, English foreign sympathies had more weight in the scale than home politics. The people wished to see Italy free and united; the Whig leaders had expressed, in season and out of season, their warm sympathy for Sardinia, and their destestation of Austrian and Papal tyranny, and had thereby gained popularity. The Derby Ministry, on the contrary, did all in their power to avert the conflict between France and Italy, did not to the last moment give up the hope of preserving peace, and were, therefore, suspected of truckling to reactionary Austria, while they only sought to curb the Emperor Napoleon's warlike tendencies for the sake of British interests.

On attentively reading Disraeli's speeches in those days on foreign policy, it is impossible to doubt that his sympathies were much more with the old French allies than with Austria; but the impression would also be conveyed that he had no idea of the genius or resolution of Cavour, who wanted to bring on the war; he was evidently not more clear-sighted with regard to Bismarck just before the outbreak of the Franco-German war; he spoke even then of the possibility of peace being maintained by wise mediation. The grand, simple foreign policy of these statesmen was so foreign to his nature, that his usual gift of divination failed him. Until the unity of Italy was an accomplished fact, he coldly called all her efforts to attain it impracticable dreams, sure to be defeated by Austria, and attributed them to the interest of the Catholic powers in securing the temporal sovereignty of the Pope. The English constituencies, in whose eyes Austria was personified by General Haynau, on whom the London draymen had inflicted lynch law for his cruel suppression of the revolts in Lombardy and Hungary, placed the Government again in a minority; on the first division in the Commons, the Cabinet was in a minority of thirteen, and thus the fate of the second Derby-Disraeli Ministry was sealed.

XXI

OPPOSITION, AND THE REFORM MINISTRY

৵৹ The reign of the new Administration (Palmerston-Russell-Gladstone) was not a very glorious one; the dignity of England was lowered under it in the eyes of the whole world, and its blundering foreign policy was accompanied by two futile attempts to solve the complicated Reform question.

The first attempt, in 1860, was so weak and insignificant, that no one could be surprised that it proved a *fiasco*. When the measure, which extended the franchise still less than the Conservative Bill of the previous session, was laid before the House, it was looked upon by both sides as a mere show; it was well known that Palmerston was against any reform, and that Lord John Russell only brought in the Bill for conventional reasons—he watched its fate with so much indifference, that he had nothing better to say in its favour than that its effects would be extremely limited. The *Times* wittily remarked that something must be said, promises must be kept, the congealed blood of Saint Reform must be liquefied once in the year. Enthusiasm, ay, even faith in the cause had long since disappeared, and now we had a cautious man proposing a cautious measure to a cautious assembly.

Under the pressure of public opinion in the country and in Parliament, and in reply to Disraeli's appeal, Russell withdrew the Bill.

During the next few years, the leader of the Opposition maintained his reputation more than ever as a keen and distinguished critic of the foreign policy of the Government; and it was not a difficult part to play, for that policy falls mainly into three great groups of blunders—those relating to the great war in North America, to the colonies, and to Poland and Denmark.

It is well known that the Ministry did not adhere with statesman-like prudence to an unambiguous neutrality during the North American civil war; they rushed hastily into a recognition of the Southern States as a military power; they did not conceal their sympathies for the "chivalrous" confederates; there were no bounds to the national jealousy for the great republic now endangered; Gladstone even went so far in 1862 as to say of Jefferson Davis, in a public speech, that he had succeeded in making "an independent nation" of the Southern States. It all the more deserves to be recorded that Disraeli, whose party almost unanimously sympathized with the slave States, observed the strictest neutrality during the whole war, in order not to increase the difficulties of the Government; he generally kept silence, and only spoke a few times, partly to criticize the vacillating attitude of the Government and Gladstone's impolitic expressions, and partly in a conciliatory spirit, to recognize as honourable the conduct of the Washington Cabinet in the *Trent* affair.

The indifference of the Whig Ministers to the colonies found about this time striking expression in the public utterance of the Duke of Newcastle (Colonial Secretary), that he "should see a dissolution of the bond between the mother country and Canada with the greatest pleasure." These words were strongly reprehended by Disraeli, and his appointment of the Queen's son-in-law, the Marquis of Lorne, sixteen years later, as Governor-General of Canada, is a striking contrast to them. The leader of the Tory party protested with still greater energy in another affair of the same kind—the proposed cession of the Ionian Islands to Greece, on the occasion of the accession of King George. That the cessation of the British protectorate was in accordance with the repeatedly expressed wish of the population, was an aspect of the question which the Imperial politician regarded as of no moment whatever. What he laid stress on was the breach that would be made in the chain of England's Mediterranean garrisons in

the way to India, and the discrepancy in the policy of Lord
Palmerston, who had, with great impetuosity, placed obstacles in
the way of the construction of the Suez Canal on behalf of Turkey,
and was now ready to weaken Turkey by the aggrandizement of
Greece. The following passage in his speech, directed against
humanitarian considerations, is significant from its reckless British
energy, and psychologically interesting:—"Professors and rhetori-
cians invent for every event a system, and for every isolated case
a principle. You will not, however, I hope, leave the destinies of
the British Empire to boys and pedants. The statesmen who construct, and the warriors who achieve, are only influenced by the
instinct of power, and animated by the love of country. Those are
the feelings, and those the methods, which form empires." It cannot be denied that the acquisition of the protectorate of Cyprus
in 1878 was an instructive contrast to the cession of the Ionian
Isles in 1863.

It required some courage in Disraeli in the same year to ex-
pose himself to unpopularity, by venturing to blame the sentimental conduct of the Government with regard to Poland. Everybody is now agreed that England's weak and noisy interference in
the domestic affairs of Russia was nothing but a mischief to unhappy Poland, as it deeply wounded the sensitiveness of Russia and
spurred on the authorities to greater cruelties; but at that time
public opinion only regarded Lord John Russell's despatches as
proofs of magnanimity, and Disraeli's criticism as evidence of
servile feeling.

Closely connected with the action of the Ministry in respect
to Poland was their still more blamable attitude in the Danish
question. First, Lord John Russell offended the Emperor of the
French by not only declining, but uncourteously declining, his
invitation to a European Congress, in which the Treaty of Vienna
was to be revised; and he thereby earned the malicious satisfaction
of France, at his bungling and unsuccessful attempts to arrange the
Danish-German question. In a despatch in 1862, he called upon
Denmark to yield to the demands of Germany, and after she had

declined to follow this advice, it was disavowed by the Prime Minister; for Palmerston, fully convinced, as it appeared, that Denmark was in the right, did not hesitate to make a solemn declaration in the House of Commons, that in case her territory were encroached upon, Denmark would not be left to herself. Her territory was encroached upon, yet Denmark found herself left entirely alone. Disraeli exposed this discrepancy in a brilliant speech, and demonstrated that there had been "the same weakness, confusion, vacillation, and inconsistency" in the Danish affair as in the other diplomatic action of the Ministry. A vote of want of confidence was proposed in the Lords, to the effect that "while the course pursued by her Majesty's Government had failed to maintain their avowed policy of upholding the integrity and independence of Denmark, it had lowered the just influence of this country in the counsels of Europe, and thereby diminished the securities of peace."

The vote was passed in the Lords, but thrown out in the Commons, through Gladstone's opposition, by a majority of eighteen. This time, however, it was the simple truth which was defeated by the majority.

The death of Palmerston brought Lord John Russell, and with him schemes of reform, to the helm in 1865. The extension of that Parliamentary Reform which Lord John Russell had called "definitive"—a term soon repented of, often ridiculed, and which gave him the nickname of "Finality Jack"—had become his favourite idea. But as he was far more imbued with a conviction of its necessity than with a passion for it as a matter of justice, all his later reform projects bore the stamp of indecision; they were brought forward rather with a view of putting an end to the everlasting reform difficulties, and to stop the mouths of the Radicals, than from a political sense of duty. The Reform Bill of 1866 was far more liberal than that of 1860—it would have created 400,000 new electors, half of whom belonged to the working classes; but it was not skilfully prepared, and, as usual, satisfied neither Conservatives nor Liberals; a section of the latter even, alarmed at the consequences of so democratic a franchise, voted against the

Bill. Disraeli's opposition was based on his objection on principle to the Americanizing of the constitution, which he had denounced in his "Vindication of the English Constitution," and often since, as well as on the patchwork character of the measure. Nevertheless, it was quite evident in the next session that his opposition was more actuated by party rancour than by considerations of principle. The Russell-Gladstone Ministry fell with the Reform Bill.

For the third time Disraeli became Chancellor of the Exchequer in a Derby Cabinet, for the third time without being able to command a majority in the Commons, and for the third time also, he was decidedly not favoured by public opinion. By degrees, as the great reform agitation increased, this disfavour grew to absolute hatred, which was mainly directed against him, as the chief opponent of the last Ministerial Reform Bill.

It was now a matter of course that the Government must take the reform question in hand, and push it forward with all possible energy. Reform Bills had been brought in, in 1852, 1854, 1858, 1859, 1860, and 1866, and had all been rejected. Lord John Russell, Lord Aberdeen, Lord Palmerston, Lord Derby, and Lord John Russell twice, had tried to untie the Gordian knot; Disraeli had profited by the mistakes of his predecessors, and was determined to stake all his skill and perseverance in obtaining a permanent result. He began, therefore, as Chancellor of the Exchequer, by making a statement, which called forth roars of laughter, that in the opinion of the Ministry the reform question was no longer one that ought to determine the fate of a Government. Without allowing himself to be disturbed by the laughter, he proceeded to state that this view was founded on the consideration that all parties had tried to carry a Reform Bill, and had all failed. Though he spoke cautiously and carefully on the whole, he could not deny himself the satisfaction of emphasizing his old doctrine, that the Whig Reform Bill of 1832 had placed the government of the country in the hands of the middle class, and had abolished the franchise of the working classes, as it had existed before 1832—a proceeding, he added, not without *finesse*, "which perhaps was natural for a party which had founded their policy rather upon liberal opinions than popular rights." He stated further that the Government, in order to avoid the previous miscarriages of the Reform Bill, intended to ascertain the prevailing views in the House by submitting resolutions to it. This was the method adopted by Disraeli in the Jews Bill, and if it was not gratifying to his vanity, it had at least the great advantage that the Government avoided the difficulty of bringing in a ready-made measure, and of having to stand or fall by it. The resolutions, intended to feel the pulse of the House, were not favourably received; their effect would have been to create about 400,000 new electors, but by various restrictions, among them a double franchise for certain classes of voters, they tried to gain over the Conservatives for the innovations. A new Bill was demanded, and in March, 1867, Disraeli laid it before the House. The result, according to the opening speech of the Chancellor of the Exchequer, would by no means be a popular tyranny; a fourth part of the electors would belong to the aristocracy, a fourth part to the working classes, and the remaining half to the middle class; but at the same time, he had to make the painful communication to the House, that three of the most important members of the Government, Lord Carnarvon, General Peel, and Lord Cranborne (the present Marquis of Salisbury), disapproving of the proposed extension of the franchise, had laid down their portfolios. This split in the Cabinet occurred at an inopportune moment, but it was to be expected, for the Bill was far more Radical than that of the Whigs, the most Radical which had been laid before the House. It was based upon the principle of household suffrage, that is, that every man who rents a house should have a vote, irrespective of the amount of rent; and the Conservative guarantees, which were to some extent to make up for these great concessions, consisted chiefly in the limitation of the franchise to ratepayers, in allowing two votes, as before mentioned, to certain electors possessing a double qualification, and on the condition that those householders only should have a vote who had rented a house for two years. The most interesting remark, in a psychological point of view, which fell from the Chancellor in defending this measure from the attacks of the ultra-Conservatives, was his reply to Lord Cranborne—then his vehement opponent, but now his thoroughly broken-in colleague—who angrily called attention to the discrepancy between Disraeli's reserved attitude towards reform in 1858, and his present revolutionary Bill. Disraeli appealed to the testimony of those still living, that even then, in the Derby Cabinet of that time, he had proposed the principle of household suffrage as the only trustworthy basis of reform.*

But it was from the Liberal party, and not from the extreme Tories, that the Bill had to sustain the most threatening attacks. Gladstone subjected it, point by point, to severe, and on the whole skilful, criticism. Bit by bit the Conservative guarantees fell beneath his axe, and to the general surprise, it appeared that Disraeli himself was the first to declare his willingness to let them go. The Chancellor did not even attempt to defend the double vote; he had, in submitting the resolution, declared this measure to be unimportant, and immediately gave way. He further renounced the restriction of the franchise to ratepayers, and the two years' possession for which one year was substituted. He even conceded the franchise to lodgers paying £10 rent, and declared that he had always in his heart been favourable to this measure. He gave way on every point on which it was necessary to give way in order to pass a Bill, even if not his original one, and by a dexterous manœuvre, which caused the defection of about thirty moderate members of the Liberal party, he succeeded in defeating Gladstone's amendment on the first reading.

The activity which Disraeli displayed during this session may, without exaggeration, be truly called gigantic; he spoke on the

* Compare the speech "Representation of the People," in "Speeches on the Conservative Policy," p. 156. The interesting collection of speeches "On Parliamentary Reform" only extends as far as 1866, but it affords a good insight into the stages through which the reform schemes and Lord Beaconsfield have passed. See, for example, pp. 82, 175, 276, 351 ff. Compare also W. N. Molesworth, "The History of England from the Year 1830," iii. p. 412, ff.

Reform Bill alone no less than 310 times, and introduced his budget with a speech, the masterly clearness of which found general recognition, and even the *Times*, then Disraeli's determined opponent, felt compelled to write a commendatory article. Thanks to this extraordinary energy, he succeeded in steering clear of all threatening dangers, and in bringing his Reform Bill safe into port. There were, it is true, but a few great outlines of the original measure left; indeed, an amendment from the Liberals, by which the number of electors was nearly quadrupled, had been adopted. But little as the Bill, as finally passed, agreed with the original scheme, there was certainly no want of accord between it and the personal views of the Chancellor of the Exchequer; for Disraeli had no fear whatever that the Bill would result in a future government by the masses; he met the forebodings of the present Marquis of Salisbury with great confidence, and twelve years' experience has proved that he was right.

By July, 1867, this important measure, which essentially changed the basis of the British Constitution, had passed the ordeal of the three readings, and was, in fact, the realization of Disraeli's old programme: the maintenance of the people's rights by Tory leadership. A passage in a speech at a banquet in Edinburgh, given in his honour, which has been often quoted and much ridiculed, throws an interesting light on Disraeli's conduct in this business. "Now mark this, because these are things which you may not have heard in any speech which has been made in the city of Edinburgh; I had to prepare the mind of the country—to educate, if it be not too arrogant to use such a phrase—to educate our party, which is a large party, and, of course, requires its attention to be called to questions of this character with some pressure; and I had to prepare the mind of Parliament and of the country in this question of Reform." *

It appears to me that Disraeli here utters, in a half-humorous form, the most serious and most deeply felt words which ever passed his lips in reference to his relations with the Tory party. He

* O'Connor's "Life of Lord Beaconsfield," p. 577.

had, as Wellington and Peel had formerly done, to pass liberal measures as Conservative leader, simply because, in this century and in a country like England, such measures only can be passed; but, unlike his predecessors, he had never shared the rigid Conservatism of his party, but from the first, he regarded it as a necessity to put an end to Conservatism of this sort, and as his mission to do it. He strikingly says, in the speech at Edinburgh above mentioned: "It is as fallacious an opinion in politics, as in science, to suppose that you can establish a party upon resistance to change; and for this reason, that change is inevitable in a progressive country. Change is inevitable, but the point is whether that change shall be carried out in deference to the manners, the customs, the laws, the traditions of the people, or whether it shall be carried in deference to abstract principles and arbitrary and general doctrines."

It must undoubtedly be regarded as a real merit in Lord Beaconsfield to have brought the old Tory aristocracy to follow then, and to follow still, a leader with views like these.

In February, 1868, an event occurred which was destined to realize Benjamin Disraeli's wildest youthful dreams. Lord Derby retired from public life, and warmly recommended the Chancellor of the Exchequer to the Queen, as his only possible successor. By a singular chance, Disraeli was summoned to the Queen by his first victorious political opponent, the son of Earl Grey, who defeated him at his election at High Wycombe, and now held an office at Court, and Disraeli left the Sovereign's presence as Prime Minister. Little as he was liked in many quarters, there was a general feeling in the country that he had honourably won the distinction now accorded to him, by his rare capabilities and persistent hard work for many years; and when he walked for the first time in his new honours from Downing Street to the House of Commons, he was greeted with enthusiastic applause, both on the way and in the lobby of the House. And yet this coveted position was literally scarcely won before it had to be looked upon as lost. The Prime Minister was, and continued to be, in a minority, just as the Chancellor of the Exchequer had been. The first serious debate was sure to cause his fall, and the Fenian disturbances in Ireland soon furnished the occasion. Gladstone, supported by the whole of his party, proposed the abolition of the Irish State Church. In vain Disraeli characterized it as a senseless half-measure, for the opinions which led to it must lead to the abolition of the State Church in England and Scotland; in vain he assumed his most unctuous tone in his repeated declarations that "the sacred union between Church and State was the chief means of our civilization and the sole guarantee of religious liberty;" in vain he finally asserted that neither the philosophers who flattered themselves that they were advancing the cause of liberty, nor the sectaries who dreamed that the downfall of ecclesiastical systems would be hastened, would derive any advantage from the abolition of the Irish Church, but only the Pope, a foreign ruler, whose authority would be substituted for that of the Queen. The Commons were favourable to the measure, and when the new elections took place, and the Prime Minister hoped to earn thanks for his Reform Bill, now for the first time coming into force, the people returned a House in which he had twice the majority against him that he had had before. Before Parliament met, Disraeli vacated his post as Premier in favour of Gladstone.

XXII

"LOTHAIR," AND FOURTH
MINISTERIAL OFFICE

❧ In looking back to the doctrines first propounded by Disraeli, and to his action during the three occasions of his holding Ministerial office, it will be found that there is but one that has been entirely dropped—the doctrine of the personal government of the Sovereign. When Sir Robert Peel came into conflict with the Queen in 1839, on his demanding the dismissal of the ladies of the Court—the Bedchamber Plot, so called—Disraeli, in spite of his theories, justified Sir Robert Peel. When, in 1853, the assumed unconstitutional influence of Prince Albert was criticized in Parliament, he said not a word in defence of "a free Sovereign," and although it is sometimes said that he has won to so unusual an extent the favour of the Queen by complaisant concession, it appears to me, as far as I am able to judge, to be always his will which the Queen carries out when she maintains her own.

Although the fall of the Tory Ministry in 1868 was occasioned by Disraeli's opposition to the abolition of the Irish Church, he had evidently not diverged in any respect from his youthful opinions as to the equal political rights of the Catholics; but, like more than one European statesman during the years preceding the proclamation of Papal Infallibility, he foresaw the approaching Catholic reaction. He foretold it at a time when Gladstone set it aside as an imaginary danger—to combat it, when too late, with the utmost vehemence—and all Disraeli's enthusiasm "for the only existing Hebrew-Christian Church" vanished before political considerations. His opposition was fruitless; the Gladstone Ministry carried the abolition of the Irish Church.

Disraeli employed his comparative leisure in once more writing a novel after a lapse of twenty years, the immediate tendency of which was to vindicate his warnings against the increasing Popish tendencies in Great Britain. "Lothair" appeared in 1870.

This novel bears evident traces of the fact that the author was now advanced in years; it is the product of fuller and riper experience than his earlier works; it contains no mere political descriptions, no attacks on living personages; it has, in fact, the virtues of age; but taken as a whole, it is a repetition of his previous writings, especially of "Tancred," and the style betrays the old man. During the years immediately preceding, a new element had crept into Disraeli's oratorical efforts, and his attitude as a Parliamentary speaker—a stamp of officialism. It is this which gives the final touches to his descriptions of character. Not that his speeches had ever lost their wit or sarcasm; he was still the same incomparable fencer in debate—as, for example, in the last session of the Reform Ministry, Mr. Beresford Hope had jestingly alluded to the "Asian mystery," and he replied with incomparable humour that when the right honourable gentleman spoke of Asian mysteries, there was "a Batavian grace about his exhibition which takes the sting out of what he has said." After this no Englishman could hear Mr. Beresford Hope's name mentioned without thinking of "Batavian grace." His wit was still sparkling enough, but his pathos, which had never been very simple, had considerably degenerated. It had always been getting more abstract, affected, and pompous, until in "Lothair," where he allowed himself full scope, it fell into the absurdities which Bret Harte has so capitally parodied.*

What makes "Lothair" psychologically interesting arises from the same position of affairs that has made the style official, namely, that the author stands at the summit of his wishes, and has realized his schemes, so that he no longer needs to take various circum-

* This simple yet first-class conversation existed in the morning-room of Plusham, where the mistress of the palatial mansion sat involved in the sacred privacy of a circle of her married daughters. . . . Beautiful forms leaned over frames glowing with embroidery, and beautiful frames leaned over forms inlaid with mother-of-pearl.—Bret Harte, "Lothair by Mr. Benjamins."

stances into consideration. "Lothair" is a more straightforward book than the "Trilogy," so called, which preceded it. It is not only without false mysticism, but, in a religious point of view, it is the most openly free-thinking work that Disraeli has written, so opposed to miracles that it might be taken for the work of a Rationalist if the fantastic author had not signed it with his fantastic doctrine, never renounced, of the sole victorious Semitic principle.

The conversion of a few fabulously wealthy members of the English aristocracy to the Church of Rome during the preceding years, especially of the young Marquis of Bute, seems to have suggested the plan of "Lothair." The hero is a young man of the same species as the heroes in all Disraeli's later novels, of very high rank, more than princely wealth, and of a religious temperament like Tancred. His sole idea on entering life is to attain clearness as to the truths of religion, and to learn which of the various orthodoxies is the true one. His ambition does not extend beyond making choice among them; to make this choice is what he understands by attaining to a view of life. He resolves to devote part of his colossal fortune to building a cathedral, without knowing whether it is to be Catholic or Protestant. The influence of his guardian, a highly educated and very worldly wise cardinal, and of an amiable Catholic family with whom he associates, makes the cathedral tend to the Papal side, when Lothair meets with "his good genius," Theodora, and all his castles and cathedrals in the air crumble away before the breath of liberty from her lips. Theodora is (like the young girl with the Jacobin cap in Delacroix's picture in the Luxembourg) at once a woman and a goddess of liberty. An Italian patriot, originally a poor street-singer, a child of the people, and an ardent free-thinker, she is the powerful feminine chief of the secret societies of Italy. For the sake of the liberties of nations, she has sacrificed her fortune, her jewels, her private life, and repose, and ends by hazarding her life as a heroine and falling as a martyr at Mentana. Theodora's spirit of liberty is as fatal to Lothair's narrowness as Venetia's superiority was to the politico-religious orthodoxy of young Cadurcis. Theodora teaches Lothair that " 'what is called orthodoxy has very little to do with religion; and a person may be very religious without holding the same dogmas as yourself, or, as some think, without holding any.' . . . 'Tell me, then, I entreat you, what is your religion?' 'The true religion, I think,' said Theodora. . . . 'My conscience.' "

And to his question whether she never needed any outward guidance, she answered, " 'I have never heard from priests any truth which my conscience had not revealed to me. They use different language from what I use, but I find after a time that we mean the same thing. What I call time, they call eternity; when they describe heaven, they give a picture of earth; and beings whom they style divine, they invest with all the attributes of humanity.' " *

It is quite intelligible that a woman holding views like these does not look upon the Pope and his temporal power with friendly eyes: " 'I do not grudge him his spiritual subjects; I am content to leave his superstition to time. Time is no longer slow; his scythe mows quickly in this age. But when his debasing creeds are palmed off on man by the authority of our glorious Capitol, and the slavery of the human mind is schemed and carried on in the Forum, then, if there be real Roman blood left, and I thank my Creator there is much, it is time for it to mount and move,' said Theodora."†

It might have been supposed that Lothair's acquaintance with Theodora would have delivered him for ever from the meshes of Catholicism. But such is not the case; through a chain of surprising, yet entirely natural events, he soon finds himself more closely entangled in them than ever. No other of Disraeli's novels has a plot so carefully constructed as this. When the revolt in Italy breaks out, Lothair accompanies the troops as a volunteer commanded by Theodora's husband, and falls severely wounded at Mentana; but when he is brought unconscious to Rome, where all his English Catholic acquaintances are staying, the cardinal and his spiritual friends find it convenient to spread a report of the miraculous rescue of Lothair by means of a Madonna revelation, and so to

* "Lothair," p. 163.   † Ibid., p. 265.

represent the matter in the Catholic papers as to make it appear that he had been fighting on the "right" side, and had received his wounds as a faithful soldier of the Holy Father. When convalescent, he happens to take up one of these papers, the style and tone of which Disraeli imitates in a masterly way, and indignantly calls its contents a lie. The cardinal coolly answers that he knew well that there were two versions of Lothair's position at the battle of Mentana, and that the one, which could only have originated with Lothair himself, was of a somewhat different character, but as this version, which was in itself extremely improbable, was not confirmed by any external testimony, there was no justification for the ill-sounding epithet which Lothair had applied to the article in question. Lothair must remember that he had been very ill, and that illness often impairs the memory. George IV thought he had taken part in the battle of Waterloo, had even commanded at it, etc. Lothair's mind, enfeebled by illness, is bound round by a web of the most delicate yet strongest threads, and his liberty annihilated; he is enticed to take part in a Catholic procession; he is gently compelled to allow himself to be wondered at and adored as one saved by a miracle; he is just about to become a helpless victim when the memory of Theodora rouses his last energies, and he saves himself by sudden and secret flight. After a journey to the East and a stay at Jerusalem, inevitable with Disraeli, he returns to England, and marries a friend of his youth.

"Lothair" is an attempt to introduce representatives of the various prevailing views of life in the present day, and to make them carry on a decisive discussion. A cardinal and a bishop represent respectively one of the chief European Churches. Theodora is spiritualistic liberalism; the artist Phœbus, a worshipper of nature, Pantheist and a zealous Hellenist, represents free-thinking, which deifies the beautiful, the Aryan principle; a venerable Syrian of Jewish descent, whose family, according to a tradition, was the first to follow Jesus, is Semiticism personified. The discussion of modern views of life on Oriental soil, is an ever-recurring reminiscence of Disraeli's own travels; it occurs in "Contarini Fleming" and in "Tancred," where the race of Ansarey, with its beautiful queen, represents Hellenic worship of beauty, as Phœbus does in "Lothair;" but it can scarcely be said to have gained in depth in the author's latest production. It strikes one as rather comic when Phœbus, the zealous devotee of the Aryan principle, ends by setting up as Court painter in St. Petersburg, in order to paint Semitic subjects (incidents from the life of Jesus) for Mongolian connoisseurs. But one wearies of this perpetual and unscientific talk about race. Phœbus is not a real human being, only an affected counterpart of Disraeli himself as a Semitic theorist. While these everlasting discussions go on, whether Hellenism or Hebraism— which, after all, do not include everything—is the more profound or exalted way of looking at life, all-uniting, all-embracing nature is lost sight of. Everything resolves itself for our author into opposing systems, political and religious doctrines or fantasies, and it is very characteristic that when at last Madre Natura does appear in his books, it is as the name of a secret and revolutionary society. One is inclined to say that she is not to be found in any other form with this enemy, on principle, of naturalism. He always loved politics better than nature, and even as a boy he personified nature in the form of the political Muse.

The exalted position of the author, the piquant fact that the late Prime Minister should once more appear as a novelist, achieved an unprecedented success for "Lothair." So great was the demand for the novel, that some of the London booksellers took 1200 copies of the first edition. A single firm in America sold 25,000 copies during the first month, and seven editions appeared in a few weeks; the book was stereotyped in two forms, translated into almost all languages, and, to quote Disraeli's own words in the preface, has been "more extensively read both by the people of the United Kingdom and the United States, than any work that has appeared for the last half-century;" * a circumstance which sufficiently proves how little opinion can be formed of the value of a book from the number of its first readers.

* General Preface to Novels, p. viii.

While Disraeli's "Lothair" and Gladstone's "Juventus Mundi," which appeared about the same time, met on drawing-room tables, and were discussed in London drawing-room talk, the leader of the Opposition was keeping pretty quiet in the House of Commons. The last Parliamentary trial of strength was so decidedly against him, that for the time he waited patiently and left the field to his opponent. Domestic and especially financial reforms followed quickly one upon another during his five years' administration, and for these undoubtedly Gladstone deserves the highest credit; but parallel with these internal improvements ran that series of blunders and defeats in foreign policy which made England an object of ridicule to every European state. Russia took advantage of the want of good faith in English statesmen to tear up the hardly won treaty of 1856. Great Britain, having lost all her influence, was unable to say a word to any purpose at the conclusion of the Franco-German war. The North American States, embittered by the want of good faith in the former Whig Ministry, compelled England to submit both the *Alabama* claims and the San Juan affair, the question of the Oregon frontier, to arbitration, and the result in both cases was unfavourable to England. The submission of the San Juan question to the German emperor ended in a diplomatic defeat and a loss of territory, and the Geneva tribunal imposed an enormous fine on England. It appeared that the Government, by its bad management, had subjected England to an international court, constituted solely for the occasion, and immediately afterwards rejected by the very country in whose favour it had decided. It appeared further that Gladstone was actually to blame for the severity of the award, for he himself stated in the Commons that he had not felt it to be his duty to read the American indictment, and was therefore ignorant of the "indirect claims" of North America. It scarcely need be said that the foreign policy of the Ministry called forth much Parliamentary criticism from Disraeli.

Still, it was not this weak foreign policy which occasioned the fall of the Ministry, but their daring and not always judicious internal reforms. It had solved the problem of secret voting, which had been a standing question for forty years, by the passing of the Ballot Bill, and thereby performed a real service; but in 1873, Gladstone introduced a new Bill for the regulation of University instruction in Ireland, which was intended to secure religious liberty, by not only doing away with the Protestant Theological Faculty of the Dublin University, but by abolition of the lectures on philosophy and modern history. It was not to be wondered at that the former measure alarmed the Conservatives and the latter the Liberals. Disraeli made a thundering speech against the Bill, and on a division it appeared that the powerful majority of a few years before had melted away. The Cabinet found itself in a minority of three. Gladstone immediately afterwards offered to resign, but his opponent decidedly declined to release him; he had had enough of holding office without a real majority that could be relied on, and preferred to allow Gladstone to heap up discontent and ill will against himself for a whole year. In February, 1874, the Ministry collapsed, with a majority of about fifty against it, and Disraeli formed a new and powerful Administration, strong in a majority for the first time in both Houses, and supported by the express personal confidence of the Queen. His life-work seemed now to be accomplished, the regenerated Tory party had become a power. When, in 1876, he accepted a peerage and passed into the Upper House, with the title of Earl and Viscount, the step was generally supposed to be an entrance on repose; it was thought that the Prime Minister's advanced age and weakened health no longer permitted him to sustain the exertion of the leadership of the Commons, and now that the object of his ambition had been attained, he himself regarded his political career as ended. This was a great mistake we all know. The deeds of Lord Beaconsfield have thrown those of Benjamin Disraeli into the shade. The interval of three years from that time to this, a short period in the life of an old man, has first given him world-wide renown. The events of these last years are fresh in the remembrance of all.

XXIII

CONCLUSION

✑ Prime Minister of England, Lord Privy Seal, Earl Beaconsfield of Beaconsfield, Viscount Hughenden of Hughenden, Knight of the Garter—this is now the style and title of the man who made his *début* as author and politician as plain Benjamin Disraeli. Let us conclude by seeking an answer to the concise question he himself asked at the outset of his career: What is he?

He is above all a great example of the steady perseverance of genius. He understands the art of striving and waiting. Few men have sustained so long a series of defeats, so much ridicule and contempt, and have been so undaunted by disaster and misfortune. The ridicule was more dangerous than the defeats; but if a striking example were wanted to demonstrate that true talent cannot be extinguished by the attacks of the press, Lord Beaconsfield furnishes that example. He has been assailed by many thousands of cutting articles, with no friendly press to defend him with anything like equal talent or zeal. He found it hard to get himself regarded as a statesman at all. The tone of the press against him is still venomous and personal, and yet, with rare coolness, he leaves not only these attacks, old and new, unanswered, but even misrepresentations of facts. At least ten times in a year the old story of O'Connell's letter of recommendation is dished up for him. From the very outset of his career, one of his apparently insignificant, but most dangerous enemies has been *Punch*. From the beginning of the fourth up into the sixth decade of this century, Leech, the cleverest and most popular caricaturist in England, furnished this paper, the tendencies of which are Liberal, with sketches of him in the most absurd situations and disguises. It is worthy of note that in 1868, when Leech's widow, who had been put on the Pension List by the Whig Ministry, died four years after her husband, Disraeli ordered that the pension should be continued to her orphan children.

For more than twenty years the press has determined public opinion about him, and yet he has pushed his way. His story is not that of the ugly duckling, who dreads and flees from persecution until one fine day it is discovered that it is innocence itself, and is rewarded by the children with bread and cakes. He has never been free from the danger of attacks, has never fled from them, and has fought for recognition as a bird of prey fights for his booty. "It came at last, as everything does, if men are firm and calm," as he says in "Sybil." What is remarkable, and almost unique, is the certainty with which, conscious of his powers and energy, he foresaw his late and distant triumphs from his earliest youth. The reader, perhaps, remembers the passage in "Contarini Fleming," where the hero sees "seated upon a glorious throne, on a proud Acropolis, one to whom a surrounding and enthusiastic people offered a laurel crown;" * and he will confess that the vision was surpassed by reality on the day when Lord Beaconsfield was received by the first men and women in the land at Charing Cross station on his return from the Berlin Congress, admired and applauded, crowned and sung by the people as the bringer of "Peace with Honour," and finally conducted to his Ministerial residence amidst an endless shower of bouquets. The presence of Sir Moses Montefiore on the occasion, at ninety years of age, gave to the celebration a sort of symbolic character, which could not fail to make a strong impression on the heart of the man who loves to regard himself as the representative of his race.

Perseverance is not a simple, indissoluble quality. It may combine many elements, and have many sources. Lord Beaconsfield's perseverance may be assigned to his imaginative character: he has had, to a surprising extent, the faculty of foreseeing his destiny, and because he foresaw it, he persevered.

He has, then, a fertile imagination; but is he a poet?

* "Contarini Fleming," p. 167.

It is the fashion to deny it, but it appears to me that the question should be answered in the affirmative. He certainly cannot be classed among the great and faultless poets, nor even among those who love and pursue their art for its own sake; he has seldom respected the forms of art, and the literature of his country is not indebted to him for any poetical or technical progress. But it is pedantic so to limit the conception of a poet that little chirping lyrical writers are included within it, while creative spirits are left out. Disraeli appeared at first to be a born satirist; he possessed a genuine Voltairean wit. If any one doubts it, let him read the little story "Ixion in Heaven," dating from the first period (1832); it is a classic model, a little masterpiece of composition, and even Heine might envy the author for the ideas. From the productions of pure wit, Disraeli gradually attained to those in which feeling and passion were the groundwork. In spite of its failings, "Contarini Fleming" called forth an appreciative letter from Goethe to the author, and a favourable criticism from Heine. But Lord Beaconsfield did not find his peculiar sphere until he created the form most natural to him, that of the political novel. It was not a generally recognized form of art, but it was that which gave the most flattering scope to his talents. Within this framework, he could give free play to his inventive faculty and his rhetoric, could entertain while he propagated his views, give vent to his enthusiasm, and discourse on politics. Rhapsodical as this form is, it is original and convenient, and is sure to be imitated when some other fictitious writer feels impelled to employ his talents in the service of the political conflicts of his time.

Is he, as he considers himself, a representative man? Can he truly be said to be a representative of the Semitic race? If the question be put in this direct form, it must be decidedly answered in the negative. For the Jewish mind has revealed itself in far more affluent and nobler forms than in Disraeli's comparatively limited mental range; while, on the other hand, he classes among the Jews many great men whose Jewish origin is wholly unproved. Extravagant eulogiums of the abilities of the modern Jews are not wanting in his writings. He is wearisome in his works with his perpetual lists of great Jewish poets, composers, actors and actresses, politicians and authors, singers and dancers, etc.; but when he descants upon the peculiar psychology of his race, one is amazed at the narrowness of his standpoint. In the "Life of Bentinck" he has tried to sketch this psychology as follows:—

"The Jewish race connects the modern populations with the early ages of the world, when the relations of the Creator with the created were more intimate than in these days, when angels visited the earth, and God Himself even spoke with men. The Jews represent the Semitic principle; all that is spiritual in our nature. They are the trustees of tradition, and the conservators of the religious element. They are a living and the most striking evidence of the falsity of that pernicious doctrine of modern times, the natural equality of man. The political equality of a particular race is a matter of municipal arrangement, and depends entirely on political considerations and circumstances; but the natural equality of man now in vogue, and taking the form of cosmopolitan fraternity, is a principle which, were it possible to act on it, would deteriorate the great races and destroy all the genius of the world. . . . They have also another characteristic, the faculty of acquisition. Although the European laws have endeavoured to prevent their obtaining property, they have nevertheless become remarkable for their accumulated wealth. Thus it will be seen that all the tendencies of the Jewish race are Conservative. Their bias is to religion, property, and natural aristocracy; and it should be the interest of statesmen that this bias of a great race should be encouraged, and their energies and creative powers enlisted in the cause of existing society.

"But existing society has chosen to persecute this race which should furnish its choice allies; and what have been the consequences?

"They may be traced in the last outbreak of the destructive principle in Europe. An insurrection takes place against tradition and aristocracy, against religion and property. Destruction of the

Semitic principle, extirpation of the Jewish religion, whether in the Mosaic or in the Christian form, the natural equality of man and the abrogation of property are proclaimed by the secret societies, who form provisional governments, and men of the Jewish race are found at the head of every one of them. The people of God co-operate with atheists; the most skilful accumulators of property ally themselves with Communists; the peculiar and chosen race touch the hand of all the scum and low castes of Europe. And all this because they wish to destroy that ungrateful Christendom which owes to them even its name, and whose tyranny they can no longer endure." *

Had Spinoza, who ought to have a voice on the question of Jewish genius, read this effusion, he would certainly have shaken his noble head. I do not know whether Disraeli would reckon him among the Communists (as a Republican he is not much better); an atheist he certainly is. But that he belonged to this reprobate set from hatred and revenge, because he was excluded from the Christian state, Lord Beaconsfield will hardly succeed in convincing any one who has read ten pages of his writings. If he did not entertain theistic opinions, and if according to him the Jews were always the first to oppose the "Semitic principle," perhaps this is rather to be traced to the eminent critical faculties of the race and their sincerity—not a peculiarity of other Orientals—than to embitterment at the stupidity of statesmen. If Jews are most eager in proclaiming to the world that the Israelites are not God's chosen people, have not received any special revelation, and that mankind is not pre-eminently indebted to them, does it not follow that their motives are disinterested? Would it not be easier for them to sacrifice their convictions to the sterile Moloch of pride of race? If, in the year 1848, Jews were everywhere found at the head of the revolts against antiquated tradition and ancient wrongs—like Daniel Manin, whom Disraeli himself once mentions, at the helm in Venice—may it not be attributed to love of liberty, twin sister of love of truth? And when later on, in some important countries,

* "Life of Lord George George Bentinck," p. 495.

well-to-do wealthy Jews, who had no need to envy the rich, instigated socialistic movements, may not this also be attributed to profound qualities, partly critical and partly philanthropic, which had nothing whatever to do with hatred of society?

The dogmatic and Conservative spirit which hovers before Lord Beaconsfield's mental vision was merely the chrysalis out of which a profoundly critical and progressive genius was developed; it budded in the prophets, revealed itself to the world in another aspect in Spinoza; but never lifted up the light of its countenance on Lord Beaconsfield. He certainly cannot be looked upon as the personification of the many-sidedness of the Jewish race; he is wanting in its idealistic tendencies. But of the persistent energy, the industry, the perseverance, the practical instincts, the quickness and the wit, the love of pomp and the ambition of his race, he is the typical representative; and he has that remarkable confidence in the superiority of the race which has preserved it pure for thousands of years. No other being like himself will arise; the civilization of the age will not permit it; he was and is only a possibility, because his audacious assertion of the "Semitic principle" fell in with the great romantic religious tendency of the age. But when I consider that, according to him, only two possibilities are open to the Jews —either to continue their life and strife within the limits of Semiticism, or to accept the all-embracing modern religion of humanity—Disraeli appears to me to be not only a distinguished representative of Judaism, but I feel inclined to call him the last Jew.

Is he a great man? Not if the word be taken in its precise and correct sense. Really great men wear quite a different aspect. The eminent philosophers of the eighteenth century were great men, because they had faith in ideas, had a religion of ideas, and because they unselfishly consecrated their lives, amidst many sacrifices, to propagating the truths they had perceived. The statesmen who were masters of all the wealth of culture of the eighteenth century, like Stein and Wilhelm von Humboldt, were great men, because, with the all-embracing eye of genius, they comprehended and looked over the heads of their contemporaries, stood far above them, and, undaunted by discouragement, strove to raise them to their own level. They were also thoroughly upright and honourable men, and no one could ever be in doubt what their opinions really were. Lord Beaconsfield is a man of a different stamp. Born during the period of reaction, he soon comprehended the age, accommodated himself to it, proclaimed its favourite doctrines in novel forms, and only to a certain extent bade defiance to the spirit of the age, because he paid homage to still stronger and more universal prejudices. From the first he was wanting in the scientific spirit; he has always been ignorant of the great idea of evolution—the common central idea of philosophy and natural science in the nineteenth century. He ridicules it in "Popanilla," where he says, in one of the satirical turns in which his strength lies: "By developing the water, we get fish; by developing the earth, we get corn, and cash, and cotton; by developing the air, we get breath; by developing the fire, we get heat." * He took up this satire again twenty years later, where the book "The Revelations of Chaos" is described. "You know, all is development. The principle is perpetually going on. First there was nothing, then there was something, then—I forget the next; I think there were shells, then fishes; then we came. Let me see, did we come next? Never mind that; we came at last. And the next change there will be something very superior to us—something with wings. Ah! that's it; we were fishes, and I believe we shall be crows. But you must read it." †

How much he was in earnest with these parodies of the doctrine of evolution appears from his well-known speech at Oxford, in 1864, in which he expressed himself with the strongest emphasis against "the most modern scientific school," and even made himself ridiculous by summing up the scientific discussions of that time as follows:—"The question is—Is man an ape or an angel? My lord, I am on the side of the angel."

It may well be asked whether he really meant this, or whether it was only accepted as the necessary sequence of the doctrine of

* "Popanilla," p. 377.   † "Tancred," p. 109.

the superiority of and revelation to the Semitic race; but if he did not mean it, so much the worse for him. This and other isolated things might be overlooked, though it is always to be regretted when a man who desires to rule his contemporaries talks like a parish clerk of the greatest scientific problems and ideas of his time.

But these expressions do not stand alone; they coincide with other results of the famous theory of race. There are many indications that one particular circumstance induced Disraeli to sacrifice his thinking faculties, namely, the great religious reaction which followed the abolition of Christianity decreed by the French Revolution. This made him think, as it did most of his contemporaries, that revealed religion was stronger than all doubts, or rather that it had such a hold on people's minds that it never could again be superseded in the future. The reaction appeared to him to be a Semitic reaction against Aryan attempts at emancipation, and in its force he found one of the strongest proofs of the indomitable superiority of the Hebrew race over the nations of Europe. In his "Life of Bentinck," he says that France, since her revolt against the Old and New Testaments, had been in a state of torpor varied by convulsions, and that England owed her prosperity to the circumstance that, in spite of her meagre and faulty theology, she had never forgotten Zion; that North America and Russia were strictly Semitic (that is, religious) countries; and that if Northern Germany had never attained the dominant position in the German Empire to which it seemed destined by nature, it was because it had never been entirely converted to Semitic principles. One is sorry for Disraeli's sake that the present powerful position of Prussia was not preceded by any Semitic tendencies; but even good prophets sometimes prophesy falsely.

When science, in the second half of the nineteenth century, emancipated itself from the swaddling bands of reactionary romanticism, the mind of Lord Beaconsfield was too deeply engraven with its peculiar stamp to admit of new impressions. The splendid scientific research, which is the pride and glory of our age, has left him wholly untouched. When German criticism began to explore antiquity, including Biblical antiquity, he either could not or would not see anything in it but a repetition of the futile attempts of the last century, and in the "General Preface" to his works we find the following sadly stupid or sadly prudent sentence:—"One of the consequences of the divine government of this world . . . must be occasionally a jealous discontent with the revelation entrusted to a particular family. But there is no reason to believe that the Teutonic rebellion of this century against the divine truths entrusted to the Semites will ultimately meet with more success than the Celtic insurrection of the preceding age." The man who could say this in the year 1870, either belonged to a past age, or did not mean what he said, and in neither case can he be looked upon as a truly great man.

Still, greatness is not an absolute quantity, and Lord Beaconsfield is, at any rate, a man of great talent and ability. He was always ambitious, and he whose first aim is to gain honour and power himself, and makes it only a secondary consideration to employ his talents and the power they have won for him in the service of humanity, will inevitably forfeit true greatness in proportion as he gains brilliance of position and renown. Like all others, he, once in his youthful days, came to the point where two ways met— the one leading to power and influence and high position; the other —that followed by better men, who seek success only in the second place, and, above all things, remain true to their convictions, and strive for this as their only direct aim. When Lord Beaconsfield came to these cross-roads, his ambition and love of power made choice for him. But scarcely was the choice made, when all the love of truth and liberty which he possessed began a long and continued revolt against it. One hears his better nature asserting itself in his utterances. He had become a Tory; but he said at once that not one of his contemporaries knew what the essence of Toryism consisted in: it was opposition to every form of noble oligarchy; it was an alliance between the crown and the people; and it was further explained, on this last point, that the power of the sovereign ought not to be increased, while the social and political wishes of the people should be legally realized. He had become a Conservative; but he immediately said, "Let us not allow ourselves to be imposed upon by those who so call themselves; they must be subjected to a rigid inquiry as to what they wish to conserve, and if it can be shown to be mere lumber, then, in the name of true Conservatism, it must be given up." He became the leader of the Protectionists; but no sooner were the Corn Laws abolished than he declared that he accepted free trade. He became the friend and greatest ally of the aristocrats; but he spoke in favour of the Chartists, and awakened sympathy for them by a novel. He became chief of a party opposed to reform; but he it was who carried the great Reform Bill, and with the declaration that he had always been in favour of household suffrage, and that he had had to educate his party. He became an orthodox Anglican, and was on all occasions the champion of orthodox Christianity as the highest truth; but his explanation of Christianity changed it into Judaism; and again, by his explanation of Judaism, he made it appear that the oppressed and despised Hebrew race was the first on earth, and made religious truth a question of natural science. He paid homage to the Church as her most devoted son; but he wrote more enthusiastically than any Radical among his contemporaries in honour of Byron and Shelley, and characterized the attitude of the Church and religious society towards them as stupidity and hypocrisy. And so it has been on every question.

He undoubtedly fell into many an awkward and many a ludicrous situation as Conservative leader. *Punch* of 1870 has a witty cartoon illustrative of his position. It refers to the efforts of the Disraeli Cabinet to extort a promise from the Sultan of Zanzibar during his visit to London, to abolish the slave trade in his dominions. Disraeli and the sultan are engaged in conversation.

"*Right Hon. B. D.* Now that your Highness has seen the blessings of freedom, I trust we may rely upon your strenuous help in putting down slavery?

"*Sultan Seyyid Barghash.* Ah yes! certainly! But remember, O Sheikh Ben Dizzy, Conservative party very strong in Zanzibar!"

The impersonality of the jest makes it even more cutting than the withering scorn with which O'Connell in his day characterized Disraeli's going over to the Conservative party. It must not, however, be forgotten that an English Conservative party, in comparison with the Continental reactionary parties, is always progressive, and that Disraeli himself always taught the impossibility of founding a party on the basis of resistance to change. And if further testimony is required to his liberal conception of Toryism, it may well be found in the fact that after the unmeasured insults which O'Connell had heaped upon him, and after he had replied to them with threats, he sought and found reconciliation with O'Connell.

"I know there are many who don't understand the sympathy which is alleged to subsist between me and the honourable member for Cork. . . . Our acquaintance was an accident. . . . What error was it in me, then a very young man, if meeting accidentally with a great man who entertained similar views, I declared my opinions with that unreserve and frankness, which I hope I may never lose?" *

The more liberty of action Disraeli has gained, the more he has returned to the sympathies of his youth. This is expressed with striking truth in the anonymous and virulent articles on him (by the editor of the *Daily News*) in the *Fortnightly Review*, August, 1878. "If a man's consistency is to be judged solely by comparing the beginning and end of his career, Lord Beaconsfield might be accounted one of the most consistent of politicians. But there is an intervening space, occupying the greater part, and the most decisively influential part of his career; and that cannot be left out of the reckoning."

A more lenient observer would have reversed the sentence, and would have said that a politician in the peculiar situation of Lord Beaconsfield, in consideration of the agreement between his starting-point and the end of his course, may claim some indulgence for the sins of the intervening period. In that interval he appears as the true disciple of the great romantic reaction. His theocratic dreams, his deification of the person of his sovereign, his aristo-

* "Benjamin Disraeli, Earl of Beaconsfield," vol. i. p. 645.

cratic tendencies, his identification of beauty with antiquity or
with the beauty of antiquity, his high estimate of forms and ceremonies, are sheer romanticism. But even as a youth he laid a mine
underneath all this, and when an old man he set a light to it.

Is he a great statesman? The rank of a statesman is generally
partly determined by the results of his career, and Lord Beaconsfield is still living, and is even now engaged in a great and perilous
political action. But it seems to me that if we apply to him the
standard of the nineteenth century, he must be considered a great
statesman. His mind and powers were under constraint so long as
only a secondary post was assigned him as Minister of a special
department under the leadership of another, and with a minority in
Parliament which was not even a large one. It has only been since
1874 that it has been possible for him to develop his long-husbanded
powers. It has not been difficult for his enemies to point out the
un-English character of a mind which, like his, acts by surprises,
and always appeals to the imagination of the masses; but even
beneath such formal measures as the proclamation of the Queen as
Empress of India, the political idea may be traced. Now that England has become a semi-Oriental power, it can scarcely be considered charlatanism for an English politician to try to work on
the imagination of Orientals. And it almost looks as if it had been
fore-ordained that it should fall to the lot of Lord Beaconsfield to
represent England during the last conflict between Russia and
Turkey. For the Eastern question may be called in an eminent
degree his affair, his cause. It was even felt to be so by those who
did not clearly comprehend it. To what extent he may have failed
in some particulars cannot now be determined, but thus much seems
certain, that he has not only achieved a great deal, but at the same
time marked out the political lines which England must follow if
she is seriously resolved to maintain her vast Asiatic colony. If Lord
Beaconsfield is not a great statesman, he has shown himself the man
capable of controlling a great political situation. This old man
of seventy-three was practically the only man in Europe in the
spring of 1878 who had courage and firmness enough to bring

Russia, intoxicated as she was with victory, to a stand. He alone seized the Bear by the ear, and dragged him to the Congress at Berlin. The considerations which tied the hands of the other statesmen of Europe were not binding on the representative of England, and the scruples which would have fettered every other English statesman were nothing to him. One must have very little acquaintance with his belief in the prerogative of a great personage to suppose for a moment that a treaty would prevent him from sending the British fleet to Constantinople, or that a clause in an Act should prevent him from thus laying emphasis on his words. Did not even Vivian Grey say: "There wants but one thing more: courage, pure, perfect courage"?

England had fallen into disrepute among the nations; her want of participation in the politics of Europe was a subject of ridicule; the fate of Holland was everywhere foretold for her. I have myself heard from the lips of more than one liberal Englishman confessions of shame at this dishonour, and the wish that England, even at the risk of staying her internal progress, might regain her place among the nations of Europe. And at the same time, Russia was turning an ever-increasing portion of Asia into Russian provinces, and threatened at last to make the position of England in India untenable. While England was not considered to be in a position to try her strength with Russia, and Europe was laughing at the exasperation of the whale with the bear, he gave a voice to the sentiments of the people. I should not wonder if Lord Beaconsfield's soul was filled with some such Old Testament pathos, as the description of the beasts of prey in the Book of Job. "Canst thou draw out leviathan with an hook? or his tongue with a cord which thou lettest down? Canst thou put an hook into his nose? or bore his jaw through with a thorn? Will he make many supplications unto thee? will he speak soft words unto thee? Will he make a covenant with thee? wilt thou take him for a servant for ever? Wilt thou play with him as with a bird? or wilt thou bind him for thy maidens? . . . Lay thine hand upon him, remember the battle, do no more."

Without firing a shot, or shedding a drop of English blood, by the energy he displayed, and by adroitly taking advantage of circumstances, he gained greater advantages for England than his Whig predecessors had gained by the long and bloody Crimean war. And even if, by this time, the glory of the Treaty of Berlin has to a great extent faded away, because its mistakes and short-comings have gradually been discerned by the multitude, still, in order to form a true estimate of Lord Beaconsfield's services, one has only to remember the amazement of Europe on hearing of English preparations against Russia, of English enterprise in import-ing the Indian troops to Malta; it saw a new spirit arising, and, still almost incredulous, became convinced that England had awakened from her death-like slumbers.

The life of Lord Beaconsfield, like the lives of all great characters, began in mystic, heroic dreams, and a youth of poetic emotion, ripening into a maturity fruitful of great deeds. When a critic tries to form a conception of and to delineate his character, he had need be upon his guard; for the subject is ever changing, and demands an ever-changing method; mere literary criticism must become psychological, and psychology must embrace the emotions of the individual soul and the spirit of the age. For his biography by degrees becomes history, and his history expands at length into a portion of the history of the world.

I had been musing on this remarkable career when, in the year 1870, I saw and heard Disraeli for the first time in Parliament. It was a few months after the French declaration of war. Disraeli de-manded that the papers relating to it should be laid upon the table; Gladstone maintained that he could not yet produce them. The debate was not in itself important. Disraeli's theories about race became intelligible on seeing the two opponents confronted with each other, for in the House of Commons he literally looked like the representative of a foreign race. While Gladstone produced the impression of the true-born, distinguished Englishman, with his noble, clear-cut profile, his piercing eye, and unconstrained man-ner; Disraeli, with his curly black hair, his dark complexion, his prominent under lip, and determined yet fiery glance, looked like a fire spirit confronted with the spirit of the ocean. When he began to speak it was evident which was the more interesting man of the two. His peculiar eloquence made an ineffaceable impression on me; I have never forgotten its spirit and energy, its fine, well-rounded periods, and the dry wit which continually called forth peals of laughter from his party.

I saw Lord Beaconsfield last in July, 1878, during the Congress of Berlin. He was staying at the Kaiserhof, opposite Prince Bismarck's palace; he was the acknowledged lion of the Congress, and when from his balcony he looked across to his great neighbour, he could pride himself on having attained a fame almost as wide. On this balcony were placed, by the attention of the landlord, six fine laurel plants, and a little stunted palm, so that Lord Beaconsfield, whose imagination had always been dreaming of laurels, and whose heroes of romance wandered among palms, had symbols of his honours and a frail symbol of the home of his race before his eyes when he opened his door in the morning.

One day, as I happened to be crossing the Wilhelmsplatz, I met him on the narrow footpath between the flower-beds, as he was going across the square to the Congress, leaning on the arm of his secretary, Mr. Montagu Corry. I was so near to him that I could look straight into his face. His steps were slow; he looked weary, ill, and almost irritable. Over-exertion was evident in every line of his countenance, and he acknowledged the deep and respectful salutations of the good citizens of Berlin with a weary and mechanical movement of his hand to his hat. But as I gazed into his pale and haggard face, I involuntarily thought of all the conflicts he had passed through, the disappointments he had experienced, the agonies and torments he had suffered, and the lofty courage with which he had triumphed over them all. I thought of his genuine sympathy with the common people whose cause he had defended, and with the oppressed race to which he was never ashamed to belong, and whose rights he compelled Roumania to acknowledge at the Congress; and I saw him all at once in a more attractive and ideal light, and, almost against my will, a feeling of sympathy took possession of my mind.